Take 5000 Eggs

Take 5000 Eggs

Food from the markets and fairs of southern France

Paul Strang
photographs by **Jason Shenai**
recipes by **Jeanne Strang**

KYLE CATHIE LIMITED

First published in Great Britain in 1997
by Kyle Cathie Limited
20 Vauxhall Bridge Road
London SW1V 2SA

ISBN 1 85626 246 4

Text copyright © Paul Strang 1997
Photographs copyright © Jason Shenai 1997
Recipes copyright © Jeanne Strang 1997

Paul Strang is hereby identified as the author of this work in accordance with Section 77 of the Copyright, Designs and Patents Act, 1988

A Cataloguing in Publication record for this title is available from the British Library

Book design by Lisa Tai
Map by John Gilkes
Printed in Singapore

ACKNOWLEDGEMENTS

Our grateful thanks to the countless people who have made this book possible: the organizers of the many events which we describe and the colourful people participating in them; the chefs and housewives who have generously shared with us their recipes; the farmers and growers for all the help thay have given us over their produce; the Chambers of Commerce for their information on markets and fairs, and the producers of the *Guide Alexandre* for the same; specifically to Erick Vedel for the background and historical input into the food of Provence and for his authentic versions of many old recipes; finally to our publisher Kyle Cathie, our editor Candida Hall and designer Lisa Tai for their enthusiasm, encouragement and skills in bringing our discoveries to the printed page.

Contents

Introduction

Eggs   Hams   **Wine**   Cheese   **Fish**   Vegetables   **Garlic**   Lime Blossom   **Spices**   Olives

Charcuterie   Pâtisserie   **Rice**   Walnuts   **Cèpes**   Chestnuts   **Peppers**   Foie Gras   **Truffles**

France remains a nation of gourmets. Despite the pressures of big business and the convenience of the supermarkets, the French have a passionate interest in the raw materials of cookery. There are fêtes and *foires* all over the country, celebrating the season for, say, garlic, or the quality of a local product, whether it be the olives of Nyons, the rice from Camargne or the ham of Bayonne. But the weekly, even daily, celebration of quality produce begins at the local market.

A French town without a market is unthinkable: such a place would be failing the prime test of any rural centre, to act as the point of sale for the surplus production of the local country people, and to enable those without the possibility of growing or rearing their own food to stock their larders.

Many towns in southern France, even some of the largest, have grown round the trade in local goods. Bordeaux, Sète and Marseille owe their commercial growth since the Middle Ages to the development of their ports, and to their ability to point regional merchandise to overseas markets. Smaller towns have acted as a focal point for the trade in local speciality produce: Sarlat, for example, in all things to do with the goose and the duck, and Carpentras in its famous strawberries.

But every town has its general market in everyday foodstuffs. Market-day can be the big event of the week: from dawn, the travelling traders arrive and set up their stalls, usually in the main square, or under a covered *halle*. The farmers come to sell their *charcuterie* in company with the specialist traders in pork and poultry products. All the traffic, pedestrian or motorized, is one-way, going in the same direction – *centre ville*.

If you have got up early enough, you see the peasant growers, their barrows, farm-carts or clapped-out *deux chevaux* laden with vegetables and fruit, and old ladies, sometimes still dressed from head to toe in the traditional black, hauling heavy bags full of their spare produce, which will yield enough pocket money to buy what cannot be produced at home. They will be expecting a good price for their eggs, butter, live chickens and rabbits, vegetables, nuts, and perhaps a few wild mushrooms found in the woods.

On long trestles, and from specially-constructed vans, anything and everything can be sold or bought: hayforks, fiendish-looking scythes, hedge-trimmers, whole chimneypots, china, fabrics, slippers, compact discs, jeans, sweets, all manner of garden produce and goodies from the store-cupboard; *confits* of duck and pork, sausages, hams, cheeses, wine, tresses of onions, shallots and garlic; everything a country family needs and much that it does not. And everywhere there are flowers: massed geraniums, petunias, portulaca, marigolds, lobelia, gladioli; and chrysanthemums – in France the flower of mourning and remembrance at Toussaint.

As well as these weekly markets, there are occasional *foires*, opportunities for the farmer to earn some really serious money from his livestock. The sheer size of these *foires* once made them happy hunting-grounds for rogues of every description, hawkers of patent medicines and those who pretended to be bone-setters or dentists.

Today, the distinction between the markets and the *foires* has largely been eroded: sometimes the monthly *foire* is an oversized version of the weekly market. Sometimes too the trading in livestock takes place in a different part of town, often under specially constructed *salles polyvalentes* which can double for other events on non-market days. Some of the rural character of the *foire* has been lost as a result. The rustic smells have disappeared from the town square, and visitors do not have to be so careful about where they put their feet. The markets have become more urbanized.

Quite apart from their commercial importance, the markets and *foires* serve another, equally valuable function. The farming day is a long hard one. The market is a chance to break the routine, to get away from the kitchen or the cattle-shed and to have a good time. There is the chance of meeting friends and relations from other villages, seeing boyfriends or girlfriends away from curious eyes, of enjoying a few too many drinks and having a too good lunch at the auberge, arguing about the price of livestock or politics. For the wives, there is a rare chance to catch up on local scandal, the elderly matrons in threes and fours chattering like magpies in a hedge. The market is still the chance to escape from the sometimes crippling loneliness on remote farms, especially for the very old who can still be seen with a few rather pathetic offerings; they have come not so much to sell as to have a chat with others, whom they might not otherwise have a chance of seeing from one year's end to another.

As more and more young people are moving into the towns, some are being replaced by 'green' producers, specializing in organically-grown fruit and vegetables. They have a growing following with a public still concerned to resist the gradual trend to intensively-produced foodstuffs, often adulterated with chemicals.

But as farms are merged in the interests of efficiency, the country population does get smaller, and the markets are becoming less exploited by farmers; but there are still the itinerant traders, called *commerçants non-sédentaires*. An old and respected profession, its practitioners have usually inherited the way of life from their fathers and grandfathers. To go from market to market, setting up a pitch every morning in a different place and packing up when the market is over, is a lifestyle different from any other. Some say it is a profession in decline, but for many it is in the blood, like being a fisherman. Today they are quite strictly regulated; there are severe rules about the marking of prices, as well as obligations to register with the tax authorities and the social security offices. On paper, the itinerant way of life offers no loopholes, but . . .

Most people think that there are bargains everywhere at the market. This is not always true. The price you will pay a farmer's wife for her eggs will be the same as you pay in the village shop, perhaps a little more, and certainly more than you will pay at the supermarket outside town. But the produce is of excellent quality. The vegetables are just picked, often from kitchen gardens where insecticides and artificial fertilizers have not been used. The eggs are fresh and guaranteed free-range from birds that have been allowed to find their own food naturally, and have not been gorged on fish-meal or their own faeces.

This is no doubt what attracts tourists in their thousands to markets. For them, these open-air displays of wonderful produce afford a welcome change from the dull show and stale smells offered by the supermarkets. A market also gives the visitor an opportunity to mix with the local community. It gives the foreigner a chance to venture a few words in a language in which he is not perhaps confident. Holiday-makers are vitally important supporters of the old-fashioned markets. Go on a winter's day and you will notice how few people there are, compared with the crowd on a warm summer's day during the holiday-season.

The South offers a complete range of specialities, and there have grown up a number of *foires* devoted exclusively to them – olives, cheeses, truffles, etc. There are recently invented ones too, like the many chestnut fairs, and the fish fairs all along the Atlantic and Mediterranean coasts. Such events are extremely entertaining and are highly charged with local atmosphere and bonhomie.

Their growth has been encouraged by the revival in traditional *cuisine du terroir*. Sometimes new products are being developed alongside the old, or new ways are being found of enjoying the old ingredients. Another feature of this kind of *foire* is the growth of *confréries* (brotherhoods) of this and that: chestnut-growers, local wine-makers, cheese-makers and so on. This is a chance for the chosen worthies to dress up in colourful costumes, have a good parade and *introniser* (initiate) new members: someone has usually written or commissioned a song specially for them.

In this book, we try to capture the spirit of some of the most colourful of the markets, *foires* and fêtes. We give recipes, all of which have been tested, using some of the produce on sale. We hope that readers will enjoy themselves as much as we have, because, even where business is to be done, the common factor of these events is that they are fun to attend.

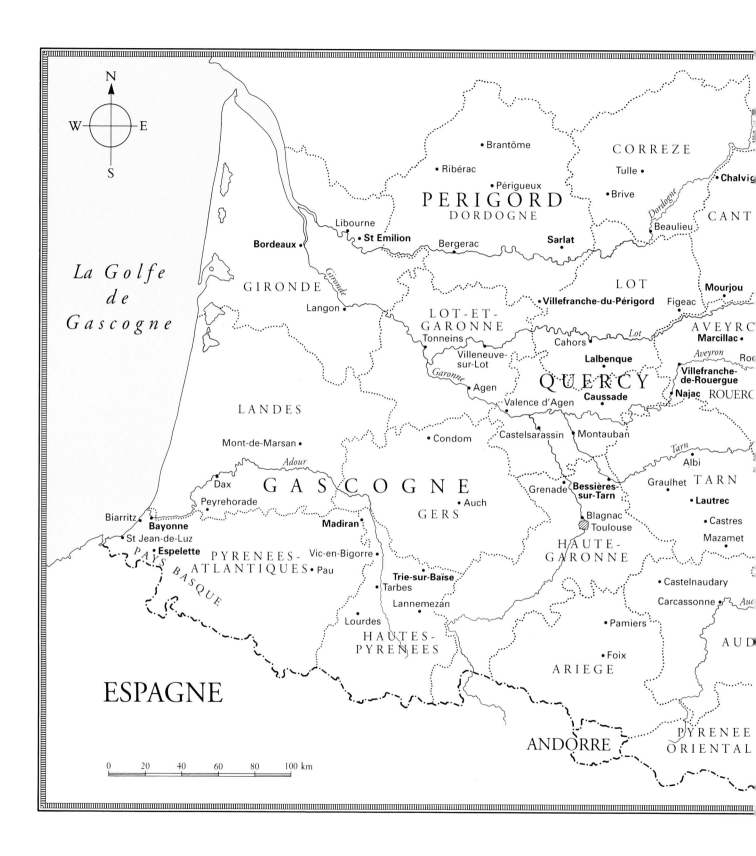

Take 5000 Eggs

I f a Frenchman needed an excuse for a gastronomic treat, what better than the arrival of spring, the end of Lent and the implied licence, even from the Church, to celebrate his freedom after forty days of fasting?

Easter Sunday lunch ranks with New Year's Eve *réveillon* as the occasion for getting out of the store cupboard the luxuries which have been put by in due season: the foie gras, the *confits*, all manner of pâtés, sausages and hams.

But perhaps the most powerfully symbolic food of spring is the egg. Nothing speaks more directly of rebirth. In the past, if the poorer peasants had no hens of their own, eggs were not affordable. It was traditional for the young men of the village to go searching for freshly-laid eggs in the early morning and to take them to the less well-off farms, where the children painted them and families enjoyed a good breakfast on Easter morning.

Eggs are forbidden food during Lent, so an omelette is a fitting celebration of its end. Every French cook seems to know instinctively how to make one. While others may debate whether to add water or cream, how hot the pan must be, whether it should be cooked in butter or oil, the French cook does not even have to think. The formula which the legendary Madame Poulard gave to an admiring customer at her restaurant at Le Mont-St-Michel perhaps withholds more than it reveals: 'I break some good eggs in a bowl, I beat them well, I put a good lump of butter in the pan, I pour in the eggs and I stir constantly.'

The worlds biggest omelette is made in one of France's sleepiest towns. Every Easter the inhabitants of Bessières-sur-Tarn welcome thousands of visitors to break the lenten fast

The late Elizabeth David believed that it is much better to make several small omelettes than one large one. This view is not shared by Monsieur Gilbert Solignac, a prominent citizen of Bessières-sur-Tarn where, for 362 days in every year, he runs a gardening and agricultural business. During the other three days, he closes his shop and acts as host to thousands of people from all over the world, all French-speaking, but from communities as diverse as Quebec, New Caledonia, Louisiana and Provence.

What brings them to Bessières, a quintessential, one-street town in the dozy countryside north of Toulouse? It is not as turbulent as its publicity proclaims, because on most days the only sounds to be heard are the rustling of the plane trees in the warm east wind, the clunk of *boules* on the gravelly sand of the square and the barking of the town's mongrel population.

The answer is proclaimed on hoardings posted at every entry to this small bourg: Bessières-sur-Tarn is the home of the Confrérie des Chevaliers de l'Omelette Géante Pascale et Mondiale – the Biggest Easter Omelette in the World – and Monsieur Solignac is president of the Confrérie. The inhabitants of Bessières always used to assemble by the river on Easter Monday to cook the traditional Easter omelette, an occasion which gradually caught on as a good way to spend a bank holiday. As the crowds grew bigger year by year, the omelette got bigger too, until what was needed was a giant frying pan. Bernard Cauchoix, the local blacksmith, was commissioned to make a cast-iron pan no less than three metres in diameter and capable of holding 2000 eggs. Elizabeth David would have been horrified.

A small committee, formed as long ago as 1955, blossomed in 1973 into the present-day Confrérie, six worthies who swore to spread the name of Bessières and to perpetuate its ancestral traditions. Year by year the Fête de l'Omelette grew.

Jean Adu, the village baker, who was originally commissioned to make two giant loaves weighing thirty kilos each, now finds he has to make six. Personalities from sport and show business were invited for induction (what the French call *intronisation*), and the Bessières omelette was soon to become televised.

The giant omelette has caught on overseas too: today the inhabitants of Dumbéa in New Caledonia celebrate the 'Largest Omelette of the Pacific and the Coral Sea'. The mayor of Dumbéa sent a team to Bessières for training, and now they come every year to Bessières as well as doing their own thing at home. The colourful costumes and music of the Pacific add a wonderful splash of colour to the Bessières fête, especially when it rains at Easter, which it often does. One year, the omelette was even made in the snow.

There is a thriving omelette branch in Granby, Quebec; and in Abbeville, Louisiana, a group of Francophone Americans have formed another offshoot. There is also a fraternal branch nearer home at Fréjus in the Var. There were once plans to make a giant omelette in Tiananmen Square in Beijing, but sadly the funds ran out.

It is the parent event at Bessières which remains the biggest and the best. At ten o'clock in the morning the Chevaliers, their friends and families assemble at the former railway station in Bessières. The town is on a line which today goes from nowhere to nowhere. Its station has recently been bought by the Confrérie as their headquarters. Bessières *gare* is a typical one-up one-down building, but is big enough to house the not inconsiderable gear of the Confrérie, including a large fridge in which the thousands of eggs required on Easter Monday may be stored. Funds permitting, the ticket office will be converted into a kitchen and the goods depot into a reception hall.

Here too gathers the village baker with his giant loaves, as well as every kind of musical performer. There is a bunch of steel-drummers, bald as convicts, with their trombone-player; a contingent from the nearby city of Albi, ranging from veterans to five-year-old boy drummers, led by an amazingly loud trumpet player who has decorated his shoes with plastic hydrangeas; a rather classier group of folk-musicians from the Auvergne; and pulsing black rhythms from New Caledonia. Leading this procession are the Cadets of the Giant Omelette, the under-fourteens with their float, on which is perched a giant papier-mâché egg containing their smallest boy cadet.

The bread is on a scale to match the omelette

At a given sign from a frighteningly bossy lady, later to be *intronisée* for her work, this oddly assorted party sets out from the old railway station for the centre of the village. The bands play all at once, which makes you feel tuned in to several radio stations simultaneously. Round the village they go until finally they arrive at an enclosure in the main square, complete with steel barrier, where an enormous fire is already burning. Nearby waits the giant frying pan, re-cast a few years ago by Monsieur Cauchoix to a jumbo four-metre size, so that it now holds no fewer than 5000 eggs. It has for its handle a giant wooden telegraph-pole.

Accompanied by a deafening crescendo of chaos, the procession of Chevaliers makes its way to the stand where the Master of Ceremonies maintains an endless programme of *animation*, interspersed with recorded pop and occasional contributions from the live musicians. Then the celebrities are *intronisés* while preparations for the omelette-making begin.

Crates of eggs, 10,000 of them in all, are brought into the enclosure, and scores of helpers start to break them into buckets, the mountains of shells being stacked against the railings. The loaves of bread are distributed round the edge of the enclosure. Everyone present will have a chance to taste the giant omelette, together with a slice of the delicious bread of Bessières-sur-Tarn. Suddenly a fork-lift truck quietly makes its entrance, raises the pan in its arms and gently deposits it over the flames. It then withdraws to a discreet distance.

The crowds are all too eager for their share of the feast

The crowd, some 10,000 strong, decides that it is apéritif time. The three cafés in the village start to work overtime. Inside each the noise is deafening. Monsieur Fischer, the husband of the lady who runs the excellent village wine-shop, dispenses luscious rillettes of goose and pâtés to all and sundry, reserving his choice foie gras for those whom he deems important visitors or fellow Chevaliers. Monsieur Fischer is also a Chevalier of the Order of the Stuffed Chicken and the Order of the Toulouse Sausage. And he has won the National Tripe Prize.

The visitors from Canada and Louisiana settle down to a bottle of Madame's champagne. They boast that their omelette is much better than the Bessières version: it contains twenty-four kilos of butter, two sacks of onions and an unspecified number of *langoustes*.

Meanwhile, the ceremonies on the podium are rounded off by a lively performance of the Chanson des Chevaliers:

Nous sommes les Chevaliers
De l'Omelette Pascale.
Dans la joie et la gaieté
Nous parcourons
Le monde entier,
Illustres représentants
De la Confrérie Mondiale.
Serment de fidélité
Ambassadeurs de l'amitié.

The big moment is approaching. More helpers appear bearing five-litre bottles of oil which they pour into the already heated pan. The Chevaliers each seize a huge wooden oar-like paddle, with which they move the oil around so that it does not catch, while off-stage the breaking and beating of the eggs reaches a frenzied conclusion, a process assisted by an outsize strimmer from Monsieur Solignac's shop. At a given signal from the *chef des chefs*, 5000 eggs are poured into the pan, to huge applause.

Now come a few moments of relative calm as everyone waits for the eggs to heat through. The seasoning is added – whole jars of salt and packets of pepper – all stirred about with the paddles. The massive loaves are each divided into three lengthwise, before being guillotined across their width. The crowd is by this time surging against the railings, impatient to get a piece of the action. Most have bought bottles of the local Fronton wine, bottled for the day of course as *Cuvée des Chevaliers*.

The stirring of the pan starts in earnest as the mixture begins to thicken. After about a quarter of an hour the omelette is proclaimed cooked, the fork-lift truck is summoned and the pan is removed from the fire. The Chevaliers then set about dividing the omelette into serving portions, which are rapidly distributed to the edge of the cooking area by the Cadets, still in their white and egg-yolk-colour costume. The helpings are dumped on to paper plates with a slice of the bread and handed over the railings, to the acclamation of the lucky recipients and the pained silence of those still waiting to be served. Not even the four-metre pan is big enough to serve everybody, so it is announced that a second omelette will be made. The head Chevalier of the Canadian branch leaps into the frying pan, which has by now considerably cooled and, on his hands and knees, scrapes the surface of the pan clean enough to take another 5000 eggs. The whole process then starts all over again, while more wine is consumed.

While the second omelette is made, it is back to the bars for the rest of the crowd, and then to the side-shows of the fête until the evening, when there is the usual *animation* and dancing in the streets. The Chevaliers proceed back to the old railway station and are allowed to don more comfortable clothes, putting away their eggy uniforms for another year. The paddles are washed and the pan scraped clean for storage in the station-master's office until next Easter.

Next morning Monsieur Solignac goes back to his business. Bessières goes back to sleep. The familar rustling of the plane trees reasserts itself, the *boules* players take up where they left off, and the mongrel population starts barking again.

As the Chevaliers' song has it:
C'est la grandeur des folies,
L'Omelette de la Confrérie.

And the arithmetic of their treasurer, Monsieur Brousse, is summed up in his own words: *Amitié + Folie = Réussite*.

And as for the quality of the omelette? Elizabeth David was, as always, right.

Soupe de vendredi saint
Good Friday soup

SERVES 4

400g (13oz) chick-peas, soaked for 24 hours

1 litre (1¾ pints) water

60g (2½oz) lard or goose fat

1 large onion, chopped

2 cloves garlic, chopped

2 slices white country bread, cut into cubes

Salt and pepper

Rinse and drain the chick-peas, then cook in salted water for 2 hours, or until tender. Heat half the lard or fat in a frying pan and cook the onion and garlic until soft and just starting to colour. Add to the chick-peas and liquidize in a blender or food processor. Reheat gently and season to taste.

Heat the remaining lard or fat in a frying pan, add the bread cubes and fry until brown and crisp. Serve the croûtons with the soup.

Omelette aux chapons
Fried bread omelette

SERVES 1

1 thick round of bread

1 clove garlic

1 tablespoon lard or goose fat

2 large eggs

Salt and pepper

Cut the crust from the bread, rub both sides with the garlic, then cut into 1.5cm (¾in) cubes. Heat the fat in a frying pan and fry the bread until crisp and golden. Set aside. Season the eggs and beat them very lightly. Make an omelette in the usual way, sprinkle it with the croûtons and roll up to serve.

Omelette géante pascale
Giant Easter omelette

SERVES 5000

Utensils:

1 good-sized dead tree cut into logs 1m (39in) long

1 fork-lift truck

1 cast-iron frying pan, 4m (13ft) wide, fitted with a wooden telegraph-pole for a handle

24 canoe paddles and as many strong men

1 strimmer

12 buckets

Ingredients:

5,000 eggs

5 litres (8¾ pints) sunflower oil

1kg (2lb) each salt and black pepper

Light the bonfire an hour ahead of time, less if it is a windy day. Load the pan on to the truck, drive it to the fire and position on top. Beat the eggs in the usual way, using the strimmer. Pour the oil into the pan when it is really hot and your 24 helpers are ready with their paddles. Tip in the eggs, season, and cook the omelette, stirring with the paddles when the eggs begin to set. Serve as best you can.

Ah! Que C'est Bon

t is half-past seven in the morning on the Thursday before Easter. A clear sky follows a brisk night, during which there has even been a touch of frost. The traders on the *quai* warm their hands with their hot breath, hug their shoulders and are happy to give Monsieur Elissalde's bar their enthusiastic patronage.

It is the first day of the Foire aux Jambons de Bayonne, and the opening moments are vital, because the hams to be displayed must first undergo the official testing without which they cannot be offered for sale. Monsieur Denis Brillant, the local representative of the Association of Butchers and *Charcutiers* explains:

'Using a spiked gadget made of horse bone, we pierce each ham in two places: one near the shin joint, and the other near the head of the femur. If the smell comes up clean and satisfying from the sampler, if the ham smells sweet right through to the bone, then the quality is good. In such a case it is immediately marked as having passed the test. Otherwise, the producer is not allowed to offer the ham for sale.'

Why is everybody so fussed? Quite simply because the hams of Bayonne are the finest produced in France, on a par with the Spanish Serrano hams and the hams of Parma and Westphalia. It is vital that no ham of inferior quality is let loose on the market as a *Véritable Jambon de Bayonne*.

Bayonne ham is no modern discovery: it has been highly prized for centuries. As long ago as the fifteenth century the

Bayonne ham is France's finest, rivalling those of Parma and Serrano. At the Easter ham fair, its excellence is monitored by the Confrérie without whose approval the name Bayonne cannot be used

governor of the Tower of London was sent a load by way of a political thank you. The husband of the wet nurse to Henry of Navarre, later Henri IV of France, is said to have visited his king in Paris and to have been horrified at the absence of Bayonne hams hanging from the beams of the royal kitchens. Back home, no self-respecting farmer was without a few hanging in his living-room: the number was a measure of his success. A ham was in those days said to be the prettiest of all domestic ornaments.

The renown of Bayonne ham is very well-documented: offers of dozens of specimens to royal brides and their grooms are recorded. Festoons of hams were normal in the house of the nineteenth-century gourmand Grimod, who was said to have four dozen at least hanging from his rafters in Paris. Prime Ministers and Presidents, Carnot to Poincaré and back,

This family sells every kind of *charcuterie* as well as ham

have sung the praises of Bayonne ham, and its fame has spread abroad to Francophone outposts in Quebec and the West Indies.

Why are the hams of Bayonne so special, when basically the same methods are used throughout the south-west of France in the production of country hams?

First it is a question of the quality of the pork. A true Bayonne ham must be made from pigs reared in one of three *départements* in the far south-west corner of the country: the Pyrénées-Atlantiques, Hautes-Pyrénées and Gers. In practice, the bulk of the production comes from the neighbourhood of Orthez, St-Jean-Pied-de-Port and the small village of Lahontan, which was once said to produce the finest pigs of all. They are called 'Bayonne' because the port of that city was the main outlet for their distribution.

The best animals are fed exclusively on grain, at least during the final months of their lives. Many are of the special Basque breed that have very dark heads, and are said to produce the most succulent meat of all. Nowadays Jean Chabagno from St-Jean-Pied-de-Port seems to be the most highly regarded breeder. His Large Whites win all the local awards, and

are highly prized by important dealers such as Montauzet and Ospital.

The excellence of the meat cannot be the sole reason for the fame of Bayonne ham. The next secret is the salting. The ham-maker has bought his meat and is about to start preparing the hams. He must now acquire some special salt made in Salies-de-Béarn, where there is a huge underground saltwater spring, which yields rock salt of an incomparable whiteness and purity. There is no question of its being refined or adulterated in any way. This salt is rubbed into the surface of the hams over a period of three days, continuous and repetitious work which is extremely exhausting. The amount of salt required, and the extent to which the meat is made to absorb it, is vital to the finished product. The skill and experience of each ham-maker is what tells at this stage. There seems to be no formula or hard and fast rule, rather what one maker described to me as a 'precise empiricism'. Chabagno and the syndicate of *charcutiers* whom he supplies favour minimum salting.

At the end of this preliminary process, the hams are transferred to the *saloirs*, the salting pans where they spend the next few months. The hams are laid on beds of coarse grey salt from the Bayonne area, and are dry-cured in this for at least six months. The industrial processors have means of shortening this period, but always at the expense of quality. The Bayonne ham-makers, unlike others in the south-west, do not use saltpetre which, though it gives a redder colour to the meat, also tends to harden it.

The hams are then washed and peppered. It is important that they are not attacked by insects when they are hung up to mature, so they are rubbed all over with grey pepper, or sometimes the special pepper called the *piment fort d'Espelette*, which we shall meet again in the autumn (see page 164). In the old days the hams were then buried in wood ash and stored in wooden boxes or crates, often wine-crates, but nowadays they are hung up in closely-stitched white cloth bags. The conditions of the drying rooms (*séchoirs*), where the temperature, the humidity and the air pressure all play a part in the perfection of the finished article, are rigorously controlled. Excessive damp, for example, can rot a ham more quickly than anything. The drying period can be anything from four months upwards, depending on size and quality. Large hams of the best kind, which Chabagno and his friends call 'Ibaïona', can be left for up to twelve months or even longer to mature; they come from pigs who have been fed exclusively on cereals for at least nine months.

Although two million hams or more are sold annually in France as Bayonne hams, there are only twenty-five exhibitors at the *foire*, which underlines the fact that many of the so-called Bayonne hams on the market come from large industrialized producers, whose hams may be of respectable quality but cannot be expected to match the standards of the artisan specialists. The latter have established a *Syndicat* for the protection of the Bayonne name, and a *Confrérie* to promote the quality of the authentic original. The hams made by the members of the *Syndicat* are marked *Marque Déposée, Véritable Jambon de Bayonne, étiquette syndicale*. These hams are always going to be expensive, but if you want to taste the real thing, you have no alternative.

The Foire aux Jambons has recently been relocated on a vacant site adjoining the main covered market of Bayonne, beside the fast-flowing river Nive. It takes place in two long, rectangular, green-and-white-striped tents, each of which has a central passageway flanked by the stalls of the ham-merchants. They all come from in or around Bayonne, but I did notice one bold Norman who had come all the way from Lisieux to sell his beautiful *andouilles* and *boudins*.

The exhibitors do not deal just in hams. They are all general *charcutiers* so, as well as the hams adorning the upper reaches of their stalls, with the powdered red Espelette pepper glowing like paprika, they offer an astonishing range of preserved goods. These are among the finest of France in quality and variety: *confits* of duck and goose as you might expect, but also of pork, lambs' tongues, pigs' ears and cheeks; belly of pork boned and rolled and cured like ham; *civets* of *palombes* (the apotheosis of the

Ah! Que c'est bon!

Le jambon de Bayonne!

– the Confrérie about to burst into song

of the ham combines marvellously with the bitter-sweet fruit of the jam.

One of the advantages of the new site for the *foire* is that it merges into the general market complex beyond. The covered *halle* shelters a wonderful display of vegetables *en primeur*, including the freshest asparagus, tiny petits pois and broad beans so young that the beans themselves can hardly be discerned under their rippling pods. Then there are the many fish-stalls, stocked with the most dazzling specimens from the floor of the Atlantic Ocean: octopus, squid and the famous local *chipirons*, as well as the more familiar langoustines, giant prawns, tuna and swordfish.

For the hungry, what better breakfast than the local sandwich, a thick slice of fried ham rolled up in a

pigeon), wild boar, beef and hare; and *saucissons* of duck as well as the more usual pork. Monsieur Estreboou from Monein offers a glass of the dry Jurançon from his native town with this, and very good the partnership is. There are also terrines of rabbit, pheasant, partridge, smoked duck and goose breasts, tins of *ttoro*, the local Basque fish soup (see page 169) and *axoa*, a sort of Basque shepherd's pie made with veal, and of course the Espelette peppers.

Some of the stalls offer cheeses, the small round cows' milk cheese called Iparla, as well as the hard *brebis* cheeses from Iraty and Ossau. Some Pyrenean cheeses are made from a combination of the two kinds of milk. It is useful to know that *brebis* cheese in the Basque country goes under the generic name of Ardi Gasna and is often eaten with the dark cherry jam of the region, or sometimes with quince jam. The hard saltiness

freshly-grilled pancake, well seasoned with pepper? Or how about a ham omelette, again from cooked rather than raw ham? Basque people tend to eat their ham cooked. They particularly like it fried with eggs and a dash of vinegar, a dish which they call *arroltz ta xingar*.

The thirsty are catered for too. As well as the wines of Jurançon, you can buy a glass of wine from the other side of the Pyrenees, or the local but unpronounceable Irouléguy, which nowadays comes in all three colours and is refreshingly delicious alongside the *cuisine du terroir*. Cider too is popular in this corner of France.

The standard of produce at this *foire* is so high that it would be invidious to single out individual *charcutiers* for special mention. However, I cannot help mentioning Yvan Lambure, who gave us so much information on the hams of Bayonne, and kindly regaled us with a mid-morning *casse-croûte* at his covered eating-place adjoining the tents of the *foire*. Yvan, as well as being a stallholder, carries on a thriving business as a *traiteur*, a term which has no exact equivalent outside France: it signifies something between a caterer and a takeaway-seller. On this occasion Yvan had set up a few trestle-tables under cover where he was going to serve quick midday meals.

He asked us to give him an excuse to take a little time off from his stall and have some coffee with him. 'Coffee' turned out to be a most delicious salt cod omelette – a Bayonne equivalent of omelette Arnold Bennett, which we washed down with the pink wine of Irouléguy. Meanwhile, he had rustled up some of his chums for a rousing rendering of the Song of the Confrérie:

Ah! que c'est bon!
Le jambon de Bayonne!
Hip! Hip! Hip! Hooray!
Le jambon de Bayonne!

Even the most commercially-minded Basque *charcutier* cannot let slip the chance to enjoy himself.

Pipérade
Ragout of onions, peppers and tomatoes

SERVES 4

3 tablespoons olive oil

2 onions, chopped

3 red or green peppers, deseeded and cut into rings

500g (1lb 2oz) ripe tomatoes, peeled and roughly chopped

2 or more cloves garlic, finely chopped

1 bay leaf

1 teaspoon fresh thyme, chopped

1 piece fresh, or ½ teaspoon dried *piment d'Espelette*

Salt and pepper

1 teaspoon sugar

4 fairly thin slices jambon de Bayonne

4 eggs, beaten

Heat 2 tablespoons of the oil in a heavy casserole. Add the onions and cook slowly until soft but not coloured. Add the peppers, cover and cook gently for 10 minutes, stirring from time to time. Add all the remaining ingredients except the ham and eggs and mix well. Cook slowly for a further 15 minutes, or until the liquid has almost evaporated.

Heat the remaining oil in a frying pan and fry the ham gently until softened and the fat is translucent.

Meanwhile, add the eggs to the vegetable mixture. Cook gently for 1–2 minutes, stirring well with a wooden spoon, until the eggs are lightly scrambled. They should remain soft and not become granular. Serve immediately with the ham slices, and fresh country bread.

Salade campagnarde
Country salad

PER PERSON

1 tablespoon goose fat or lard

100g (3½oz) jambon de Bayonne (1–2 slices)

Salad leaves in season

Walnut oil dressing

1 egg

Freshly ground pepper

Heat the fat in a frying pan and fry the ham very gently. Toss the salad leaves in the dressing and arrange some on each plate. Lay the ham on top of the salad. Heat the remaining fat in the pan and fry the eggs. Top each salad with the fried egg and season with pepper but no salt.

Cows' Week

F ew large-scale cattle-farmers in the south of France have enough pasture on their farms to provide food for their herds all the year round. Each cow needs a hectare of grass and for the most part the farms in the Midi are relatively small. Furthermore, the grass dries to dust in the summer sun, while in the mountains snow can cover the pastures from October through to late spring.

For the cattle specialist, it is an advantage to have two landholdings: a home farm in the lowlands, and summer pastures in the mountains of the Pyrenees or the Massif Central, where even in the hottest months there is enough rainfall to ensure plentiful grass. This means that in the late spring the cattle have to be transferred to their summer home in the mountains, and in autumn they have to be brought back again to base. This migration is called *transhumance*, which means literally 'change of terrain'.

Cattle require the best-quality pasture, which is why the western hills of the Massif Central are so suitable. In the Cantal the grass lies on the slopes of old extinct volcanoes; it gives a unique flavour to the milk and cheese made from it. Further south in the Aubrac, the subsoil is of basalt rock, which gives a particular *goût du terroir* to the local dairy produce. While the farmers of the Cantal are justly proud of their own famous cheese, and that of its sub-variety, Salers, the Aubrac farmers insist that there is nothing like their own cheese, Laguiole, which is made exclusively from the milk of the Aubrac cattle.

The time-honoured transfer of cattle to and from mountain pastures is known as 'transhumance'; the commune of Aubrac holds a special fête in spring to greet the arrival of the herds

There is indeed a breed of cow called 'Aubrac', which is easily distinguished from the other breeds living on the Massif. It has short but very tough and stocky legs and an almost square head with a short muzzle; the chest is broad, and the back gives the appearance of having been squashed flat; the hide is a delicate café au lait colour, the eyes ringed with darker and then lighter circles. The horns are of medium length, tipped with black points and gently turned. The tail is long and thin.

The breeding of the Aubrac cattle is very much an Aveyronnais speciality, limited to the farms which are within reasonable migration distances from the Aubrac hills. When you consider the logistics of moving up to three hundred head of cattle on foot over distances of up to 200km, you realize that (in the days before lorries were invented) the twice-yearly transhumance took on the character of a folklore ritual; a

celebration of the changing seasons and the hugely different lifestyles which man and beast would enjoy (or suffer) for the next few months. Even the cattle can tell instinctively when the season of transhumance is approaching; if it is delayed they become restive and stop giving milk.

The village of Aubrac is as tiny as the mountain spaces to which it gives a name are vast. The Aubrac hills stretch from the upper valley of the Lot in the south to the gorges of its tributary the Truyère in the north. To the west they shelter the town of Laguiole, famous for its cutlery as well as its cheese, and in the east they look down on the motorway to Paris. They rise to over 1100m above sea-level and 1000m above the rivers into which they drain. Even today this is sparsely-populated country, wild

and desolate at all seasons, but especially in the winter when the *bise*, the bitter north wind, blows and the temperature falls to -6°C (-20°F). In days gone by it was wilder still, the home of brigands and cut-throats. It was so dangerous for travellers that one worthy knight in the Middle Ages constructed a hospice, which is now the parish church of Aubrac and called La Dômerie, as a sanctuary for them. The Aubrac was also one of the last outposts for wolves in France, though a herd of cattle knew how to deal with a lone wolf by surrounding it and killing it with their horns. Even today, a walker in the hills should not allow his dog to get among a herd of Aubrac cows.

Students of the south-west will not be surprised to learn that Aubrac was on the pilgrimage route from Burgundy to

St Jacques de Compostelle, and was also a staging post for soldiers from the court of Aquitaine in Poitiers travelling to St Gilles on the Mediterranean, the port of embarkation for the Holy Land. It was considered a sufficiently important crossroads for the invading English in the Hundred Years War to make it one of their outposts; the so-called Tour des Anglais stands beside the church, almost dwarfing it, as a reminder.

With the end of the wars and Crusades, and the decline in the pilgrimage to St Jacques, Aubrac lapsed into obscurity; until the end of the eighteenth century it was home to huge flocks of sheep which did much to deforest the area. Cattle took over from the sheep and the teams which looked after them from May to October built primitive mountain quarters called *burons*, or in the local patois *mazucs*, which served as a summer home and as a dairy, with cheese made under the same roof from the cows' milk. These single-storey buildings were covered with heavy stone slabs called *lauzes*.

The typical *buron* would contain a small sleeping-area for the men, a larger area where the cheese was made, a sty for one or more pigs which would be fattened on the whey from the cows' milk, and an inner sanctum, well away from

the warmth of the summer sun, where the cheeses would be matured in the dark.

A *buron* would typically service about three hundred cattle. If the farmer had more than this number he would put the surplus out *en pension* with an adjoining owner, paying usually by allowing the neighbour to keep some of the cheese as rent. Conversely, if he did not have enough cattle to exhaust the land, he would take in a neighbour's cows on a similar basis. The quality of pasture in these parts varies considerably. Generally, the higher ground is to be favoured, for though it may contain a high proportion of virtually bare rock and drains more quickly in summer, the grass is better. Lower down there tend to be peat bogs called *vergnes*; but these do have the advantage of remaining moist throughout the year. The landholdings are called hereabouts *montagnes*, which is rather confusing.

Today the number of working *burons* has declined almost to the point of extinction. The extremely spartan lifestyle is not attractive to modern farm-workers. Furthermore work in the *buron* was guaranteed only for the 140 days of the summer season. There used to be a *foire* at Aubrac at the end of each season at which the *buron*'s employees could offer themselves for the following season; if the owner agreed to take them on, he paid a deposit of five percent of the season's wages by way of guarantee. This still left the winter unprovided for, and most of the *buronniers* were obliged to go to Paris to find work in the bars and cafés, many of which were run by their local countrymen.

The owner-farmer did not direct the operations of the *buron* himself. He normally sent one of his more trusted employees to act as manager. This man was called the *Cantalès*, and at the end of the season he returned to the home farm to resume other duties. It was his responsibility so to manage the *montagne* that there was a rotation of pasturing. In this way the whole area was regularly manured. In particular, he was in charge of dosing the milk with rennet, and salting and maturing the cheese. Responsible to him was the *Bédélier*, whose particular duties were to look after the calves, the rearing of which was just as important to the absentee owner as the amount of cheese produced by the *buron*. The *Bédélier* needed a good memory, because although cow and calf were both branded on arrival at the *montagne* with the same mark so that they could be paired, their coats soon grew and covered up the distinguishing marks. The *Bédélier* had in the meantime to

remember exactly which calves belonged to which cows, so that mother and child could be correctly paired up once milking was completed.

Then there was the *berger*, who was in charge of the milking and the delivery of the milk back to the *buron*. He also helped to make the cheese and looked after the pigs. Finally, a young lad completed the team of four as a general dogsbody-cum-apprentice.

To survive a whole season in a *buron* must have required a particular kind of temperament. The job was relatively well paid, but it would have had to be, and the team of four earned every penny. They had no company but their own; they slept on straw; their diet consisted of a bowl of bread and milk after the morning milking, with any luck sweetened with a little sugar or chocolate which they had to provide themselves; a bowl of soup at ten o'clock after the cheese had been started; sometimes there were also a few potatoes and perhaps a little fat bacon. At two o'clock, before the afternoon milking, they had another bowl of milk and at bedtime a cup of soup. None of the butter or cheese made at the *buron* was consumed on the

You can record this event without leaving the bar

retired *buronnier*. These hermit-like herdsmen were pious church-goers, though. Their prayer to the Virgin ran: 'Keep us in God's name from all harm; from sickness and the storm; and from the wolf with the evil teeth. Give us a good summer, that we may make a little cheese and that the master may be pleased.'

The migration of much of the country population to the towns and the mechanization of farming have all played their part in the decline of the *buron*. Just as important, the relatively small *buron* unit does not have the resources to comply with national and international rules on health and hygiene, although the cheese-makers of the *burons* have always striven as hard as possible for the highest standards in this respect. Modern laws prevent cheese made in the old way from being sold except to private buyers. Many farmers have therefore preferred to pool their resources and have set up a Co-operative, equipped with the latest in modern technology. The milk is collected daily by the Co-operative and the cheese is made and marketed by them. They are careful, however, to simulate as far as possible the old techniques of the *buronniers* and all Laguiole cheese from the Co-operative is still made from unpasteurized milk.

Today, the Commune of Aubrac has officially 40 residents, but the population of the village itself does not reach double figures. Nevertheless, because of its name and historical associations, it is the site chosen by the Laguiole Co-operative and other local sponsors for the fairly new Fête de la Transhumance. Its first year was 1987 and the organizers were both delighted and amazed that they managed to attract 500 visitors. Ten years on, the figure is nearer 30,000 if the weather is fine, which is not always the case – one year it snowed. The fête is timed to coincide with the traditional transhumances which saw the cattle arrive at Aubrac around May 26th, St Urbain's day. By this time the snow on the hills will have melted, giving way to carpets of wild narcissi, golden buttercups and shy violets. Warm clothes are however essential, especially if the *bise* is blowing.

premises, because this would diminish the amount of produce sold, which in turn determined the pay of the *Cantalès*. Twenty-five litres of wine were provided for the *buron*, and this supply was to last the whole season. There was only the occasional treat, such as the Fête de St Jean on Midsummer Day or the Feast of the Assumption on August 15th, when the *Cantalès* himself would take over the cooking and make *aligot*, a delicious speciality of the Massif in which mashed potatoes are softened with cream and plenty of garlic and then mixed with Laguiole cheese in its unfermented form, called *tomme*, (see page 31). On the evenings of those fêtes, the *buronniers* would make for the local village, and their return in the small hours of the morning *n'était jamais triste*, in the words of a

After a well-deserved break, the herds make their way into the mountains for the summer

By nine o'clock in the morning a fair amount of traffic has already found its way up the twisting mountain roads, even coaches. Parking is provided a short distance out of the village, so as to keep traffic out of the main square. Later in the day, there will be so many cars and buses that the hills begin to look like Epsom Downs on Derby Day.

The order of events is simple. From ten-thirty onwards there will be a succession of herds driven at roughly half-hourly intervals into the village to rest and drink, and to be fêted and honoured by the Mayor and the local sponsors. Each herd then heads for the hills, rejoining on the way their calves from whom they have been temporarily parted,

and who have been parked nearby. Although the modern transhumance is today carried out in motorized cattle-trucks, all the herds passing through Aubrac on fête day are driven on foot. They vary in numbers from about twenty to seventy, and may represent only part of the herd going to any given *montagne*. Heading each herd is the 'queen', the old lady of the party, elaborately decorated with the *tricolore* or with a horse's tail planted firmly on her forehead. Somewhere in the pack will be a magnificent bull, sumptuously garlanded with flowers and perhaps wearing the flag of Languedoc, a yellow Maltese Cross on a red background. At the back will be a pony and trap, driven by a couple in peasant costume, bringing the luggage required by the *buronniers* for their summer stint in the hills.

Distractions at the fête include a tombola, at which the first prize is an Aubrac cow. More modest prizes include cowbells and cutlery from Laguiole. Two meadows on the edge of the village are laid out with 200 or so stalls, offering local produce. There is Laguiole cheese of course, and also the *aligot* which is made from it; charcuterie of every kind, *saucisse à l'huile* in glass jars, ducks' necks stuffed with foie gras and the local salami-type pork *saucissons*. You can fish for trout in a tank, or buy anything you care to name made of cow-horn – Aubrac cow-horn of course – and an assortment of cowbells will always attract a good crowd. Wonderful strawberries and cherries remind you that in the Lot valley they grow the finest in France.

Honey is much prized in the mountains, so much so that the bee-keepers practise a kind of transhumance of their own, carrying their hives from one flower-supply to another, depending on the progress of the season: acacia to lime-blossom to chestnuts, and so on. The technique is to load the hives on to a lorry with its engine running. The engine is then revved up and this apparently sends the bees to sleep, so that they can be handled more easily on arrival at their next resting-place. Honey was highly valued in the old days because it was a substitute for sugar, which was expensive and highly taxed. Its purveyors today will also sell you flower pollen in jars (good for the prostate, I was assured) and a wine called Hydromel which comes in a dry form as well as sweet, and which makes a rather good aperitif, sharpened with lemon zest.

The word 'apéritif' is like a bell tolling for lunch, which can be had on a plastic tray, sitting down in a huge tent. You would do better à la carte off the stalls. How about some *farsou*, a savoury pancake stuffed with spring onions, chard, and any available herbs? Or some hot sausages, real sausages made from 100 percent pork? There are plenty of wine stalls too: Philippe Teulier displaying his delicious local red Marcillac; or there is Monsieur Forveille's red Entraygues, another local

Making *aligot* – the apotheosis of potatoes and the good cheese of Laguiole

wine; or a range of Gaillac wines offered by a group of producers from that region; or some wines from Gascony, which have travelled further even than the cows.

While you eat and drink you can enjoy music and dancing from a group called 'La Bourriou del Castel' hailing from Sévérac-le-Château. The programme will likely as not include a dance for four men with canes instead of swords, and a noisy stamping sort of dance which was said to have been performed in the fields at harvest-time to clear the quails from the path of the harvesters' scythes.

By this time the crowd has grown to enormous proportions and it becomes difficult to move easily in the main street. As one bystander put it: *Il y a vachement beaucoup de monde ici.* You should nevertheless make a point of securing a ring-side place for the arrival in the square of at least one of the herds. Perhaps you will be lucky, and have the benefit of a patois song describing life in the *burons* from old Monsieur Capou, one of the herdsmen. Someone complained to Monsieur Capou that she could not hear the words, and he promised to get another set of teeth before next year.

This fête has managed to rescue the traditions of the old transhumances from the edge of oblivion. It works so well because it does not just reproduce the trappings of folklore, but conveys the message which is still within the memories of so many people present. At a time when there are just three working *burons* on the Aubrac and seven in the whole of Cantal, is it too much to hope that just one or two people at this fête might be inspired to try their hand at *buron* life?

Lou Farsou
Spring pancake

'To be made when the first dandelions appear and when the hens start to lay again.'

Marie Rouanet in *Appolonie* (Plon 1980)

SERVES 4

150g (5oz) salt belly of pork, cut into small cubes

2 tablespoons goose or duck fat

2 tablespoons each parsley, chard, dandelion leaves and spinach, chopped

2 cloves garlic, finely chopped

2 cabbage leaves, finely chopped

150ml (¼ pint) milk

3 eggs

50g (2oz) flour

2 tablespoons breadcrumbs

Pepper and a little salt

Fry the pork in 1 tablespoon of the fat until golden.

Combine the greens, garlic and cabbage with the milk and eggs, beat well 'with the energy of springtime', add the flour, breadcrumbs and seasoning, and mix together. Add the pork and its pan juices.

Heat the remaining tablespoon of goose fat in a 20cm (8in) frying pan, tip in the mixture and cook over a medium heat for about 4 minutes. It must cook through but not be allowed to burn. Loosen the pancake with a palette knife and slip it out on to a plate. Turn it over on to another plate, then slide it back into the frying pan and cook for a few minutes on the other side.

Aligot
Purée of potato and mountain cheese

SERVES 4

700g (1½lb) floury potatoes

60g (2½oz) butter

4 tablespoons double cream

4 tablespoons milk

2–3 cloves garlic, chopped

Salt and pepper

250g (9oz) *tomme fraîche de* Laguiole or Cantal, thinly sliced

Boil or steam the potatoes in their skins and peel them. Mash them as finely as possible to a smooth purée in the pan.

Over a low heat beat in first the butter, then the cream and milk, and keep beating until the mixture is really light – this will take time and effort. Stir in the garlic and seasoning, and when the purée seems heated through, drop in the cheese all at once. Continue beating and lifting the mixture as if you were adding egg whites to a soufflé. The cheese has to melt. At a certain point the purée becomes a little tacky and shiny, and comes away from the sides of the pan in an almost pouring consistency. The *aligot* is then ready, and should be eaten immediately.

Blessed Are the Winemakers

Every Whit Monday St Bourrou is fêted. Impossible, you will say. Saints' days are fixed and Whitsun falls on a different day from year to year. Ah, but the difference between St Bourrou and all the other saints is that he never existed. He is an imaginary patron saint of the winegrowers of Marcillac. *Bourrou* is the Occitan word for *bourgeon*, the new shoot of the vine. In this part of the world, the hill country of the northern Rouergue not far from the famous Abbey of Conques, the winters can be hard and long, and the reappearance of growth on the vines each spring is indeed something to give thanks to God for. St Bourrou had to be invented for the occasion.

There is nothing irreverent about this fête; it is more genuinely religious in feel than many another celebration where the Mass has become a mere overture to just another day's jollification. The essence of the St Bourrou fête is simplicity, genuine gratitude to God for the newly-sprouting vines and a rural, almost archaic lack of the modern trappings of stage production. St Bourrou is a creation by the people of Marcillac for the people of Marcillac. It is not a promotional event. Not one bottle of wine is sold. It is a village party.

Few people – even today, when travel and communication are so easy – know Marcillac, either the wine or the place. It is the centre of a remarkable area of the Rouergue called Le Vallon, a miniature river system rising in the limestone *causses* behind the city of Rodez and running north-west

On Whit Monday the Fête of St Bourrou in the Rouergue celebrates the burgeoning spring growth of the vines of Marcillac and serves as a reminder to the children of their duty to the vineyards

into the river Lot. Whether you approach from the dusty chalky *causses* to the east or the comparatively lush parkland to the west, the discovery of the canyons of the Vallon comes as a breathtaking surprise. To left and right, and into the distance as far as the eye can see, the steep green of the hillsides and the occasional parcels of terraced vines clinging to them contrast vividly with the rich purply red soil from which the name 'Rouergue' derives – it means red earth.

Marcillac town lies in a bowl. It has given its name to the wine of the area, which nowadays enjoys full *Appellation Contrôlée* status. Its character and flavour may well come as a surprise, reminding you in a way which no other wine in the world can of red- and blackcurrants, freshly crushed. It is made entirely from one grape variety which is found nowhere but in the south-west of France. This grape is usually known as *fer*, or

fer servadou, but in Marcillac it is called *mansois* after its Occitan name *saumencès*. The grape is part of the composition of many wines in the south-west, but Marcillac is a 100 percent *mansois* varietal wine. It is the pride and joy of the Marcillac *vignerons*. It forms the basis of the 'Ten Commandments' which are laid down by the local Confrérie des Vignerons, and which new members pledge to uphold when they are enthroned at the St Bourrou fête. For example:

> *Thou shalt swear faith to the mansois grape, and equally to our local gastronomy;*
> *Thou shalt set aside Sunday for tasting our wine, and every other day as well, naturally.*

Pride in the local wine is the more remarkable because thirty years ago it was nearly forgotten. Almost wiped out by the diseases of the nineteenth century which destroyed all the vines of the south, Marcillac lost out in the general revival of the 1950s because its traditional market, the industrial areas of Decazeville and the coal-mines nearby, had fallen on hard times and were eventually shut down. Marcillac made its comeback much later. Even today, production is but a fraction of what it was in the heyday of the nineteenth century, when every available square metre of the local hillsides was terraced

and planted with vines. Nevertheless, the vine is virtually the only crop which really succeeds in the difficult terrain of the Vallon, hence the fanatical devotion of the local population to the small but vitally important wine industry. For the inhabitants of the Vallon, the Fête de St Bourrou is an act of faith in their future.

This is why so many of the local children, sons and daughters of the local growers, are involved in all stages of the fête, right from early morning when the procession begins to form in the narrow streets of the small town. A single grower symbolically leads five children, all in traditional local costume, with two musicians, an accordionist and a player of the *cabrette*. These are followed by about forty youngsters, the larger teenagers leading until the last of them are pairs of boys and girls perhaps five years old. The lads are dressed in black *Auvergnat* hats with red kerchiefs, black jackets, blue jeans and trainers; the girls wear straw bonnets, tied firmly with black ribbons under the chin to prevent their being blown away in the breeze, and decorated with flowers.

Following in the procession are tractors decorated with vines, pulling decorated carts in which sit old-style *vignerons*, everyone's idea of what a winegrower must have looked like in the days when all the work in the vineyards was done by hand, and the grapes were trodden by feet after being carried back to the presses in huge baskets. These were worn on the necks of the pickers like the yokes of oxen; the steeply terraced vineyards did not permit the passage of carts.

The procession is accompanied throughout by growers wearing sprigs of vines in their buttonholes, the rear being brought up by a cart bearing an outsize papier-mâché bottle with the all-important legend MARCILLAC AOC. On the cart is perched an unbelievably pretty six-year-old who smiles and waves to everybody along the way.

Finally comes the soberly clad brass band, boys and girls in black jackets and grey flannels, playing remarkably well in tune, except for one performer on the euphonium who has lost his sheet music somewhere along the street.

There is a pause in a side-street before setting off down the main thoroughfare of Marcillac, while a girl who has accidentally emptied her basket of flowers on to the ground is detached from the procession and escorted away in tears. Watching and applauding bystanders fall in behind, swelling the numbers until there could be a full two thousand following the parade up a steep hillside towards the tiny church of Notre Dame de Fontcourieu.

The church is also called by the locals Notre Dame des Bourgeons. It is small and pretty, built in the red sandstone so typical of the region and set on a green slope surrounded by walnut

While the procession moves through the town, one float-driver snatches a sly chance for refreshment

and plum trees. Its porch gives on to a wooded glade, and through the surrounding greenery there are flashing glimpses of the sunlit valley beyond. An altar is laid out in the shade and the pews brought out of the church for the crowd to take part in an open-air mass of thanksgiving for the new grape season. The brass band and a choir stand by the church door while the members of the Confrérie des Vins du Vallon take up position at the other end of the glade. The local brigade of gendarmerie is in close attendance. The altar, dressed with vines, is flanked by the banners of the Confrérie, and two *fouaces*, a local version of

hearth-cake, are close by with bottles of the local wine, to symbolize the elements of the sacraments. The children have been allotted their own space beside the altar.

The band, fortified by a large percussion department including two kettle-drums and glistening music-stands, strikes up the 1812 Overture, without the benefit of a cannon but well-rehearsed and enthusiastic all the same.

The service is an informal affair, though at least seven priests may be in attendance. The Prior of the church takes charge; he is quite a show-man and conducts the proceedings with aplomb as well as a patent sincerity. His sermon may be based on the parable of the fig tree or on the miracle at Cana in Galilee. '*Dieu laboure le coeur, l'homme travaille la terre,*' he says, and calls St Bourrou '*la fête des fruits nouveaux; avec Dieu il y a toujours la possibilité d'une vie nouvelle.*' The crowd is respectful but muted, and the women sing their responses much more lustily than the men, some of whom, including members of the Confrérie, remain adamantly silent throughout. Holy Communion follows, but not before the Prior turns to the choir of children and impresses upon them their importance as the *vignerons* of the next generation.

The thanksgiving mass is conducted under the shade of walnut and plum trees outside the small church

The 'going out' music is the theme from Exodus, spiritedly rendered on the massed saxophones of the Vallon. One might expect everybody to go back to town the way they have come, because apéritif hour approaches. Instead, they file on up the hillside along the narrow lane which continues beyond the church, past flanking elderflower trees, and meadows full of purple vetch where the hay has not yet been taken. Their destination turns out to be a grass plateau with space enough

for all to circulate. Here a temporary platform is constructed for the speeches of the dignitaries and the *intronisations* of new members of the Confrérie.

The crowd is welcomed by the Grand Maître of the Confrérie. It is time for the ceremony. The Grand Maître demands trumpets, and sure enough trumpets sound, the kind you see in medieval paintings: no valves and plenty of uncertainties, but courageously handled by two musicians dressed up as *confrères*. The Grand Maître then calls up the drums, and two rotund and senior *confrères* beat passionately on a pair of tambours.

Now for the *intronisations*. Five local notables, all of whom have had a hand in the organization of the event so far, have been selected and are invited on to the podium. The Ten Commandments of the Confrérie are solemnly intoned and the five worthies solemnly promise compliance.

The formalities are over and it is now time for the *vin d'honneur*. The members of the Confrérie circulate among their friends in the crowd. They are easy to pick out in their regalia, a brilliant scarlet cloak with a green neck-band and mauve cuffs, topped with a soft red hat with mauve trimmings. Round their necks they wear the inevitable *tastevin* on a green and mauve band. One of them is André Metge, who has run the local Co-operative of growers since its beginning in 1968. The members are responsible for the production of about two-thirds of all Marcillac made, and are the generous providers of the wine offered to all present. There is more music and folk-dancing on the podium, which includes a demonstration of the *bourrée* by some local tinies. The girls, slightly older than the boys, drag their small partners through the steps. The boys shuffle hesitantly, not always in time to the music, but their enthusiasm is obvious. Meanwhile the crowd is enlarged still further by the descent out of a vivid blue sky of a party of hang-gliders who have dropped in for a quick glass – the Aveyron's own flying winemakers perhaps.

Monsieur Metge's good wine shows no sign of running out, so there is time to meet some of the independent growers: Philippe Teulier, for example, whom many would describe as the *locomotive* of the wines of Marcillac. Philippe's innovative techniques include spraying his vines by helicopter, a time-and-labour-saving idea in an area where the vines are grown on terraced slopes which even mountain goats might find hard to negotiate. Then there is Philippe's close friend, colleague and rival, Jean-Luc Matha, swashbuckling and moustachioed.

These two men and Pierre Lacombe are the only three independent winemakers of Marcillac who cultivate their vines as a monoculture. All the dozen or so other producers grow other crops as well, or have other sources of income. Jean-Marie Revel, for example, keeps sheep whose milk he sends to the cheese-makers of Roquefort, while Francis Costes is a successful potter when he is not tending his vines.

The built-in clocks which all Frenchmen keep in their stomachs now remind them that the magic hour of *midi* has already passed and, since there is no solid sustenance to be had on that pleasant hillside other than a piece of *fouace*, it is time to go back into Marcillac in search of more substantial fare. Gradually the trek downhill starts to gather pace, and everyone disperses to their homes or to the bars and restaurants of the town, already full to bursting-point. A lively *bourrée*, performed in the main street by a folk-dancing group, seems to mark the end of the old-style festivites. Soon the modern fête will take over, plastic, noisy and soulless.

Still, there is always the Fête des Vendanges in October to look forward to . . .

Santé!

Lapin aux herbes
Rabbit stuffed with fresh herbs

Stuff the rabbit with an enormous bunch of fresh herbs – as many of those listed as you can lay your hands on.

SERVES 4

1 rabbit, about 1kg (2¼lb)

Salt and pepper

1 large bunch of fresh herbs, such as thyme, parsley, basil, sage, mint, tarragon, rosemary, chervil, marjoram, savory

3 onions, finely sliced

3 tomatoes, peeled and sliced

3 thin slices belly of pork

2–4 tablespoons water or stock

2 tablespoons double cream

Preheat the oven to 220°C, 425°F, gas mark 7. Season the rabbit inside and out and place the herbs inside. Put the rabbit in a roasting tin and cover with the sliced onions and tomatoes. Lay the slices of pork on top. Season again.

Pour a little water or stock into the bottom of the tin and roast for 45 minutes. Reduce the heat to 180°C, 350°F, gas mark 4, and continue roasting for another 45 minutes. Baste from time to time, adding a little more water or stock if necessary.

At the end of the cooking time, remove the herbs, and place the rabbit on the slices of pork in a heated serving dish. Arrange the onions and tomatoes round the dish. Pour the cream into the roasting tin, scrape up the bits off the bottom and mix together to form a sauce. Pour it over the rabbit.

Serve with new potatoes, sautéed until golden, adding a little chopped garlic just before serving.

Fricot des barques
Boatmen's beef

This recipe is from Erick Vedel. It is a dish that was greatly enjoyed in local taverns by nineteenth-century bargees working on the Rhône, after perhaps a return trip from Avignon to Lyon, which could take up to three weeks each way.

SERVES 4

1 large onion, finely chopped

1 large bunch flat-leaf parsley, stalks included, chopped

3 anchovies *au sel* (6 fillets), rinsed and chopped

2 tablespoons capers, chopped

2 bay leaves

900g (2lb) boned gîte de boeuf (topside or leg of beef)

Salt and pepper

2 tablespoons olive oil

Preheat the oven to 150°C, 300°F, gas mark 2.

Mix together the onions, parsley, anchovies and capers and crumble in the bay leaves.

Trim the meat and cut it into slices 2cm (¾in) thick. Season lightly. Coat the bottom of a casserole with the oil, and place a layer of beef on it. Spread some of the onion and herb mixture on top, then add another layer of beef followed by another covering of the onion mixture. No liquid is required – this dish makes its own juices.

Cover the casserole and cook for 1 hour. Reduce the heat to 140°C, 275°F, gas mark 1 and cook for another hour. Baste the meat with the juices and continue cooking slowly for up to another hour, or until the beef is tender.

Grand Vin

'Alléluia! St Emilion! A-LLE-LU-IA!' The voice of Alain Querre rings out through the loudspeakers over the sun-bleached roofs of the small but important town. He is standing on the top of the medieval Tour du Roy, with his colleagues from the Jurade of St Emilion, waving to the crowds. The words of his stirring speech riccochet against the ramparts of the town, which glow like gold in the late afternoon sun.

This is the climax of the Fête du Printemps which is held in the middle of June each year to proclaim the quality of the wines of the previous vintage, and to celebrate the safe flowering of the vines for the harvest to come. Alain Querre is the *Procureur Syndic*, the public voice, if you like, of the Jurade of St Emilion, an association of wine-growers devoted to maintaining and improving the quality of their wines, and to spreading their fame throughout the wine-drinking world.

The Jurade takes enormous pride in its antiquity. Its foundation goes back eight hundred years, to the time when Eleanor of Aquitaine married Henry Plantagenet, thereby annexing the West of France to the English crown. This made Eleanor the most powerful English queen since Boadicea.

Her second son John has had a raw deal from the historians. His father had learned how to reward loyalty, especially from those living close to the war-torn interface with the subjects of the French King. He had already promised the people of St Emilion a large degree of autonomy in return for their

support, and in 1199 John Lackland granted St Emilion the so-called 'Falaise Charter', confirming the right of the townsmen of St Emilion 'to hold in full ownership a Commune with all the liberties and free customs, and the power to administer it through magistrates and Jurats elected by and among themselves'. This was the origin of the Jurade, who were given charge of the commercial interests of the community.

Their powers were later extended by Edward I in 1289. Short of being able to mint their own money and of having the right to administer the death penalty, the Jurade of St Emilion were able to govern their little town entirely as they pleased.

The wines are today world-famous, ranking with the finest you can buy. Even in the Middle Ages, St Emilion, unlike the

At the annual Fête du Printemps the

800-year-old Jurade de St Emilion

celebrates the world-famous local wines

with pomp and circumstance

rest of Bordeaux, was producing highly-prized wine. As legislators and administrators it would have been surprising if the Jurade had not spent much of their time on their principal crop, wine. Composed almost entirely of wine-makers, it enforced a rigorous policy of quality control. The barrels of wine had to bear the city arms, which could be applied only with the blessing of the Jurade; they determined when the harvest should begin, curbed the sale of inferior wine and punished abuse and fraud. All stages of the making and maturing of the wine were supervised by the Jurade; they inspected cellars, checked the barrels and it was their chief vintner who himself applied the branded city arms to the barrels, a kind of early *Appellation Contrôlée*. Any wine considered unworthy was destroyed, and the Jurade issued certificates without which wine could not leave the city. This policing enabled them to maintain their pre-eminence over the wines of the rest of Bordeaux into the eighteenth century.

Sadly, come the Revolution of 1789, the Jurade was one of the babies thrown out with the bath-water of the *ancien régime*. The collapse of its authority helped the newly-emerging châteaux of the Médoc to assert a primacy in the market-place which lasted for more than a hundred years. During the last great vintages of the pre-phylloxera era of the 1860s and 1870s, it was the growths across the river which fetched the highest prices, and although Château Cheval Blanc won prizes in Paris which started to put St Emilion back on the map, it was not until after the Second World War that St Emilion, with its

splendid vintages of 1947 and 1949, once more reached the front rank where it had previously belonged.

Nor surely was it chance that St Emilion's renaissance coincided with the revival in 1948 of the old Jurade, not as a body with constitutional powers but as a wine-makers' watchdog and marketing tool. It was re-created by a band of dynamic growers determined to rehabilitate St Emilion. They included Jean Capdemourlin and Alain Querre's father, Daniel, both owners of distinguished châteaux as well as important wine traders in nearby Libourne.

Alain explained to me that, in those seemingly far-off days after the Second World War when he was still a lad, the problem for St Emilion was that, although there were some justly famous wines, there was also a great deal of poor sour stuff being produced in the district. This led to widespread fraud. Alain recounted to me the case of one dealer who bought up a parcel of sour wine produced in St Emilion, and at the same time bought up a parcel of fruity wine from the Midi. Both wines were bought for very little money. The

After mass the procession of the Jurade leaves the church . . .

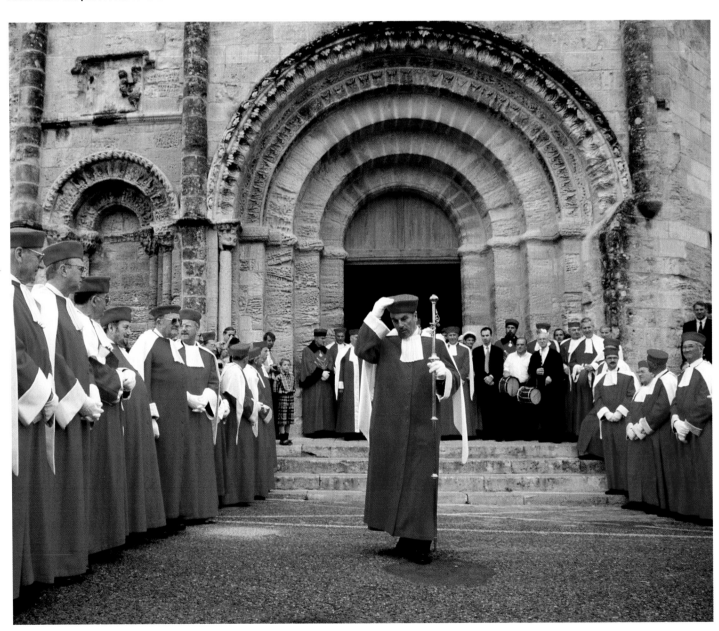

dealer sold off the sour St Emilion to the vinegar makers for next to nothing, as wine from the Midi, but the Midi wine he sold on as St Emilion at full market price. The law could prove nothing: his books were perfectly in order, but for the dealer the profit from being able to sell on one of his wines at St Emilion prices was substantial.

Alain's father, Daniel Querre, came to the conclusion that there was only one way to halt this kind of practice, and that was to stop the production of bad wine in St Emilion, so that all wine produced there would be worthy of sale under the name. 'If your meat isn't rotten, it doesn't attract the flies,' Alain explained.

. . . for the Cloisters, where new members will be sworn in

It was clear that this would involve the re-imposition of some kind of discipline among growers, the kind of control which was exercised in the old days by the medieval Jurade. It would also involve established growers in submitting their wines to the kind of test which might suggest that their wines were not necessarily as good as they were cracked up to be. The Querre and Capdemourlin families were gradually able to persuade such local notables as the Abbé Bergey, the local priest and Member of Parliament, and Monsieur Dubois-Challon, part-owner of Château Ausone, to join forces and draw up a code of conduct for all wine-growers. Not surprisingly, the old Jurade was chosen as the ideal medium to persuade a naturally conservative wine fraternity to join in the plan. So it was that the old Jurade was revived. Having established the rules, the new Jurade, though having no legal jurisdiction, asked the Government organization which polices the *Appellation Contrôlée* system to give the new rules legal effect and to enforce them. The Jurade levied a tax on the growers to pay for this, and also to enable young *vignerons* to go to wine-school at Talence in Bordeaux.

The position of the modern Jurade is curious in some respects because it has no statutory or official function. Alain Querre stresses the importance of its relationship with the Syndicat Viticole de St Emilion. The Jurade acts rather like a roving promoter for the Syndicat and its members. It plays an important archival and promotional role. It has branches, supporters' clubs, in Great Britain, Belgium and the United States – three of its principal export markets.

The pageantry of the Fête du Printemps begins at ten o'clock on Sunday morning at the Maison Guadet, a rendezvous just outside the town's ramparts where the Jurats don their ceremonial robes, heavy scarlet cloaks with white capes, cuffs and gloves. Preceded by a brass band in medieval costume, they process towards the Eglise Collégiale where there is already a good crowd waiting to enjoy the spectacle and go into Mass. The Jurade is often joined by representatives of other wine-confréries, from Ste-Croix-du-Mont, whose primrose-yellow costumes contrast vividly with the scarlet of the home team; or the Côtes de Blaye, in sombre black, just touched off here and there with red, and a gold braid band round their hats; or the brilliant bottle-green of a team from Castillon.

The service is a full-length Mass, with very good singing. The text of the sermon usually manages to relate the local wines to the Glory of God, a combination to which the priests of St Emilion are well-accustomed. One year, the English contingent included an Anglican vicar, who was allowed as a special dispensation to give the sermon in English. It was not until afterwards that he confessed to me how difficult it had been for him to follow his notes, scribbled late the previous evening on the back of that day's tasting sheet.

After the long service, most of the celebrants are glad to get back out into the sunshine, where they and the Jurade are welcomed by flute and tambours. The Jurats make their way to the Cloisters behind the church, where the *intronisations* are made. This part of the ceremonial used to take place in the town's famous underground monolithic church, carved entirely out of the rock, but this church will be closed for some while to enable substantial repairs to be made.

The town is not short of other suitable locations for pageantry. The Cloisters are ideal for the *intronisations*, not as romantic perhaps as by candlelight below ground, but the sight-lines are a great deal better and everyone can enjoy the spectacle. Visitors can appreciate the cloistered shade while the Jurade and their distinguished visitors sweat it out beneath a canopy in the centre of the garden.

By the time fifty or more volunteers have pledged eternal support for the wines of St Emilion, everyone is ready to taste some. The cafés and bars are not unprepared, while the Jurats, their guests, the overseas teams and the newly-enthroned worthies repair for lunch to the recently restored Salle des Dominicains, a splendid banqueting hall. Aperitifs are taken in its charming garden, which backs on to the vineyards of Château Villemaurine. A short fanfare from the band urges everyone inside for lunch, a formidable repast always

The wines of St Emilion are serious business – until it is time to enjoy them at the Salle des Dominicains

consisting of at least five courses and giving the chance to taste a dozen or so top-class St Emilion wines.

Once this feast is over, the prudent will take the chance to walk off some of its effects before the Jurade processes to the Tour du Roy, an imposing donjon on the west side of the town, from the top of which the Jurats can be seen by all. As Alain Querre reaches the climax of his speech, paying tribute to the founding fathers of St Emilion in 1199 and to those whose efforts have revived and sustained it in recent years, the assembled Jurats greet the acclamation of the crowd and a flight of doves is released into the blue afternoon sky. The Fête du Printemps is suddenly over.

Lotte au vin rouge de St Emilion
Monkfish in a red wine sauce

SERVES 4

2 tablespoons olive oil

12 pickling onions

2 teaspoons sugar

150g (5oz) salt belly of pork, diced

2 large onions, sliced

4 cloves garlic, finely chopped

3 shallots, chopped

Salt and pepper

Pinch of cayenne

Pinch of quatre-épices

Bouquet garni including fennel leaves

1 bottle St Emilion or other good red wine

4 tablespoons flour

25g (1oz) butter

250g (9oz) cèpes or other mushrooms, sliced

2 monkfish tails, weighing 400g (13oz) each, boned and cut into
  2.5cm (1in) cubes

Croûtons of fried bread or puff pastry fleurons (optional)

Heat the oil in a pan, add the pickling onions and cook slowly for 20 minutes, sprinkling with the sugar halfway through, so that they take on a little colour. Then add the pork, sliced onions, garlic, shallots, seasonings and bouquet garni.

Heat the wine in another pan. Make a roux with the flour and butter and gradually add the wine, stirring until smooth. Add this to the other pan and cook for 20 minutes. Add the mushrooms and monkfish. Season, cover and cook over gentle heat for a further 25 minutes. Remove the bouquet garni and serve garnished with croûtons or pastry fleurons.

Macarons de St Emilion
Almond biscuits

MAKES 20–24

110g (4oz) ground almonds

200g (7oz) vanilla sugar

3 tablespoons sweet white wine

White of 1 large egg

Granulated sugar

In a non-stick pan, mix the almonds and vanilla sugar together and stir in the wine. Heat this paste until the sugar has melted, stirring continuously. Leave to cool.

Preheat the oven to 160°C, 325°F, gas mark 3.

Whisk the egg white until it is stiff and gradually mix it into the almond paste.

Cover one or two baking sheets with greaseproof paper. Place teaspoons of the mixture on the sheets, well spaced out. Flatten them gently into neat rounds and sprinkle the tops with a little granulated sugar. Bake for 30 minutes until they are crisp. Cool on a wire rack.

Sheep May Safely Graze

ach year Magali and Jean Lemercier load their 2000 merino ewes and rams into trucks and drive from Le Crau near Arles to the Pont de la Griotte at Die, Magali clad in a full-length waterproof and rubber boots – showers in the mountains can be monsoon-like. This is a twentieth-century transhumance, the ovine counterpart of the migration of cattle which we have seen in the Aubrac. Sheep are still driven up into the mountains in this way all over the southern half of France – to the Pyrenees, the Cevennes and the Alps.

In former times, the journey was made on foot and took several days, the farmer having to negotiate stopovers in advance, where the sheep could rest and feed. Today, the journey as far as Die takes some four hours, plus an hour to load and unload at each end, but how, except by truck, would Magali and Jean be able to shepherd all these animals to avoid motorways and railway-lines, or to keep them from invading lovingly-manicured gardens along the way?

Die, however, is not the end of the journey, for this attractive ancient town lies in the valley of the river Drôme, and the final destination of the Lemercier flocks is in the mountains of the Vercors, a day and a half's journey to the pastures some 1000m above the town. Die is hemmed in by mountains. There are no other bridges across the river for many miles upstream or downstream, so Die has been a traditional halting-place for the transhumance for many years. Its historical association with the sheep migration is celebrated round the third week in June.

Sheep are taken from the scorched plains of Provence into the Alps for the summer; some flocks are driven through the streets of Die, providing an excuse for a week-long fête

A week-long fête seeks to tie in various aspects of Mediterranean culture, and to establish Die's links with Provence as well as the mountains. It is run by an organization called simply *Drailles*, the old word for the tracks habitually taken by the migrating sheep. It offers poetry readings in the Provençal language, exhibitions and, above all, music of all kinds. You can choose between Mussorgsky on the piano, a group called 'Jazz Rock Trad' and a cross-over style called Rap-Provence, performed by 'Los Trobadors' in the Cathedral. Such cultural events remain strangely peripheral to the transhumance itself, sadly unintegrated with it. For most people, the transhumance itself is the thing.

But first the sheep must be allowed to feed and rest overnight, to recover from their long cramped journey by lorry. They do not seem to need to be told what to do or where to go – most of the ewes are four years old or so, and need no prompting. Leaping deliriously from their transporters, delighted at their new-found liberty, they race towards the one bridge across the river Drôme, jumping for joy over imaginary obstacles, as if in anticipation of the mountain-top gourmandise to come.

The town of Die is compact. It huddles within its ramparts round its cathedral, which goes back to the eleventh century. The motorist hurrying past will be despatched round the ring-road, and will not realize that the streets are so narrow that in some places you can almost shake hands with your opposite neighbour out of your first-floor window.

A crowd assembles early, lining the narrow streets and leaning out from balconies. The shop doors are firmly shut against possible invasion of the sheep, only the cafés doing such good business as to make all risks acceptable. As all eyes are fixed on the stretch of road leading into town, a juggler on

painful-looking stilts entertains the crowd; local dogs strain at their leads in anticipation of a good nip at lambs' legs; and the gendarmerie eye with more hope than expectation the tapes that are supposed to rope off the sheep from the spectators.

The crowd crane their necks to get the first glimpse of approaching herds. The sheep are scheduled to arrive at eight o'clock, but by a quarter to nine there is no sign of them. Suddenly it seems as if a fawn blanket is gradually drawn over the road beneath the shady avenue of plane trees. It is of course the sheep, and as they get nearer, their bobbing heads and shoulders suggest a field of corn being blown in the mistral. In front can be made out the figure of Jean Lemercier. The procession, piped into town by a rustic band, slows perceptibly as it approaches to enthusiastic applause.

The rams wear bells: the larger the bell, the more senior the ram, age also being distinguished by the one, two or three tufts left unshorn on their backs. Accompanying the sheep are a few donkeys, brought along by one of the farmers 'for company; there was a bit of space in one of the lorries'. There is also a splendid white horse for the use of the shepherd in the mountains, and a few goats which will keep him supplied with milk and cheese through the long summer days.

Now the street seems to be a sea of sheep and humans. The people are mixed up in the flock, sometimes trying to get to the front, sometimes following behind, chatting to Magali who brings up the rear with a trio of sheepdogs. The clanging of the sheep-bells, the yapping of frustrated lapdogs and the applause of the bystanders bounce off the walls of the old stone houses, as the snake-like file of ewes, goats and rams makes its way as far as the old west gate. At this point the procession is almost as long as the street itself, about five hundred metres. At the end of it, a difficult left wheel, almost an about-turn, leads the party back to the market-place where the street widens out and allows plenty of people a good view. Round trot the sheep to the north of the cathedral, where the cafés are doing wonderful business. The street narrows again and the ancient

"Not far to go now"

rue de l'Armillière leads back to the east, near to where the animals entered the town. They do not leave by the same road, but slip down a precipitous side street through the old east gate. This is a solid medieval fort, flanked by two massive circular stone towers and pierced by a narrow archway.

The transhumance procession now heads for open country. North from Die the suburbs do not stretch far towards the mountains. This is just as well, because it needs the permanent vigilance of the skilled dogs to prevent their charges from demolishing in five minutes a year's loving work by a rose-enthusiast who has left his front gate open. The dogs are so busy looking after the sheep that they fail to spot one of the donkeys making short work of a local farmer's Jerusalem artichokes.

A good metalled road leads from Die to the village of Romeyer, past plantations of walnut trees which provide an important local crop. There are many orchards, and immaculately hoed vegetable gardens; lime trees too, not the kind that drop sticky nectar but the more graceful variety whose voluptuous perfume is such a pleasure on midsummer evenings. As the sheep pass through a rocky defile, the goats form a group of their own, snobbishly keeping to themselves and not mixing with the sheep. The bells of the rams suddenly take on an added reverberance, and the echoing shouts of the herdsmen, bouncing off the rocks, suggest that the open spaces of the high mountains are not far away.

The road is good but the scenery is getting more rugged

They are though, and the party must stop for lunch, a field having been booked for the purpose at the hamlet of Les Planeaux. Plenty of enthusiasts have followed the flocks, and some have brought picnics. The horse snorts his disapproval of so many townies pretending to be countrymen, and the boldest of the donkeys soon learns to cadge from the children.

From here there will be one more overnight stop on the way to the mountain tops. The walnut trees give way to beech and ash, cultivated farms to equally cultivated forests. The hillsides are steep, with stunted trees clinging to almost vertical slopes of scree, the mountains topped with pinnacles, sometimes like large fingers pointing into the sky, sometimes like giants' teeth, or a church steeple. Earth and sky draw closer together, and all the time, night and day, rest-periods and journeys alike, the bells jangle without competition except for the occasional mewing of a marauding buzzard.

The last morning sees the arrival of the sheep at their destination, the mountain-top pastures of the National Park of the Vercors beyond the pass called Chabrinel. Here they will stay until the first snows of October, with their one lonely shepherd who will have little or no company during the summer. Magali assured me that he was quite happy in his solitude. He had a well-built *cabane*, and *'tout confort'*; why, he even had drinking water. I asked whether he had family of his own. Magali told me that he was a confirmed bachelor, and when I asked her how he occupied himself during the winter months, she replied with only the shade of a smile: 'I expect he makes up for lost time.' Is this what Proust meant by *temps perdu*?

Carbonade de mouton
Lamb and bean casserole

This recipe is from Erick Vedel.

SERVES 6

1kg (2¼lb) lamb from the shoulder or leg, cut into bite-sized pieces

Salt and pepper

3 tablespoons olive oil

110g (4oz) salt belly of pork, diced

2 onions, quartered

1 tomato, peeled and quartered

4 carrots, halved and cut into lengths

1 small turnip, cut into chunks

1 celery heart, cut into lengths

300g (11oz) white haricot beans, soaked overnight

2 cloves garlic, crushed

3 bay leaves, crumbled

2 cloves

2 pinches freshly grated nutmeg

200g (7oz) black olives

250ml (8fl oz) dry white wine

Preheat the oven to 180°C, 350°F, gas mark 4.

Season the lamb with salt and pepper. Heat the oil in a large ovenproof casserole and brown the pieces of salt pork over a good heat. Add the onion and stir until it begins to colour, then put in the lamb. When it starts to brown, about 5 minutes, add the vegetables, stirring occasionally.

Rinse and drain the beans and stir into the pan with the garlic. Add the bay leaves, cloves, nutmeg and olives. Pour in wine and enough water to cover the meat.

Cover and cook until simmering, about 20 minutes, then check the seasoning and reduce the heat to 140°C, 275°F, gas mark 1. Cook for about 2 hours, or until the meat is tender. Try this with Artichauts Barigoule (see page 116) .

Daube de mouton Issaly

Rich lamb casserole

Madame Issaly is a fine winemaker, and certainly one of the best country cooks of the south-west. This is her recipe. Start preparing this a day and a half ahead of time.

SERVES 4

110g (4oz) salt belly of pork, cut into cubes

A good piece of pork rind (optional)

1 pig's trotter, split in half (optional)

1kg (2¼lb) boned shoulder of lamb or mutton, cut into chunks

1 onion, chopped

2 carrots, chopped

2 tomatoes, chopped

3 large cloves garlic , chopped

½ bottle red wine (Mme Issaly's of course)

2 tablespoons walnut oil

1 bouquet garni

25g (1oz) flour

Salt and pepper

Pinch of quatre-épices

Place the belly of pork in a pan of cold water with the rind and the trotter. Bring slowly to the boil and cook gently for 30 minutes. Drain and discard the water.

Place the lamb in a large shallow dish with the pork, rind and trotter and all the other ingredients. Stir to combine well and leave to marinate for at least 6 hours in a cool place.

Preheat the oven to 180°C/350°F/gas mark 4. Place the lamb, pork, vegetables and marinade in a large casserole. Either the pot must have a concave lid which you can fill with water, or you will need an enamel plate which you can fill with water and use instead of a lid. It must fit tightly. Push all the ingredients well down into the casserole so that they are covered by the liquid. Bring slowly to the boil on top of the stove, then place the casserole in the oven and cover, filling the lid with cold water. After 10 minutes reduce the temperature to the lowest possible and cook for 3 hours, topping up the liquid in the lid from time to time. Remove from the oven and leave to cool.

Next day, remove as much of the fat as possible and discard the pork rind and trotter. Preheat the oven to 180°C/350°F/gas mark 4. Place the casserole in the oven to reheat for 10–15 minutes, then reduce the temperature to the lowest possible and cook for another 3 hours, watching the water level in the lid as before.

Coupo Santo

During the worst times of Christian persecution in ancient Rome there was a Pope called Marcellin, who was martyred at the hands of the Emperor Diocletian. In his ministry there was a humble priest also called Marcellin. He too was canonized, and in the small Provençal village of Boulbon he is a good deal more revered than his illustrious superior. It is said that he was thrown into a deep dungeon, where he fell on some sharp pieces of broken pottery. An angel appeared and picked him off the ground as he clutched a fragment of an amphora which was stained with his blood. He raised it to heaven, offering it to God in pious thanks. A miracle duly supervened and the fragment was transformed into an amphora flowing with wine.

Just to the north of the village of Boulbon, which lies in the valley of the Rhône between Tarascon and Avignon, a small chapel dedicated to the humbler of the two Saints Marcellin can trace its foundation back to the eleventh century. The western façade houses an ancient stone slab of that period, primitively but beautifully carved with the hand of Christ raised to heaven and a sacrificial lamb. The entrance porch is on the southern façade, which was rebuilt in 1175. Six steps lead down inside the chapel, and the altar is to the right as you enter. The church is the proud owner of a famous retable from the fourteenth century, which is in the Louvre. Its north side houses the tomb of the former lord of Boulbon, called Archimbaud. Otherwise the chapel is pure undecorated

Romanesque, its simple porch recalling that of St Guilhem-le-Désert not many miles away to the west.

St Marcellin's association with various liquids has many spin-offs for the parishioners of Boulbon, or so they believe. He can stem the floodwaters of the Rhône, and there are the town records of Tarascon to prove it; he can either bring rain or prevent it falling in excess, and the good wines of Boulbon are said to derive at least in part from the benevolent efforts of the Saint. There is a local adage which runs: *S. Marcellin, bon per l'aigo, bon per lou vin.* ('Good for water and good for wine.') Though Boulbon is no Chambertin, and its name is not likely to be seen on the shelves even of supermarkets, it does produce a great deal of honest plonk on which the locals rely for a living.

It is not known when the inhabitants of the village first asked their priest to bless their wine in the name of St Marcellin. Some say it is an update of an old pagan tradition going back even beyond the Christian era. Certainly the parishioners of Boulbon have celebrated the name-day of the saint for hundreds of years, seeking his blessing on a bottle of their best wine, which they take to the church for that purpose. Afterwards it is returned to pride of place in their homes, and consumed only on the rarest of occasions, when the help of the saint is needed in time of trouble. It must in the meantime oxidize rather horribly.

The modern form of this ceremony has been much developed since the acquisition by the parish of Boulbon of some supposed relics of the saint. First a tooth of his, encased in a carved bust of the saint and kept in the parish church of St Anne, was acquired in 1730 in circumstances which none can now account for, and certainly there is little to guarantee its authenticity. This bust is called *le petit Saint Marcellin* to distinguish it from *le Grand* which is a much over-restored statue standing in the saint's own chapel. The second set of relics are kept in a gilded copper chest. These were acquired direct from the Holy City for a large sum of money in 1882, and thus their genuineness is beyond question.

On June 1st, the village of Boulbon

commemorates its patron saint with a

blessing of wine in the tiny parish

church, each member of the congregation

holding up a bottle to be blessed

St Marcellin's day is on June 2nd, but his blessing on the local wine is sought on the day before. For some unknown reason, it has always been this way. It is in the evening, at seven o'clock and, notably, it is confined to men only. Whether this is also a relic of some previous barbaric age, or whether the locals regard their best wine as something not to be shared with the ladies, is not clear. But traditionally this has been an all-male event, and will continue so until someone gets a rocket from the European Court of Justice.

Until six o'clock on the appointed day the streets of Boulbon are as deserted as they always are. The village shop may have its occasional customer, the parish church its occasional confessant, but mostly it is the dogs and cats of the village, and the swifts that swoop among the buildings, that provide what animation there is. But suddenly a gathering of men starts to form outside the church, each of them carrying a bottle of red wine. Some of the bottles bear a special label announcing *Bourboun*, the Provençal version of the village name. Others are quite obviously plonk from the local shop, while quite a few have come from the *caves* of their owners, filled from the cask and partly corked for the occasion. There are boys of all ages, from toddlers upwards, many equipped with a plastic water bottle containing red wine, for although women will not be admitted to the ceremony, boys can be. The women don't seem to mind; they are quite happy just to come along for the preliminaries and the procession to the chapel.

Soon the little square outside the parish church of St Anne fills with people. They all know each other; this is a very

Women may not take part in the service, but peer in eagerly from the relative cool outside

domestic kind of celebration. There is much kissing by way of greeting (three kisses in this district) and exchange of gossip. Dress is quite informal, no collars or ties, but many caps and berets to give the occasion just a little importance and respect.

The ecclesiastics then arrive. You would imagine the parish priest to be a rubicund, jolly fellow, short, tubby and beaming with *joie de vivre*. The *curé* of Boulbon is quite the opposite: short yes, but thin as a rake, white-haired and really rather unhappy-looking. Fortunately, it is not he who is going to officiate at the ceremony, for with him is a large well-built man with flowing white locks and a bushy beard.

While the crowd waits expectantly outside, the ecclesiastics go into the church. As the church clock chimes seven they emerge, bearing the precious relics of the saint, while an acolyte carries the richly embroidered banner of St Marcellin. They set off up the street in the direction of the chapel, which is about a kilometre away. The crowd falls in behind them, some of the children getting a lift on the backs of their fathers. The walkers are rather silent and respectful. Soon they leave the roadway and take a path which leads up to the chapel, set discreetly among trees at the foot of a rocky hillside.

The first problem is to get everybody inside the chapel, which is relatively tiny – perhaps another reason for excluding women? Through the narrow doorway and down the steep steps into the interior the crowd files, two or three at a time. Once inside they fan out to fill every available space: all round the altar, in the transepts and down the nave of the chapel. The priests are of course by the altar, with the mayor of the village, and surrounded by the cameras and gaffers of the television crews, the whole church lit by powerful arc lamps which soon begin to make the heat inside the chapel almost unbearable.

Then the singing starts. The hymn to St Marcellin has thirteen verses. The first one or two are taken up in unison by a few voices, but as the rest of the audience joins in, the character of the singing changes gradually from that of Gregorian Chant to that of a football crowd in full throat. The music gets slower and slower too, until by the thirteenth verse it is more like a dirge. You might think that everyone had opened and drained their bottles, so drunken does the singing sound. It has a strangely primitive and dramatic enthusiasm, primeval almost in its fanaticism.

Just when voices are getting hoarse, the priest begins. First a little mutual back-slapping by the mayor and himself, and then an address in Provençal, which to the unitiated seems as if it might be about the divine nature of the grape. Although the priest manages to keep his speech fairly short, the shoulders of parents carrying their children so they can get a good view are beginning visibly to ache, sweat pours down the brows of the sardine-like congregation, cameras gradually stop flashing, and everyone clutches their bottles to remind themselves that they have not left them somewhere. Perhaps the women are better off than anybody: outside the chapel they are able to peer in through the windows and get the best view of the strange proceedings inside.

At last the sermon comes to an end, there are a few more choruses of the same old hymn, and then the climax: the priest asks everybody to raise their bottles to him and he then blesses them *en masse*; every man and child uncorks his wine, takes a good swig, and then corks the bottle again. The doors of the chapel are opened, and to more singing of the same old hymn everyone files out into the relative coolness of the evening. It is time to go home to *la soupe*.

Vin cuit

Concentrated sweet red wine

Unfermented juice from freshly-picked grapes

Quinces (optional)

What is today sold commercially as *vin cuit* has little to do with the traditional Provençal version, which contains nothing but pure grape juice and perhaps a few quinces.

Grape juice is drawn off the *vigneron*'s vats before it starts to ferment, and is heated outdoors in a huge cauldron over a wood fire, and skimmed regularly. The quinces may be added if wished. Glowing embers are added to the cauldron at this point to give a smoky flavour. The liquid is simmered till reduced by one third, the fire dies, the cauldron is covered and left to cool overnight.

Next day the juice is filtered off into a barrel which is stored in the cellars where the rest of the *vigneron*'s wines are fermenting. Must from these wines (the juice which still contains fruit and pips) is added, so that the cooked juices are activated by the yeasts. The *vin cuit* is racked several times over a period of a month by which time the fermentation has finished. It is left on its lees for a further two or three months before bottling.

A Vintage Port

The spirits of César, Marius and Fanny, immortal characters from the pen of Marcel Pagnol, live on in the old port at Marseille. Le Bar de la Marine and the many like it clustered round the waterfront have changed no doubt; the number of fish restaurants, some more authentic than others, has proliferated; and the camcorder-bearing Japanese and cigar-smoking cabin-cruiser owners would have caused a few eyebrows to go up in what was once a predominantly working-class *quartier*. But the fish brought in from the warm waters of the Mediterranean have not changed, neither have those who fish them.

Every morning throughout the year the stalls are set up on the Quai des Belges, ready to receive the night's catch. From nine o'clock onwards the fishing boats arrive one by one,

Though it is not the largest fish market

in Marseille, the old port flourishes

because the produce and those who sell it

are more vibrant and colourful than

anywhere else in Provence

threading their complicated way through the luxury yachts and sailing boats which today are the port's main customers. The port is rectangular in shape, the long north side having been substantially rebuilt in the 1950s – it was blown up by the Germans during the war because it was thought to be a warren of resistance fighters. The southern side is largely unchanged, the buildings, some of them centuries old, painted in delicate pastel shades. The short east side, where the market is held, is unremarkable, except that off it leads Marseille's famous main street, La Canebière, which these days is rather dull. Its endless shoe shops remind the footsore visitor of Oxford Street in London.

The old port itself retains a great deal of character. The church of Notre Dame de la Garde tops a steep hillside, facing across the water another up-and-down quarter where the streets are mostly stepped, and so closed to traffic. Down on the quay the atmosphere seems not wholly French: there are overtones of Naples and even Sicily, enough to underline the long history of Marseille as a Phocaean-Greek and then a Roman settlement, between them responsible for importing the olive and the vine to France for the first time.

This transalpine quality is accentuated perhaps by the city's reputation for lawlessness and corruption. For the tourist, this lends a certain *frisson*, though the locals are more realistic, reminding you at every turn to watch your bag or wallet. A waiter told me that the most shocking offenders were the children; the younger they were the worse they were, he said, but perhaps it was always thus in Marseille. The police seem as mistrusted as the criminals. One stallholder, eyeing me and my notebook with some suspicion, asked me point-blank if I was a *flic*, and when I said no, I was a writer, he said jokingly, but no doubt reassured: *'C'est la même.'*

It is hard to believe that this is the same Provence as that found in the country markets inland, though the fish market in the old port is in the same genre. It is not, however, the most important fish market in the town, let alone along the Mediterranean coast, as you might expect in the centre of the third city of France. The biggest markets are at Sète and Martigue, and even in Marseille there is a bigger market on the road to l'Estaque. These markets are principally for the trade, the commercially organized fishing-fleets on the one hand and the important wholesalers on the other. There the boats are more like barges, and the buyers arrive in smart refrigerated container-lorries rather than battered *camionettes*.

Here in the old port business is more intimate, as it must have been in Pagnol's time. Each boat is small, a family affair. They set out for the fishing grounds at two in the morning. It is not a question of dropping your nets and hoping for the best: each of the hundred and forty-six registered fishermen knows the best places for each species, and they will decide in advance what to go fishing for. This in turn determines what

equipment they take with them and what techniques they use to land the fish. This explains why a boat may arrive with a very limited assortment of fish, although overall the market is large enough to offer a complete range.

Typically, the wife of the family will have stayed at home, but it is often she who minds the stall in the market while the men mend the nets and bail out the boat ready for the next night's trip. A fish-wife may have only half a dozen *langoustes* to offer, but what magnificent specimens they will be, their feelers as thick as canes. An old-timer may have nothing but eels and perhaps a few mussels, or the archetypal loud-mouthed vendor may rely on a catch of grey mullet,

Fishing is a family business in the old port. The men

go out with the net and the women do the

marketing. The catch is small, but the quality is

superb. Langoustines do not however come cheap

though she will try to lure tourists into buying one of her *yeux de Ste Lucie* to keep in their purse. These small, beautifully coloured red stones from the sea-bed are reputed to bring luck as well as keep the eyesight sharp. Saint Lucy is the patron saint of good vision, I was assured.

The most striking impression of this market is the variety of fish you have never seen before. Small fry of all shapes and colours for soup, or for deep-frying in oil; a large orange fish called *linette*, with a gaping mouth, the only exhibit of one very large fisherman who cuts thick steaks off it for his customers; tiny fish called *girelles* with green and orange stripes, and not exactly cheap either; huge conger eels, called in Provence *fiélas*; a flattish fish called *sar*, oval and scaly, and weighing up to 2–3 kilos, and its smaller relative the *pageot*, more pearly in colour and a speciality of the port's restaurants; *grondins*, here called *galinettes*, larger than in the north, their needle-like fins even more prickly and their protruding hooded eyes like dormer windows; small mackerel-like fish called *sévérous*; and the expensive *marbré*, with its vertical stripes which make it look as if it has already been on the barbecue; the *vive* with diagonal stripes and a nasty bite, essential though for a true bouillabaisse, as is the ugly John Dory, called *St Pierre* in the south; and perhaps most important the fearsome little *rascasse*, bright vermilion in colour and to be handled with great care, but without which a bouillabaisse is simply not a bouillabaisse.

As well as *langoustes* you will find crabs, and also small spider-crabs called *favouilles*, which make a delicious soup; the prickly sea-urchin, the rubbery sea-snails so soothing when accompanied by the garlic-and-oil emulsion, *aïoli*; and the unprepossessing *violets*, which must be among the ugliest denizens of the sea – once cut open they reveal a creamy-yellow interior like scrambled eggs, highly prized by the local gourmets; mussels of course, but also tiny *tellines*, crustaceans the size of a finger-nail, from the mouth of the river Rhône, which are delicious heated so they open, served sprinkled with a puréed garlic, oil and lemon dressing and some parsley.

There are more familiar fish too; no plaice, halibut or turbot, for these are cold-water fish, but plenty of sea bream (*daurade*) which come in two varieties, one with orange stripes and the other a dullish plain grey; the biggest monkfish you have ever seen, here called *baudroie*, which are just as esteemed for soup-making as their more famous tails are for sophisticated cookery; red mullet, very much a Mediterranean speciality, the smaller ones being called *rougets de roche*, and the full-sized ones *rougets barbus*.

The fishermen and their wives are just as colourful as the produce they have to offer. Usually they look as if not even a force 10 gale would blow them over. I asked one rather lean fisherman how fond he was of fish; he told me that his mother, who had just had her 89th birthday, ate fish without fail every day of her life. One tanned and muscular sixty-year-old told me he was not hopeful for the future. As in so many other trades which have been taken over by the *gros légumes* (a picturesque phrase to describe smart operators who combine something of the business executive and the fat cat), there are few young people taking over from their parents in what is nearly always a family enterprise.

Another old fisherman, his face as craggy as the coves in which he fished, said life was hard because the rules on quotas were rigidly enforced against the small businesses, while the big operators seemed to get away with impunity; they were also decimating the fishing-grounds by taking even the smallest tiddlers for fish-meal.

The fishermen do not mind performing with pleasure for an audience which may have no intention of buying anything – four elderly Marseillais sitting on a bench and looking as if they never move from it, missing nothing and perhaps fantasizing about the *friture* they are not going to have for lunch; or a trio of women from the old *quartier* adjoining the port who have come just for a good natter and to enjoy the morning sunshine.

But however much the fishermen complain, they will have sold all their catch by lunchtime; this is a market that attracts the buyer who knows what he wants. The produce is fresher, though more expensive than up the road on the Route de l'Estaque. Here, all the fish are alive on the slab, communicating with their baleful eyes and contorted body language their slow pain. Even those which do not quite survive the morning have that look in the eye which second-

class specimens have long before lost. It is here that Jean-Michel Minguella, whose starred restaurant Miramar makes perhaps the best and certainly the most expensive bouillabaisse on the waterfront, buys his raw materials. If the demand for quality survives, then perhaps the livelihood of those that supply it may also.

Thon à la Chartreuse
Tuna with tomatoes and lemon

Both the recipes in this chapter are from Erick Vedel.

SERVES 4

700g (1½lb) fresh tuna

3 tablespoons extra virgin olive oil

200g (7oz) onions, halved and sliced

500g (1lb 2oz) tomatoes, each cut into 8 segments

½ lemon, thinly sliced

2 bay leaves, crumbled

1 small chilli, halved and deseeded

200ml (7fl oz) dry white wine

Preheat the oven to 180°C/350°F/gas mark 4.

Skin and bone the fish and cut into slices 2.5 cm (1in) thick.

Coat the bottom of a casserole with the oil and spread a third of the onions over it, followed by slices of tuna and some of the tomatoes, more onions, some of the lemon slices and the bay leaves. Add a second layer of tuna and the rest of the dry ingredients. Pour in the white wine and top up with enough water just to cover the fish.

Cover and bring to the boil over a medium heat, then either reduce the heat to a simmer, or transfer the casserole to the oven for about 1 hour, or until the fish is cooked. Test for seasoning during the cooking, adding a little salt if necessary. This dish can be eaten warm or cold.

La Quinquebine
Salt cod with leeks

A Friday dish from the Camargue, morue *(salt cod) became a popular local dish, as it was one of the primary means of payment that Camargue salt-sellers received from the Atlantic fishermen.*

SERVES 4

450g (1lb) salt cod, soaked overnight

4 tablespoons olive oil

2 onions, sliced

4 leeks including green parts, sliced lengthways and cut into
  2.5cm (1in) pieces

2 cloves garlic, crushed

3 bay leaves

1 sprig of thyme (optional)

Freshly ground black pepper

Rinse and drain the fish, then place in a pan of cold water. Bring it almost to the boil, then poach for 5 minutes. Drain the fish, then remove the skin and bones and flake the flesh.

Heat the oil in a casserole, add the onions and leeks, cover and allow to cook gently for 10 minutes until they have softened but not coloured.

Stir in the flaked salt cod, the garlic and herbs and continue cooking for about 5 minutes. Season with black pepper before serving.

On Sale in Two Cities

The streets of French cities are lined with shops which seem to sell everything but foodstuffs. Where do the housewives do their daily shopping? Not always in the out-of-town hypermarkets, which you can reach only by car, and which are not worth going to without one. In any case, many older shoppers, whose husbands have taken the family car to work, don't drive.

Bordeaux, for example, is ringed with suburban markets. But in the city centre, where the permanent population is substantial, the answer to the housewife's problem is supplied by the covered markets. Like the supermarkets they provide a complete choice of perishable foodstuffs; and because Bordeaux is the trading centre for the whole of Aquitaine, the range of goods on offer is vast and of especially high quality.

The source of much of this merchandise is the wholesale Marché de Brenne. It is immense, not hard to find in the bleak hinterland behind the main railway station, but difficult to get to. Three low sheds, each half a kilometre long, house the trading operations of some two hundred or so fruit and vegetable wholesalers. The market is an early-morning affair: by eight o'clock it has been completely cleaned and tidied, a mere handful of traders staying to store away their unsold produce for the morrow. It is here that the restaurateurs of the region will buy their raw materials, as well as flowers to decorate the tables of their dining-rooms. Retailers of all kinds buy at Brenne, and dealers with a few minutes' spare time on their

It is difficult to imagine France without its markets; in these two very different cities you can find colourful street markets and covered ones; both guarantee superb quality and choice

hands pack up those twee little parcels of vegetables – say, three carrots, an onion and a couple of turnips – to be found on supermarket shelves.

Nearby is the meat market, called the Complexe de Viande. Here is traded some of the finest meat and poultry in France: the milk-fed lamb from Pauillac, still hand-reared by specialist producers; the choicest beef from Bazas on the border with Gascony. Unsurpassed too are the free-range *poulets fermiers* of the Landes and Chalosse farms.

Brenne is not intended for the private consumer. Bordeaux has a few small street markets, but most of the locals go to the covered markets, perhaps Les Capucins at the southern end of town, near the churches of Ste Croix and St Michel. It has a convenient first-floor car park and is by far the largest of the markets, filling three buildings. The smallest of these is a

cash-and-carry for bulk-buyers. Here you can buy all manner of cooking utensils, tablecloths and napkins as well as a range of foodstuffs: tins of *confit de canard* containing twelve pieces or more, five-kilo cans of tomatoes, outsize bags of croûtons, jars of haricots and chestnuts to last you a lifetime, vinegars, fish soup to see you through the whole of Lent; sauces of every kind: hollandaise, béarnaise, chasseur, diable, marchand de vin; fish and meat stocks, and tins of demi-glaze, up to one and a half kilos; dried cèpes in half-kilo bags, olives and gherkins in five-kilo jars and armfuls of *sarments de vigne* for the barbecue.

Of more interest to the daily shopper are the buildings opposite. One is given over largely to poultry and meat, with a few flowers and vegetables. The other is much busier and here the emphasis is on fish. The variety on display is astonishing: shiny black mussels, the small *bouchots* as well as the larger kind; *langoustines* whose price, never cheap, depends on their size; the kind of clam called *palourdes*; *amandes* and *bulots*, which are also called sea-snails; giant prawns, calamares, cockles and shrimps – the range of shellfish would put most fishmongers to shame. The sea fish are more familiar. There are stalls dedicated solely to the oyster, those from nearby Arcachon being specially featured. There may also be a couple of stalls devoted to mushrooms, depending on the season.

The vegetable stalls carry a colourful range of what is in season, at prices a little more than you might pay at the weekly

market in a typical country town, but then you would expect to pay more here. In June, the choice of fruit is mouth-watering: peaches, yellow or white, at knockdown prices; tiny perfumed *fraises des bois*, firm, fat cherries, the dark red, slightly triangular-shaped ones called *burlats*; and orange-fleshed charentais melons from Roussillon in the deep south.

The market spills out into the open air towards Place de la Victoire. The prices are even more competitive here and represent the best value in town, though you may have to buy more in bulk than you really need. In the warm June sunshine there is much more of a feeling of community and camaraderie among the stallholders than there is in any market under cover.

Take the Marché Victor Hugo, for example, further north and much nearer the centre of town. Here, as one retailer put it, 'each stall is personalized, each trader seeking to set himself apart from the others.' The atmosphere is a world away from Les Capucins. So are the prices. This is an up-market shopping mall for the relatively well-heeled, living and working in the

BORDEAUX: *left:* Brenne; *above:* Capucins; *right:* Victor Hugo

centre of the city. No longer wet concrete under foot by the fish stalls, but clinically clean marble everywhere, and not a scrap of rubbish to be seen.

There is no shortage of competition: four fruit and vegetable stalls, selling only the highest quality produce, four charcuterie traders, some of whom have their base elsewhere. Georges Millepied, for example, specializes in produce from the Basque country, while Paul Berdeu boasts wonderful poultry from the Chalosse and the Béarn. Monsieur Borgiovanni has veal from Gascony as well as Pauillac lamb, while Jean-Pierre Dumartin is another Basque specialist in Bayonne and Serrano hams.

One of the two fish stalls is presided over by Régine and Jocelyne, dressed in white lace country-style bodices (see photograph below). One attracts customers with a remarkable Edith Piaf impersonation, nostalgically reminiscing about the pleasures of Paris, while the other gets on with the business of filleting a plaice. Again, there is the dedicated oyster stall, a flower-seller with magnificent giant gladioli and lilies, the inevitable *viennoiserie* and, thank goodness, a bar where the foot-weary may rest and enjoy a cool glass of Stella. Air-conditioned throughout, and with its own underground car-park, the Marché Victor Hugo clearly supplies a demand, but it is not the place you would come to for a bargain.

Even less so is the Richard Rogers-like Marché Grands Hommes, with its escalators and transparent lifts. It is a miniature shopping precinct close to the opera house and built on three floors. The upper two are given over to boutiques:

there is an oriental carpet shop, an architects' studio and a beautician's as well as the usual designer-clothes shops. There are cafés to serve the exclusive *tout-Bordeaux* clientele, but no lavatories. The lowest floor, a kind of semi-basement, is given over to food, as designer-inspired as the rest of the place. The charcuterie stalls include branches of Bizac from Périgueux and Les Ducs de Gascogne from Gimont; the butchers will offer you the most temptingly delicious cuts of meat but at prices which make the Marché Victor Hugo look like a bargain basement. An exclusive coffee shop doubles as an *épicerie fine*, but you would still be hard put to find anything as vulgar or as necessary as a bag of salt anywhere in this building.

Above: **Grands Hommes, Bordeaux**

If Bordeaux has an air of faded glory, Toulouse exudes vitality and a sense of growth. Even during the *crise*, there has been a feeling of continued expansion and prosperity. Its vibrant cosmopolitanism is reflected in its eating habits. Comfortably placed between Languedoc and Gascony, it enjoys the best of both. Looking east down the Autoroute des Deux Mers, it challenges Castelnaudary and Carcassonne with its own version of cassoulet, while the proximity of Gascony to the west enables it to waddle in the glory of the goose and duck. As the centre of pork production in the south-west, Toulouse has not surprisingly given its name to a famous sausage. For fruit and vegetables it has to look no further than the rich fertile orchards and kitchen-gardens of the Garonne basin, where all manner of produce is grown *en primeur* for the markets of the world. For fish, it can draw on the best from the Atlantic and Mediterranean.

The large diversity of foodstuffs available in Toulouse is not to be sought in shops, except in the suburbs and in a handful of *épiceries fines* and specialist boutiques in the city centre. Everyday food is bought and sold on the streets and in the excellent covered markets of Victor Hugo and Les Carmes. If you are on the left bank, there is an attractive open-air market at the beginning of Avenue Etienne Billières, just by the new metro station of St Cyprien-République, but by far the biggest concentration of produce is to be found on the other side of the river, along the Boulevard de Strasbourg, going north from the Place Jeanne d'Arc and the bus station. This market can extend northwards for half a mile or so on busy days, nearly all of it devoted to fruit and vegetables, with just the occasional *charcuterie* van, spice stall and dairy stand. It is a market where the sellers are professionals who use the street as a shop, turning up several

While Bordeaux sometimes seems to be resting on its historical laurels, Toulouse

(opposite) is bursting with vigour and life. Perfectly positioned for agriculture and

seafood, its inhabitants get the pick of the produce of the south-west

times a week with whatever they have managed to buy wholesale or direct from growers. They say that the number of these traders throughout France is in decline, but you would not think so to judge by the level of activity on the Boulevard de Strasbourg.

Toulouse is home to one of the trio of famous cassoulets, so it will be no surprise to find here dried white haricot, coco, Soissons, Vendée, red beans and michelet beans, the cream-coloured haricots from Tarbes always fetching the highest prices. There is also white garlic, mauve garlic, and the pretty pink garlic from Lautrec. Reflecting a preference for more highly-seasoned cooking, there are sweet peppers of every colour, green and red chillies and the red peppers of Espelette (see page 164). There are potatoes for every purpose – Nicola and Bea from Brittany, Bintje and Mona Lisa from the north, and the Roseval and Charlotte salad potatoes from Noirmoutier on the Atlantic coast; and plum tomatoes – the knobbly Marmande tomatoes, anonymous round tomatoes and those simply labelled *pays* but always indicating which *pays*. The olive stall may offer up to two dozen different kinds, stuffed and spiced with every flavour imaginable.

Then there will be the mushroom-sellers, offering chanterelles and morels from the late spring onwards, cèpes of every size and quality in autumn, from every corner of southern France, and more exotic varieties such as grey *tricholomes* from the Loire, yellow-gilled ones called *equestres,* looking distinctly dangerous, and *trompettes de mort,* the variety so often passed off as truffles by unscrupulous *charcutiers* and restaurateurs.

For your meat and fish you will have to go to one of the covered markets in the Place des Carmes or the Marché Victor Hugo. The latter is not unlike its Bordeaux namesake, but it is several times the size and has the added attraction of a number of modest restaurants at first-floor level where cheap and cheerful food, well and freshly-cooked, is available to restore tired shoppers.

Betty's cheese stall, Toulouse

Victor Hugo houses no fewer than twelve fishmongers, one of whom, Bellocq, owns Attila, the best of the first-floor restaurants where you need to turn up no later than quarter to twelve to get a table. Everything that comes out of the sea is in this section of the market: octopus, squid, cuttlefish and *chipirons,* to name a few of the visually less prepossessing items; all you will need to make a Mediterranean bouillabaisse or a Basque *ttoro* (see page 169), as well as piles of *langoustines,* giant prawns, spider crabs, outsize *tourteaux, langoustes* and lobsters. The freshness of everything is even more amazing than its variety.

There are no fewer than twenty-one butchers, two of them devoted exclusively to lamb. This is not counting the *charcutiers* and *traiteurs,* the tripe dealer or the specialist poultry and game merchants where you will find fresh magrets, sometimes pheasant and partridge (though they are rare in France) or the special pigeons that make such wonderful *salmis* when simmered in red wine and armagnac.

There are shops selling nothing but pasta or flowers, and a lone Portuguese retailer specializing in produce from his native country, to remind you of the large numbers of families who have over the years emigrated from the Iberian peninsular to France to seek work. You will find a fairly serious wine merchant to sell you wines from nearby Fronton and the Côtes de Gascogne, and a number of bars where energy can be restored by the glassful. Irresistible too are the cheese stalls, particularly Betty's. Betty, blonde and immaculately white-overalled, is one of the colourful characters of the market. She has no other shop, relying entirely on her market stall which closes like everyone else's at lunchtime. She will stock between two and three hundred cheeses at any one time, and they all come from the best makers in the land. Her Roquefort, for example, is matured by Carles and is personalized for her. She imports from other European countries: Stilton from England and mozzarella and ricotta from Italy. She says she would like to have more of these, but producers find Brussels' red tape a deterrent. All her family love the pleasures of the table, and she is pleased that her daughter is studying to be an oenologist at Montpellier.

If you have forgotten something for Sunday lunch, the *traiteurs* at Victor Hugo will have few problems tempting you to delicious extravagance, for the market is open on Sunday morning. You could buy a multi-course *menu gastronomique* here without difficulty. If your ambitions and your purse are more modest, for none of these things comes cheap, or if you feel like a picnic in the gentle countryside out of town, you will find all you need in the huge open space surrounding the Cathedral of St Sernin, where there is a market every Sunday morning. Even if you are not in a buying mood, a visit is a must if you love Romanesque church architecture, because St Sernin is one of the finest examples of the genre. Fortunes have been spent on its restoration.

The most beautiful square in the city is the formally laid-out Place du Capitole, the heart of Toulouse, and the best place to enjoy the famous rose-coloured brick with which the older parts of the city are built. Nor is there any shortage of cafés, where a half-hour after shopping can be most enjoyably spent just watching the world go by. On Wednesday, the acres of space in the centre of the *place* are given over to a miscellany of the cheap and nasty, but sometimes on other days of the week, people will come in from the country to sell a few cheeses or other home produce. If you can find the rich Ariège cheeses from Bethmale or Moulis, for example, be sure not to miss the chance. Farmhouse examples are hard to come by.

Ragoût d'asperges
Poached asparagus

SERVES 4

32 thin green asparagus spears

500ml (17fl oz) chicken stock

1 large onion, finely chopped

2 tablespoons goose or pork fat

150g (5oz) salt belly of pork, diced

2 tablespoons flour

Salt and pepper

Pinch of nutmeg

Clean and scrape the asparagus, cutting off and reserving the tips.

Simmer the stalks in the stock for 30 minutes, then strain and reserve the stock.

In a wide pan, soften the onion in the fat. Add the pork and continue to cook for 15 minutes. Add the flour, blend well, then gradually stir in the stock to make a sauce, adding it little by little. Simmer gently together for 10 minutes. Add the asparagus tips and poach in the sauce until just cooked, but still quite firm – about 12 minutes.

Season, add the nutmeg and serve, either as a dish on its own or as an accompaniment to plainly roasted poultry.

Huîtres au gratin
Oysters baked with cheese

SERVES 4

24 oysters, shucked and put in the deeper half of their shells

110g (4oz) fresh breadcrumbs

4 tablespoons milk

5 shallots, finely chopped

Salt and pepper

200g (7oz) cheese, Cantal or Cheddar, grated

Preheat the oven to 230°C/450°F/gas mark 8.

Arrange the oysters in their shells in a shallow gratin dish large enough to hold them in one layer. Soak the bread-crumbs in the milk and add the shallots. Cover the tops of the oysters with this mixture. Season, allowing for the saltiness of the cheese. Sprinkle the cheese over. Bake the dish in the oven for 7 minutes or so, until the cheese starts to crispen.

Serve piping hot with *pain de campagne* and a crisp, chilled white wine.

Moules à la bordelaise
Mussels Bordeaux-style

SERVES 4

2kg (4½lb) bouchot mussels

60g (2½oz) butter

75g (3oz) shallots, chopped

4 tomatoes, peeled, deseeded and finely chopped

300ml (½ pint) dry white wine

3 tablespoons fresh breadcrumbs

½ teaspoon *piment d'Espelette,* or a blend of paprika and cayenne

2 tablespoons chopped parsley

Scrub and debeard the mussels under running water, discarding any that are slightly open.

Melt half the butter in a pan, add the shallots and soften over a gentle heat. Mix in the tomatoes, then set aside.

Place the mussels in a large pan with the wine. Cover and place over a high heat for a few minutes, shaking the pan. As soon as the mussels start to open, take the pan off the heat and remove the empty half-shells of each, placing the filled shells in a large serving bowl. Keep warm in a very low oven while finishing the sauce.

Carefully strain the liquid from the mussels into the shallot and tomato mixture and stir in the breadcrumbs, *piment d'Espelette* and the remaining butter, cut into small cubes.

Reheat gently, then spoon the sauce over the mussels and serve immediately, sprinkled with parsley.

Lotte à la gasconne
Monkfish Gascon-style

SERVES 4

2 monkfish tails, each weighing about 450g (1lb) on the bone, or
   350g (12oz) filleted

2 tablespoons seasoned flour

50g (2oz) butter

2 tablespoons cooking oil

100g (4oz) button mushrooms, halved or quartered

1 large clove garlic, chopped

1 tablespoon tomato purée

120ml (4fl oz) medium dry white wine

½ tablespoon armagnac

Salt and pepper

1 tablespoon chopped parsley

Skin and fillet the fish if not already done. Cut it into 5cm (2in) pieces and toss in the seasoned flour.

Heat the butter and oil in a frying pan over a medium heat. Then put in the fish, mushrooms and garlic. Turn the fish to seal it on all sides, then add the tomato purée, wine and armagnac. Reduce the heat and stir gently to blend the sauce, seasoning to taste.

Leave to cook slowly for a further 5 minutes – not too long or the fish will become leathery.

Sprinkle with chopped parsley and serve with plain rice.

Poulet en cocotte Tzouano
Chicken casserole from the Languedoc

SERVES 4

1 young chicken about 1.3 kg (3lb)

Salt and pepper

5 large cloves garlic

1 bouquet garni

1 tablespoon goose fat

5–6 slices salt pork or green streaky bacon

12 button onions, peeled

125g (4½oz) wild mushrooms

1 tablespoon chives, chopped

1 glass dry white wine

55ml (2fl oz) chicken stock

12 small new potatoes, scrubbed and cut into walnut-sized pieces

1 tablespoon butter

1 teaspoon flour

Preheat the oven to 170°C/325°F/gas mark 3.

Season the chicken inside and out. Put the unpeeled garlic cloves and bouquet garni inside and truss for roasting.

Heat the goose fat in a large casserole and brown the chicken all over. Remove the chicken and put in the salt pork, cut into cubes. When it has coloured a little, add the onions and mushrooms. Cook together for a few minutes, then add the chives. Pour in the white wine and stock and put the chicken back in the casserole on top of the other ingredients. Cover and cook in the oven for 40 minutes.

Add the potatoes and cook for another 10 minutes, then remove the chicken, garlic and bouquet garni. Peel the garlic and crush to a purée with the butter and flour. Add this to the juices in the casserole, stir well and replace the chicken. Check the seasoning and cook for a further 15 minutes.

Serve the chicken surrounded by the vegetables and pass the sauce separately.

Selle d'agneau de Pauillac
Saddle of salt-marsh lamb

SERVES 8

1 saddle of young Pauillac lamb

Vegetable oil

Salt and pepper

150g (5oz) butter

1kg (2¼lb) potatoes, peeled and thinly sliced

250g (9oz) cèpes or field mushrooms, thinly sliced, or 75g (3oz) dried cèpes, pre-soaked

150g (5oz) breadcrumbs

4 tablespoons parsley, chopped

4 cloves garlic, chopped

Preheat the oven to 220°C/425°F/gas mark 7.

Brush the lamb with oil and season liberally. Butter a large ovenproof gratin dish and fill with alternate layers of the potatoes and mushrooms, seasoning each layer. Finish with a potato layer and dot the top with 50g (2oz) of the butter.

Set the saddle of lamb on the top rack of the oven with the gratin dish immediately below, so that the meat juices drip on to the vegetables. Roast for 30 minutes. Melt the remaining butter and mix with the breadcrumbs, parsley, garlic and salt to taste. Coat the lamb with this mixture, then return to the oven for a further 20 minutes.

Remove the lamb and leave in a warm place to rest. Brown the potatoes in the top of the oven for 15 minutes or so.

The Divine Bulb

There is scarcely a village shop in southern France which does not stock garlic. Certainly at every market there will be plentiful supplies of all the main cultivated varieties: the new season's white, mild, juicy, large-cloved and usually the least expensive; the purplish kind called 'violet', the most widely grown, of high strength, quite good for keeping; and the third and most expensive kind, the pink garlic from Lautrec. There is also wild garlic, tiny and amazingly pungent, and still the favourite of many peasant cooks, but this is rarely seen except on the smallest of stalls from a *petit producteur*.

Garlic is the most characteristic condiment in the cuisine of southern France, not always in the huge doses often mentioned, but sometimes by way of subtle suggestion only – perhaps just a single clove to wipe the bowl before salad is put in it. But who could imagine a succulent leg of lamb without spikes of garlic inserted before roasting, or cassoulet without a few garlic cloves added to cut the dish's richness? Or an *aïoli*, which, without garlic, would be just another mayonnaise?

Garlic does however call for some respect in its use. First, you may never see a garlic press in a southern kitchen; the oils released by a press will oxidize and spoil the flavour of the garlic and the dish for which it is intended. Instead, as Erick Vedel, the Provençal historian-cook from Arles demonstrates, put a teaspoon of lemon juice in the bottom of a saucer with a pinch

'Peace and happiness begin, geographically, where garlic is used in the cooking.'

Marcel Boulestin

of salt, and into it grate against the prongs of a fork the cloves of garlic to be cut up or puréed. The lemon juice will both preserve the garlic from oxidization and ensure that, even eaten raw, it will not cause indigestion. Erick says that garlic puréed in this way even makes a good stuffing for an avocado pear.

In the main areas of production, there are specialist *foires* for the bulk sale of garlic to wholesalers and restaurants, as well as private buyers. At Uzès, for example, you may find a buyer who has been nominated by an entire village to buy in bulk for a syndicate of residents. Uzès is a fun event, because it comes on the last day of the traditional midsummer festivities at the end of June, and visitors can enjoy the whole town as well as the garlic stalls. The circular medieval centre of the town is a wonderful spot to linger under the plane trees with a glass of cool wine; but you will find only the odd garlic-seller there. Most of the action is at the western end of town, just outside the Tourist Office. If you ask here for details of the garlic fair, they will, in the typically well-informed way of such organizations, likely as not ask you: 'What garlic fair?'

There are usually about twenty stalls, each of them groaning under the weight of their seemingly impossible burden of garlic, the stems tied loosely together; sometimes there are woven tresses but these are dearer. The growers often offer quantities of shallots and onions along with the garlic.

Guy Champetier comes from Beaulieu in the neighbouring *département* of Ardèche where he is a *vigneron* as well as a garlic-grower. He conducts his business under the trees in the area between the two limbs of the Avenue de la Libération.

His produce ranged in a semi-circle, he puts up a basic kind of scaffolding which serves to carry no less than 2,000 kilos of his garlic. He is well known to the dealers who buy bundles of it from him by the bagful – the kind of black plastic bags you put your rubbish in. The garlic is first weighed on Champetier's weighing machine which he has brought with him, and which will carry loads up to sixty kilos.

Other garlic fairs (see the list on page 180), include the important one at Piolenc, a short drive from Uzès across the

This is due, according to Docteur François Delga, the mayor of Lautrec and also senator for the Tarn, to its higher sugar and lower water content, the result of the local growing conditions. Pink garlic will keep for up to a year, longer if it is a good year. There are vintage years in garlic as well as wine.

Docteur Delga is a stout advocate of the medicinal properties of garlic. Children are taught in school at Lautrec that it is a stimulant – did not the construction workers on the Pyramids chew garlic? And an insecticide – did not their ancestors hang necklaces made of garlic cloves round the necks of their children to deter fleas? It has always been known as an aid to digestion and it is now, fashionably, a protector of the cardiovascular system because of its anti-clotting properties.

Garlic can also be used industrially in the manufacture of paper and glue, which seems a waste of a valuable culinary commodity – certainly the pink garlic of Lautrec should stay in the kitchen. It may cost marginally more than other varieties but it is well worth the price because its cloves, stored in a cool place, will keep you supplied throughout the winter and enable you to make the delicious soup on page 78.

Four thousand tons of Lautrec garlic are produced each year by three hundred producers on 1000 hectares covering the ten communes within the canton of Lautrec and eight of its neighbouring communes. This represents 10 percent of the whole of France's garlic production. Two hundred of these producers belong to a syndicate to protect the local variety of pink garlic which, so legend has it, Spanish *colporteurs* (travelling salesmen) in the seventeenth century used as payment for their board and lodging in Lautrec.

River Rhône, where they seem to specialize in double tresses. On the eastern slopes of Gascony, where the hills descend gradually into the Garonne Valley, there is a big *foire* at Cadours. But it is the *département* of Tarn that has the most attractive one of all.

On the first Friday of August the village of Lautrec holds its annual garlic fair, an event which draws hundreds of visitors – local residents, farmers and holiday-makers. Lautrec lies fifteen kilometres from Castres, built spectacularly on a promontory overlooking the plain. The approach from the west gives a romantic view in the early morning of the town's windmill, silhouetted in the mist against the sun.

The fair is a promotional event aimed at publicizing and selling the locally-grown pink garlic, whose main attractions, apart from its pretty appearance – the skins are streaked with pink – are its smallish plump cloves, its flavour, and especially its longevity. It keeps longer than the white or purple varieties.

A parallel group – SICAIL – was set up to breed from this special strain of pink garlic. The researchers produced two new clones, *Goulurose* and *Iberose*, the latter being particularly useful because its strong flower stem enables the dried 'heads' to be tied together into the tresses here called *manouilles*.

Lautrec is today classed as an IGP (*Indication Géographique Protégée*) which permits the use of a *Label Rouge de Qualité*, a guarantee of extra quality. These growers have continued to promote and protect their product. They do not mind knocking the competition; visitors will be offered a car-sticker with the injunction *Non à l'ail de Chine*.

Although garlic is on sale at the weekly Friday market in Lautrec (from eight o'clock in the morning between the last week of July to the end of the following March – and you must get there early), the fair at the beginning of August is special. First there is the annual garlic-growing competition. Each professional entrant has to submit thirty of his one-kilo tresses to be judged on the size of the heads, colour, uniformity and fine appearance of the tied bunches. There is quite an art in the stringing of these, and you will probably find at one of the stalls ranged under the trees along the ramparts of the medieval village the Carayol family of growers demonstrating with much jollity how it is done. Grandfather trims the heads neatly, Geneviève binds the tresses while her husband Michel collects the money from the customers.

The second competition is theoretically open to anyone and is for the most artistic 'sculpture' of any subject, created out of pink garlic. There may not be many entries, perhaps eight, ranging for example from a model of a lighthouse, standing two metres high, entirely covered in heads of garlic with its flashing beacon on top, to a full-size model of Marie Antoinette in crimson dress, the lace on her décolletage and skirt simulated by heads of garlic; or an extremely ambitious galleon in full sail, the hull made from heads of garlic, the rigging from plaited stalks, and most impressive of all, the sails entirely constructed out of the wafer-thin skins which cover the garlic clove.

The judging of the two competitions takes place during the morning on the ramparts where the exhibits are laid out. After judging, the strings or sacks of garlic are for sale. There is also seed garlic for the next year's crop alongside farm machinery for those with a fat wallet or bank manager.

All too soon it is *midi* and the crowds flock back to the market-place in the centre of Lautrec where benches are set out under the shade of the arcades. The doors of the fifteenth-century covered market open and strong men carry out cauldrons of the soup for which we give the recipe. The visitors line up and are offered a plastic bowl brimming with the delectable, creamy local speciality, accompanied by a beaker of vin rosé, both free by courtesy of the local farmers.

For those who stay on after recovering from the August midday heat, there can be a stroll round the pretty village or a climb to the top of the village to the windmill, fully restored and in working order, to watch a demonstration of flour milling. Then for those who want to linger in Lautrec for the evening there is a giant cassoulet and the inevitable *bal*.

Rugby players thrive on garlic

L'Aïoli

Poached fish with vegetables and a garlic mayonnaise

There are two versions of this dish; one an ordinary Friday lunch dish; the other a grand festive affair traditionally served on important feast days.

SERVES 8

garlic mayonnaise:

6–8 cloves garlic

Large pinch of salt

4 egg yolks

600ml (1 pint) extra virgin olive oil

Lemon juice (optional)

for an 'ordinary' aïoli:

1kg (2¼lb) salt cod, soaked for 24 hours

1kg (2¼lb) new waxy potatoes, unpeeled

750g (1lb 10oz) young carrots

for the 'grand' aïoli, as above plus all or any of the following:

1 can of prepared snails (about 24 snails)

4–6 hard-boiled eggs

450g (1lb) haricots verts

1 cauliflower

8 tiny artichokes

450g (1lb) beetroot

First prepare the mayonnaise – all the ingredients must be at room temperature. Crush the garlic cloves with a little salt, mix in the egg yolks, then start adding the oil, a very little at a time, beating continuously. Only when the *aïoli* begins to thicken can the oil be added more steadily. It should become very thick. Add a little lemon juice if wished. If the mayonnaise curdles, begin again in a clean bowl with another egg yolk and trickle in the curdled sauce drop by drop, beating all the time.

The accompanying fish and vegetables should be served slightly warm. Poach the salt cod for 5 minutes. Heat the snails in their liquid and drain. Steam or boil the vegetables and serve the potatoes in their skins, the carrots cut in lengths and the cauliflower in florets. Arrange the fish and each of the vegetables in separate serving dishes and pass the bowl of *aïoli* separately. A cool Provençal rosé usually accompanies this dish.

Soupe à l'ail rose de Lautrec

Pink garlic soup

SERVES 4

1 litre (1¾ pints) water or stock

4–8 garlic cloves

55g (2oz) vermicelli

2 teaspoons mustard

2 large or 4 small eggs, separated

Salt and pepper

200ml (7fl oz) sunflower oil

Bring the water or stock to the boil, throw in the chopped garlic and vermicelli, and simmer until the pasta is cooked, about 7–10 minutes.

Meanwhile, beat together the mustard, egg yolks, salt and pepper, then gradually beat in the sunflower oil until the mixture thickens.

Allow the garlic broth to cool a little, or add a little cold water to hasten the process, then vigorously whisk in the egg whites. Dilute the mayonnaise with a ladleful of the broth, then gently pour it into the soup and stir well. Check the seasoning. If it has cooled too much, reheat very gently.

Serve with slices of fresh country bread.

Heaven-Scent

Lime trees of various species grow all over Europe, but the climate of Upper Provence suits to perfection the highly-scented variety called *tilia platyphllos*. In particular the *petit pays* Les Baronnies, which lies between the river Eygues and Mont Ventoux, has made something of a speciality of harvesting lime blossom. Here the variety is called *Bénivay*, after one of the villages in the area.

The first question from the uninitiated is: 'What do you do with lime blossom?' Old recipes may tell you how to use it as a flavouring in pastries, sweets and ices; it is also an ingredient in some perfumes. But its principal use nowadays is to make the kind of infusion which the French call simply *tilleul*. The result is a deliciously fragrant tea made from soaking the dried flowers, and the pale green bracts which grow at the base of their stems, in boiling water. The liquid turns a pale green and is then poured off into cups. Alternatively, it can be made in special porcelain double containers called *tisaniers*.

A good *tilleul* is a wonderfully relaxing, soothing drink after meals and also an ideal nightcap. It is sedative rather than stimulating. It is said also to be good for migraines, indigestion and giddiness, as well as helping to reduce the viscosity in the blood.

Tilleul is drunk all over France, though not as widely as it once was: most farms would have their own tree from which they harvested and dried their own crop to last a whole year. If you do not have a lime tree, you can buy *tilleul* at the pharmacy,

Tilleul, an infusion made from lime blossom, is drunk all over France, but the village of Buis-Les-Baronnies has made it a speciality, with a *Tilleul* Fair held annually in mid-summer

or sometimes at local markets. It is the latter for which the crop from Les Baronnies is destined; in this region 90 percent of the entire commercial *tilleul* production of France is grown.

At the centre of this *petit pays* is the peaceful and very picturesque village of Buis-les-Baronnies on the little river Ouvèze. It is ringed by an avenue ending in the deeply shaded Place des Quinconces where Napoleon had plane trees planted in 1811 as a tribute to his newly born son, procociously created King of Rome. At this point the road follows the river, from which it is separated by a raised wall or *digue*. It is here that on the first Wednesday in July the Tilleul Fair takes place as part of the town's annual celebrations; by this time the first flowers will have blossomed and been dried ready for sale. Higher up the valley, the flowers bloom later and there will be smaller *foires* in due course at La Charce and Villefranche-le-Château.

At Buis the *foire* starts early; the growers arrive from seven o'clock in the morning. An hour later the *digue* is crowded with vans, some with trailers, others with roof-racks piled high with *tilleul*. By nine o'clock business is well under way. The heady, exotic scent of the flowers is almost overwhelming.

The growers have packed their *tilleul* into large bundles called *bourras* or *trousses*, large pieces of sacking tied at the corners with webbing, each weighing between fifteen and twenty kilos. I learned that the flowers and their bracts have to

be picked when fully open, but before the flowers drop and the *boules* (seed-pods) form. The flowers only last ten days so you have to choose the right moment fairly swiftly. One of the growers I talked to said he had fifty trees but he only picked two of them, because the price at the *foire* did not justify taking on hired labour for the harvest. Another grower said he could only pick enough to fill two *bourras*. Much depends on the weather and what time can be spared from other farming activities; many growers also have cherry-orchards which

bring in a much better return, and, if the cherries ripen at the same time as the lime flowers, the latter get left on the trees.

A tree will start flowering after six years but does not crop properly until it is twenty years old. It will yield between forty and sixty kilos of blossom, but picking is hard and finicky work, backbreaking as well as repetitive. There are also hordes of insects which the pickers have to contend with. It takes four kilos of blossom to make one kilo of dried *tilleul*. The drying is done in a warm place, often the farmhouse attics or barns, away from direct sunshine. The quicker the drying, the better the appearance of the finished *tilleul*. The process usually takes five or six days. If the flowers are not sufficiently dried, they will be rejected at the *foire*, because they will not keep.

There is nothing to stop anyone from buying a *bourras* of *tilleul*, but in practice the few buyers are all dealers. They park their lorries under the plane trees and spread huge sheets on the ground. Near each lorry, suspended by a rope from one of the plane trees, is an old-fashioned weighing-machine of the type called *balance romaine*. One lorry driver told me that his firm exported *tilleul* to pharmacies in Germany, Switzerland and Belgium, and that the average price in recent years had been about fifty or sixty francs per kilo. The price was largely determined by the size and appearance of the bracts more than the flowers. The Bénivay variety was noted for its extra-large bracts, and this in turned explained the demand for the *tilleul* of the Baronnies district. His own view was that the smaller bracts made the better tea, and they were 10 percent or so cheaper too.

The actual buying is conducted by the firm's *courtier*, who can be seen walking up and down inspecting the produce and negotiating a price. If a deal is struck, the *courtier* hands the seller a bought note, and the seller then has to heave the sold produce over the railing to the buyer's weighing machine. Once weighed, the contents of the bundles are transferred to the buyer's own *bourras*, and the final purchase price established. The seller is then handed a voucher which he exchanges for a cheque at the buyer's accounts department (a

table by the *digue*). One of the buying firms is from nearby Vaison-la-Romaine, and the blonde lady cashier invites me to see round her firm's *atelier* when the day's trading is over.

Meanwhile, preparations are under way in the gardens of the Mairie for the inevitable *intronisations* into the Chevaliers du Tilleul des Baronnies. As may be imagined, the Chevaliers are dressed in pale-green robes with capes in a darker olive-green, and they wear black hats trimmed with lime blossom. The new members of the order are tapped on the shoulder with a branch of lime tree and given a glass of Le Castillou, a local drink made from lime flowers. On page 87 is the recipe I was given by Etienne Albert from the hill-village of Beauvoisin, who later dispenses quantities of this very refreshing liquid to the public from huge plastic *bidons*. After the ceremony, the lady *animateur* leads all present in a spirited rendering of *Coupo Santo*, with lyrics by the Provençal poet Frédéric Mistral.

The event had been billed as the Foire du Tilleul et de la Lavande and I ask the newly enthroned Mayor of Buis about the lavender, because I had seen no sign of any, though Provence is famous for its lavender fields. He tells me that the *foire*, which started in 1808, no longer included lavender although it had been kept in the title; there were lavender fêtes locally in several other villages. A few days later, when I was in

nearby Nyons for the Olivade, I visited a lavender distillery and was told that picking often did not start until later in July.

The Mayor introduces me to Jean-Verlaine Delaye, who had given up farming to help run the Syndicat des Producteurs de Tilleul. He is also in charge of the Comité de Promotion des Plantes à Parfums Aromatiques et Médicinales de la Drôme Provençale. To the public this means a little museum in Buis called La Maison des Arômes, which has been open since 1989 to promote the perfumes and fragrances from local plants. He confirms to me that the Bénivay variety of *tilleul* has the biggest bracts, and it was these which contained the sedative ingredient of the eventual tea. Some buyers use Baronnies *tilleul* to strengthen the flavour of inferior produce imported from other countries, which is made up into sachets. The message seems to be: don't buy *tilleul* sachets.

In the Baronnies, I learn from Jean-Verlaine that lime trees were planted widely during the reign of Henri IV at the instigation of his wise minister Sully. They can live for up to 400 years, but will degenerate if not pruned and cared for. The pruning is done at the time of the harvest. The harvest is like an old-fashioned *vendange*, the whole family taking part with as many friends and neighbours as can be persuaded to join in; a mini-fête of its own in fact. Everyone in the Baronnies has at least one tree which they have inherited from their ancestors, and there are today about 36,000 trees, on average about seventy to eighty years old. Nobody is planting any new ones because of competition from abroad, the labour costs which make anything but a family endeavour unprofitable, and the tendency to concentrate on more lucrative crops such as cherries and apricots.

In the Baronnies lime trees are never cut down, but in the Roussillon, for example, a second bark under the outer one, known as *l'aubier de tilleul*, is cut into strips and used as a diuretic. Lime timber can be used to manufacture ropes, and Jean-Verlaine reminds me that the French word *tillier* means 'to transform into fibres'. Lime wood is easy to use, so it is much in demand from artisans working in inlay and marquetry, from sculptors and pencil-makers, even from boat-builders, the makers of moulds for hat-makers, and lute makers. It might even be possible to commercialize oil produced from the *boules*.

I ask Jean-Verlaine about the song which was sung at the *intronisation*, because I remembered hearing it at the bottle blessing in Boulbon (see page 48). He tells me that the melody was Catalan in origin, but is now sung all over Provence. He describes it as *un hymne tendancieux*, which I take to mean that it has a hidden significance, private but exclusive to the people of Provence, expressive of Occitan solidarity. It has become an all-purpose and ubiquitous Provençal hymn, sung on all possible occasions to whatever words can be made to fit.

During the afternoon, I take up the invitation of the blonde cashier to visit her *atelier* in Vaison. The firm is called Herbissima, and deals in all manner of plant products. I see machines for cleaning, chopping and blending herbs to be made up into packets of *herbes de Provence*. She tells me incidentally that lavender should never be included in this mixture, although in blends marketed by others it is sometimes listed as an ingredient. She also shows me bundles of cherry stalks which are macerated to produce a diuretic, and gentian roots spread out in the open air for drying. I also see *tilleul* unsold from the previous year, which will be jobbed off to be made into sachets; this is apparently common practice, and underlines the benefit of buying loose produce from the pharmacies or the market-sellers, rather than sachets from an unknown source.

This *foire* is so enjoyable because it is both different from any other and so extraordinarily beautiful as a spectacle, in the setting of Buis. Although *tilleul* is only tangential to the culinary repertoire, it yields nevertheless a traditional harvest for man's enjoyment – and in Les Baronnies of a quality not surpassed anywhere else in the world.

Pavé romain d'Orange

Orange and almond gâteau

This recipe was generously given to me by Gérard Blaise,
the well-known Maître-Pâtissier *of Orange.*

SERVES 8

180g (6oz) unsalted butter

3 tablespoons lavender honey

2 large eggs

35ml (1½fl oz) milk

110g (4oz) icing sugar

250g (9oz) self-raising flour mixed with 1 teaspoon baking powder

100g (4oz) candied orange peel, chopped and tossed in flour

2 tablespoons Grand Marnier

2 tablespoons marmalade, quince or other fruit jelly

Sugar

50g (2oz) chopped almonds

Preheat the oven to 180°C/350°F/gas mark 4. Cream together the butter and honey, then beat in the eggs one by one. Beat in the milk, sugar and finally the flour and baking powder. (Alternatively, mix all together in a food processor.) Beat until the mixture is smooth, then fold in the chopped orange peel.

Line a 450g (1lb) bread tin with non-stick baking parchment and spoon in the mixture. Bake for about 1¼ hours, until the cake is light brown on top and shrinks slightly from the sides of the tin. Remove from the oven and, while it is still hot, sprinkle the top of the pavé with Grand Marnier. Leave to cool for about 10 minutes, turn out on to a wire rack and remove the paper.

When the cake is cold, prepare a glaze by melting the marmalade or other jelly with a little sugar and a tablespoon of water. Brush the top and sides of the cake with glaze, then dip it in the chopped almonds, pressing them firmly on to the cake. This cake keeps well and can be served in thin slices with a *coulis* of raspberries and crème fraîche.

Le Castillou

Lime-blossom cordial

SERVES 4

1 litre (1¾ pints) water

25g (1oz) dried *tilleul* (flowers and bracts)

40ml (1½fl oz) sirop de cassis

40g (1½oz) caster sugar

Juice of 2 lemons

Bring the water to the boil, add the *tilleul* and leave to infuse for about 5 minutes. Strain, and allow the liquid to cool. Add the remaining ingredients, mix well and allow to rest. Drink well chilled.

Oiling the Huiles

The olive goes back in history as far as man himself. The seafaring Phoenicians brought it to Marseille, where successive Greek and Roman colonizers promoted its growth. It has survived because it is tough and can live to an incredible age. Like the walnut, it takes several years before it becomes a useful producer, but there are trees in Provence which go back to Roman times; pruning and loving care can achieve almost Faustian miracles.

It can endure the longest of droughts, but its weakness is the cold. Below -8°C it will almost certainly die because its roots are close to the ground. It is no surprise to find it hugging the coasts of the Mediterranean, but its success as far north in Provence as the Drôme is unexpected, until one realizes that parts of that beautiful area are well sheltered from the mistral, as well as enjoying a particularly hot and dry summer. The small town of Nyons is not only a thriving centre of production, but even enjoys its own *Appellation Contrôlée* for its excellent fruit.

Nyons is home to its own Confrérie de l'Olivier which holds two fêtes annually, one to honour the new season's oil in January or February, the other, called 'Les Olivades', to celebrate the fruit itself in summer.

Everyone knows that there are green olives and black olives; fewer people know that the green olive, harvested in the autumn, is quite simply an unripe black olive. At Nyons they grow a variety called Tanche, which is hardier than most and thus more likely to survive at this latitude. It alone may be used in AOC quality oil

Olives are at the heart of Provençal cooking. The fruit is eaten raw or cooked in countless dishes, and the fragrant oil is the basic cooking medium of the entire Mediterranean basin

from Nyons. It ripens to a rich shade of brownish-black, is slightly wrinkled and of medium size. The stone is small and the fruit is firm. It is harvested around the New Year. The smaller specimens are destined to be made into oil by a process largely unchanged for centuries. The choicer specimens are kept for preserving in brine. The oil is made by pressing the fruit between plates which look like old gramophone records. It is filtered through thick straw mats and then the oil and water contents are separated, nowadays in centrifugal drums.

It takes 14 kilos of olives to make a litre of oil, so it is little wonder that olive oil is so expensive. The price is further determined by acidity: the lowest in acidity is called *Extra-Vierge* (less than 1 percent); then comes *Vierge fine* (maximum 1½ percent) and then *Vierge* (3 percent). After that, oils are, shall we say, variable?

No fête would be complete without its *intronisations* and Nyons certainly has those; it also has one of the most hilarious town bands you could wish to hear. But the best features of a visit are the permanent exhibition at the Co-opérative du Nyonsais, which contains a shop offering everything possible connected with the olive. There are also a number of mills in the area, one of which is just by the old bridge in the old part of town. Here was explained to me the process of preserving olives for consumption throughout the year. The techniques for green and black olives are quite different.

Green olives are individually pricked and bathed in an alkaline solution based on potassium or sodium, or both, with as little air contact as possible. This takes an hour or so. The olives are then rinsed several times and the water is changed daily for three to five days. Sometimes the last soaking is in a 5 percent brine. For long storage, a fresh brine is made by boiling up water, and adding 10 percent of its weight in salt and quantities of wild fennel, thyme and bay leaves, which are left to infuse until the liquid is quite cold. The olives are then stored in jars, covered with the brine and sealed.

Black olives are put in a large bowl with any favourite herbs, and sprinkled with salt until they are covered. They are shaken daily for a week and the liquids they exude are drained off. For long keeping, they are then stored in air-tight jars in a cool dark place. Before serving, the olives are put into a serving bowl, and sprinkled with a little pepper and a few drops of oil. When stirred around they will look attractively and professionally shiny.

Olives could well be adopted as a symbol of the Midi. They are to be found all over the south at every market, to be eaten on their own in their plain salted state, stuffed and flavoured with every imaginable spice and herb, or used in countless dishes. Their oil varies almost as widely in flavour. In general, French oils are lighter in colour and milder in flavour than oils from Italy or Spain, and there is almost the same range of style as well as producer rivalry as will be found in the winegrowing areas of the south.

Olivade de fromage blanc
Purée of olives and cream cheese

SERVES 4

110g (4oz) black olives, stoned

1 small onion

250g (9oz) fromage blanc

6 tablespoons extra virgin olive oil

1 tablespoon chopped chives

Salt

Crush the olives almost to a purée in a food processor. Chop half the onion finely. Mix the olives into the cheese and then slowly stir in half the oil. Add the chopped onion and most of the chives. Turn into a bowl and beat with a wooden spoon, slowly adding the rest of the oil until you have a mixture you can spread on rounds of toasted bread. Season to taste.

Cover with the remaining half onion cut into rings and a thin layer of oil. Chill for 24 hours. Remove the onion rings and serve on bread croûtons, sprinkled with chives.

Meet The Growers

The village of Madiran is a microcosm of Gascony. It has its annual summer fête in the middle of August. The high spot for many village fêtes is the 15th which, as well as being the Feast of the Assumption, is the last of the summer *jours fériés*, with none other until All Saints' Day, the herald of winter.

But both Madiran and its fête have something special. The village is the centre of a small but progressive vineyard with an active Syndicat to promote the wines, and they have grafted on to the fête an opportunity for visitors to taste the wines of thirty or so local producers in an atmosphere of jollity and celebration. More important, it is an opportunity for customers and those in the wine trade to meet a good proportion of the better growers in the area, and for tourists and holiday-makers to make acquaintance, perhaps for the first time, with the wines of Madiran.

On the last Monday in June each year, the Syndicat des Vins de Madiran et Pacherenc-vic-Bilh organizes a competition to which it invites wine writers, media personalities, chefs, gastronomes and journalists. The object is for all these worthies to join in blind tastings to select the best two-year-old red wine, the best five-year-old red wine, and the best dry and sweet white wines called Pacherenc. So there are four different categories. The five best in each category are declared and published, and the winners attract a great deal of press and professional attention; there are no other rewards. It is a condition of entry that all participants take part in the Fête des Vins in August; failure to do so will automatically disqualify them from entering their wines the following year.

During the annual mid-summer village fête at Madiran, the Winegrowers' Association invites both serious connoisseurs and holiday-makers to enjoy themselves tasting the local wines

Many will wonder what the wines of Madiran and Pacherenc are, and where they are made, for they are relatively little known outside their area of production. On the other hand they are considerably more than local country wines, some of them having successfully competed against the best wines of Bordeaux for honours in international competitions. They are new, in the sense that the vineyards were only replanted for the most part in the early seventies (after their total destruction by the phylloxera disease at the end of the last century); they are relatively limited in area, extending to only 1,500 hectares in all; and they buck the fashionable trend towards wines which are fruity and can be drunk young. The red wines at least, which represent nearly 90 percent of the total production, are big, well-structured and full-bodied, and they need some years in bottle before they show their best.

Geographically, the Madiran vineyards are halfway between the Armagnac district and the Pyrenees; remote and beautiful in gently rolling countryside where the principal crops are maize and sunflowers. The village boasts a mere five hundred inhabitants, but its fête is worthy of a small town four or five times the size, and it attracts huge crowds. The growers for their part are anxious that the event should be more than an opportunity for the public to drink too much, but they are also keen to keep the festive nature of the occasion. Naturally they want to promote the wines, but to do so in a holiday atmosphere. In recent years the growers have been allotted a special area away from the fête proper. Behind the former priory, which is now a hotel, is a large *parc*, around which all the growers' stands are ranged, well-equipped for refrigeration and lighting. Admission is open to all, but there is an entrance charge of fifteen francs which buys you an engraved tasting glass. This is your entry ticket, and with it you may taste as many wines as you wish and come and go as you please, so it is important not to lose it.

In 1995, the organizers instituted for the first time a preliminary tasting on the evening before the *jour férié*. Your glass entitles you to admission on both days. It really needs two days to do justice to the wines of so many growers, and, in theory at least, a little forward planning on the part of the taster may save a great deal of confusion as the event proceeds. The tasting started at half-past eight in the evening, just as it was beginning to get dark. There was a good but rustic band, which included a washboard and two sousaphones, playing delightfully retro music without amplification, which meant that you could carry on a conversation with the winemakers without being deafened. Long trestle-tables were laid out for a barbecue (fifty francs), and at about ten o'clock everyone started to queue up for their first course, melon and charcuterie. There followed the predictable steak and *frites*, then ices.

When the evening had finished shortly after midnight, the main festivities in the village were still in full swing. Sportsmen had already been at it for two days with competitions for ball-trap, tennis and *pétanque* and, while the wine-fanciers were busy with their tasting, everyone else was enjoying a country-style buffet in the main square. Dancing started at ten in the evening and went on until well into the early hours.

The 15th is of course the big day. It starts with Mass in the village church at ten o'clock, and at least an hour before that a band of youngsters, calling themselves Les Dandys de l'Armagnac, had assembled to welcome the visiting dignitaries. This group all wore Plaimont tee-shirts; Plaimont is one of the largest and most successful wine co-operatives in the south-west, and it produces Madiran as well as a range of other wines.

The local riding school also presented a team of children on horseback dressed in blue and white riding gear. As the church bells summoned the faithful, the members of the Viguerie Royale gathered. These are the respected growers, or in some cases the fathers of the respected growers, who assemble in picturesque robes like those seen at other wine fêtes, here in vivid scarlet with green scarves and cuffs. There was also a well-fed team calling themselves Les Gourmands du Queyran. The church is large for

The red wines of Madiran are famously full-bodied, well-structured and award-winning

such a small village, but it was bursting at the seams, and many were denied entry, including a *vigneron* in his red fancy dress who had arrived late and was obliged to spend the duration of the Mass outside chatting to holiday-makers. Meanwhile various traders had set up stalls in the streets of the village. There were some superb cheese stalls offering real unpasteurized cheese from the Pyrenees, and visitors would do well to buy some to take in with them to the tasting. There were some interesting *charcuterie* stalls too, with local mountain sausage and ham, while others were selling preserves of *confit* or pâté, or jams and honey.

Mass is over by eleven and it is time for the procession of all those in fancy dress through the narrow village streets. Preceded by the horses from the riding-school (one of which left a pile of manure in the street in which a lady *vigneronne* in flowing robes nearly lost her balance as well as her dignity) they gradually made their tortuous way to the wine-tasting area. Here they proceeded to conduct a tour of all the stands to greet the growers, who were of course all friends or relations. This was a signal for the morning's tastings to begin, and hundreds of visitors flooded through the entrance, each bearing their fifteen-franc glass.

The public are naturally curious to taste the wines of the competition winners. In 1995, Jean-Marc Laffitte had won two awards for his white Pacherenc, in both dry and sweet categories, and many wanted to know exactly what Pacherenc was. As he filled their glasses he explained that it was a traditional white wine of the area which had nearly disappeared altogether during the middle of this century. It is made, usually, with a good dose of a local grape called arrufiac, which is found nowhere else but in this corner of France. Nowadays, the growers also use some other grapes, and these enable them to be in control of the style of the wine, rather than leaving the choice to the weather. Most of them are therefore able, in all but the worst years, to produce both a dry and a sweet Pacherenc. It is still a rare wine, few *vignerons* having more than one or two hectares of the appropriate grapes.

Martine Dupuy an up-and-coming young winemaker

Jean-Marc's dry Pacherenc came in two versions, one oaked, the other not. There was no gainsaying the quality of his sweet Pacherenc, easily one of the best wines of the day. Jean-Marc is one of the better-known growers in Madiran, as is André Béheity, the handsome, green-eyed publicity organizer for the Syndicat. He had won the prize for the best five-year-old red wine. In between stints at the gate, a job which was taken in turn by many of the growers present, he was happy to dispense his traditionally made 1990, which was clearly still full of potential for development .

But the star of the show was undoubtedly (and for reasons not wholly attributable to the quality of her wine) Martine Dupuy, a young winemaker only two years out of college, where she had gained a degree in oenology at Toulouse. Her father and, after his death, her mother had been making wine at Domaine Labranche-Laffont for many years. Her mother Yvonne is still in charge of work in the vineyards, while Martine looks after the winemaking and the marketing. She did not win any prizes for her Pacherencs, although they were very good. She makes two reds, and it was her

wine from her old vines, some of which go back to before the phylloxera, which carried the day with the judges. In a *vignoble* whose wines are famous for their virility, and whose winemakers are as macho as their products, Martine already knows how to stand out from the crowd.

Come lunchtime, you can have a full sit-down lunch, but if fifty francs is more your mark than one hundred and fifty, grab a bottle of good Madiran and make for the covered *halle* in the village where the brochettes, sausages and chops are excellent, and you can have fun joining in the non-vinous activities. You may find that the heart-throb tenor last heard at the pig-squealing at Trie (see page 96) has moved on up the road to Madiran, and that his intonation has not improved.

Alternatively you may prefer to go back to the winegrowers, clutching your precious glass, as it is now time for the usual *intronisations* of various celebrities. The tasting continues, ignoring this event, for the growers are now doing a roaring trade. On a hot day they are hesitant to bring too many supplies, but business can be so good that they send for reinforcements. By this time the professionals will have done all the tasting and buying they want, and it is the turn of the public, with several hours experimenting and deliberation behind them, to put their money where their glass once was. Few go home with an empty boot.

One of the striking features of this fête is the feeling of solidarity and camaraderie among the growers. There is nothing aggressive about their rivalry, nor do you hear anyone utter a nasty comment about another's wines. Perhaps this is because they have a ready market for their wine, and no difficulty in selling it; the vineyard is so small and most of it never leaves the district. Whatever, it is good to see them touring each other's stands and cracking jokes.

You may be tired of wine-tasting by now. You may even have tickets for the tombola, the draw for which is shortly due. Otherwise you have a choice of modern dancing in the village or something more leisurely in the gardens of the priory. At midnight a firework display will crown the day's festivities, and thereafter the rest of the fête is given over to the rockers and ravers.

Jarret de boeuf en estouffade
Slow-cooked shin of beef

SERVES 8

Shin of beef, cut in one piece, about 3kg (6¾lb), on the bone

5–6 tablespoons flour

4 tablespoons goose fat

2 large onions, coarsely chopped

3 large carrots, coarsely chopped

2 sticks celery, coarsely chopped

3 tablespoons armagnac

1 bottle of Madiran or other sturdy red wine

1 bouquet garni

Salt and pepper

1 tablespoon Dijon mustard

350g (12oz) field or other wild mushrooms

Preheat the oven to 180°C/350°F/gas mark 4.

Coat the beef all over with the flour. Melt the fat in a large roasting tin over a brisk heat, add the beef and brown it on all sides in the fat. Transfer the beef to a casserole with a tight-fitting lid and one which is just wide enough to contain the joint. Brown the onions, carrots and celery in the roasting tin. Flambé with the armagnac and, when the flames have died down, add the wine, scraping all the bits off the bottom of the pan. Bubble fiercely for 5 minutes, then add the contents of the roasting tin to the casserole. Add the bouquet garni, seasonings, mustard and enough water to cover the meat well.

Bring the casserole to the boil on top of the stove, then cover and place in the preheated oven. Cook for 10 minutes, then reduce the temperature to the lowest possible setting and leave to simmer for 4 hours.

Remove the beef and take the meat off the bone, cutting it into serving pieces. Carefully spread any bone marrow over the pieces and discard the bones. Discard the bouquet garni. Purée the gravy and vegetables in a blender or food processor and return to the casserole with the pieces of meat. The liquid should be the texture of a good gravy. Bring back to the boil, then cover and return to the oven at the lowest possible heat for at least another 4 hours.

Before serving, add the mushrooms, cut into pieces, and cook for another 30 minutes. Serve with jacket potatoes.

Granité au vin de Madiran
Red-wine water ice

SERVES 6

150g (5oz) sugar

110ml (4fl oz) water

½ bottle of Madiran

Juice of half a lemon

Juice of half an orange

Melt the sugar in the water and allow it to simmer for 5 minutes to form a syrup, then leave to cool.

Pour the syrup into a plastic bowl or container, add the wine and the strained fruit juices and stir well. Freeze at the lowest setting of the freezer. After about an hour, stir the partially set sides into the middle. Continue to freeze, stirring from time to time, until you have a fine mush of frozen granules. This is likely to take longer than usual, because the alcohol in the wine freezes at a lower temperature than other liquids.

Serve in chilled wine glasses with crisp, sweet biscuits.

A Porker's Life

Imagine four grown men, crawling around on all fours, imitating the sound of a sow giving birth, a piglet enjoying its food, two pigs copulating and a full-grown animal being slaughtered, and you might think you were in a place for the mentally deranged.

Not so. You would almost certainly be in a little town called Trie-sur-Baïse on the second Sunday in August, witnessing the champion pig-squealers of the world in competition. It is important to understand that this unique event does not involve any pigs at all, merely human beings imitating them. The winner is the person or team (yes, multiple entries are allowed) adjudged by a highly-qualified panel of experts (farmers, *charcutiers*, chefs and gastronomes) as giving the most realistic portrayal of the sounds of the pig at the most important occasions in its life; as determined by the Mayor of Trie-sur-Baïse who makes the rules.

Trie is a small and remote town of just over a thousand souls, tucked away in a forgotten corner of Southern Gascony. Tuesday is market-day, no common or garden kind of market, but one which includes a lively trade in pigs. The pig-squealing contest is therefore a natural bolt-on to Trie's summer festivities. The competition, like the pig-market itself, is held in a large covered space, 200 metres or so long and 30 wide, like a railway goods yard without the rails. It is called, not surprisingly, the Place des Porcs, and there is just the slightest hint of the denizens in the aromas rising from the concrete

On the second Sunday in August,

the small town of Trie-sur-Baïse organizes

a riotous and truly mad-cap competition

– for the person or team best able to

imitate the squeals and snorts of a pig

floor. This should not deter the tourist, any more than it would worry the local country-people, because the farm pig has a unique place in the affections of the small farmer in the south and in the calendar of the peasant family.

Of all farm animals the pig is the most important in the south-west. Unlike the cow and the sheep, the pig is good for very little else than the table, and the various ways of preserving every part of it ensure a good supply of protein throughout the winter. The best cuts may be preserved in lard as *confit*, the legs made into dry-cured hams, the belly salted either dry or in brine to provide the necessary weight for soups and stews. Left-over bits are used for sausages, often preserved like *confit*, or for salami-like *saucissons* or *saucisses sèches*. The trotters and ears all go into the brine-pot, and the blood into black puddings and a curious kind of garlic-flavoured pancake called *sanguette*.

Small wonder that over the years the slaughter of the family pig became something of a festive ritual: if a farm were lucky enough to have two pigs, one would be killed towards the beginning of winter and the other just before Lent. In poorer households the earlier date would be chosen so that the larder would not be bare over the cold months of January and February. But there is no pleasure taken in the act of slaughter itself. Indeed, to minimize the suffering to the unfortunate beast and the loss of a friend to the family, an outsider would usually be engaged to do the ghastly deed. Combined with the anticipated relief from hunger was the feeling of deprivation inherent in the concept of sacrifice.

The essentially rural audience

delights in watching competitors give

their most authentic rendition of

a sow giving birth, a pig relishing its

food – or even meeting its death

Veteran competitors include this

seventy-five-year-old man from Lot-et-

Garonne, who gave one of the most

amusing, convincing and touchingly

sentimental performances of all

Experienced connoisseurs from the farms

of Gascony make a point of being the

first to arrive and secure front row

seats. They have a better understanding

of these strange sounds than even the

Italians have of *bel canto*

The imitation of the sounds of such a creature provide an entertainment which is not as bizarre as it might seem, because it is within the folk-experience of so many local people. The shared enjoyment of such a fête brings an essentially rural audience together in a way which a more sophisticated show might not. It is something with which they can so easily identify, with its elements of nostalgia and necessary gratification of the pangs of hunger.

Or so it would seem, judging from the huge crowd attracted to this fête. Unlike many events for which preparations are

ever, especially when used to amplify the cries of the would-be pig. At one end of the covered area, the platform for the performers, and at the other trestle-tables with benches laid out for an anticipated eight hundred lunches; in the space between a bar selling pastis, beer and *floc* (the local aperitif made from grape-juice laced with armagnac); a few small stalls round the edge mostly dedicated in one way or another to the cult of the pig; a stall of regional *charcuterie*, including a range of joints preserved in wood ash, and an old photograph stall including many rustic old piggy postcards.

obviously being made days ahead of time, you would not guess until about eleven o'clock in the morning of the day itself that anything unusual was about to happen at Trie-sur-Baïse. The only hint of the fun to come is the decoration of every shop, each window illustrating the trade within in piggy terms. No merry-go-rounds, dodgem-cars, shooting-booths, tombola-stalls or other trappings of the modern fête; only the ubiquitous sound-system, here destined to be louder than

Until recently, the morning was given over to a display by the local *charcutier*, who each year attempted to break his own world record for the longest sausage in the business. This seems now to have been discontinued. Nowadays the festivities begin with lunch, an ever-lengthening column waiting patiently to collect their trays, each containing some raw ham, *boudin noir*, sausages and, of course roast pork, all of which may be outshone by some really delicious sauté potatoes, reeking of garlic. To follow, a solitary raw apricot, but to go with it all as much roughish country wine as you can manage. The composition of this menu reminds you that, traditionally, lunch out in the countryside meant an endless parade of protein.

By apricot-time, the *animateur* arrives. Every fête has one; he is the fellow who keeps up an endless barrage of chat, occasionally interrupting proceedings when he cannot think of anything to say, to introduce famous visitors or invite members of the public to make fools of themselves. A tongue-

not all of them have the courage in the event to go up on to the platform and grab the microphone, so some fall by the wayside. The contestants come from far and wide, Switzerland, Marseille, Aix-en-Provence, and some of them have never even seen a pig, so there is hope for any intrepid reader who fancies a go.

Always there is last year's winner, there to defend his title; but there are many worthy challengers, including those who have won in previous years; more especially the younger talent who carried all before them the year I was there. Also

twisting competition for example, more likely than not to be won by a foreigner whose innocence of the perils of French enunciation makes him an easy winner. A competition for the wearer of the piggiest tee-shirt will inevitably involve little children as well as grown-ups; the field will be divided into two classes so as to ensure at least one prize for one of the tinies.

Soon it is time for the start of the big event. But first, the preliminary round. Usually there are about fifteen entries but

competing was the self-appointed *garde-champêtre* of the town, a previous winner over several years, and Josef, a seventy-five-year-old veteran from the Lot-et-Garonne, who gave one of the wittiest and at the same time most touching performances of all. These men remind you that the contest is not just about imitating the cries of the pig, but expressing its pain as well; and the sorrow of the farmers who were saying good-bye to it for the last time.

But the great moment is now at hand, and the *animateur* is about to introduce the day's celebrity: the south's answer to Delia Smith, a well-known food expert called Maité. Alas, Maité is detained, and may be late; so it appears is the main contestant for the pig-squealing final, the four men from near Grenoble, who, in the first round, had given a collective performance worthy of the best theatre.

Eventually all are in place for this breathtaking final; six contestants, all of them with something original to contribute on the amazing theme of the Life of the Pig.

The quartet from Grenoble gives an incredible performance, even more lifelike than the first time round, playing very much to the gallery the episodes of sex and slaughter. But it is the previous champion who really offers the most serious challenge to the young team.

In the end the Jury decide, under Maité's chairmanship, that the *mise en scène* of the quartet carries the day and they are duly proclaimed the winners. They receive a handsome trophy, which suitably celebrates the excellence of the pig over all other farm animals.

The fête is not at an end, because the usual festivities will continue until well beyond midnight; but the pause at this point, before everyone reassembles for a giant cassoulet and dancing, makes one reflect yet again on what draws such a crowd to such a bizarre happening. Is it the need to satirize an episode which is otherwise a painful one in the calendar? Is it more simply another manifestation of the celebration of violent death which seems endemic to modern entertainment?

This is however only the first stage. In order to raise the excitement, as well as to introduce a little variety, other events may be planned; for example, the medal for the person who can consume the largest quantity of blood-pudding, although it has to be said that in 1995 this event failed for want of entrants. Not so the pig-racing, for which many intrepid breeders had entered thirty or so likely candidates. This event was run as a treble; three races, for which the public were invited to nominate the winners of each heat. The successful were to earn handsome prizes – whole hams and succulent sides of pork, as well as quantities of the good wines of Gascony. At the last moment of the course the pigs were made to turn a sharp left-handed bend to the finishing post. Alas, most of them decided to turn round and go back whence they had come, which caused a deal of confusion, as well as gross upsets of form.

Or is it simply a need to find an escape through celebrating an already familiar ritual, a need for colour and the revival of lost traditions? When the elusive moments of a transient fête such as this linger in the memory, may they not nurture and enrich the imagination of those who have taken part, even at this very basic level?

Rôti de porc froid glacé
Cold glazed roast pork

The virtue of this method is that the pork does not shrink in the cooking as it does with dry roasting. It also remains moist. Make sure the butcher gives you the bones and rind.

SERVES 6

1.25kg (2½lb) loin of pork, boned and rolled

2–3 cloves garlic

Salt and pepper

1 onion stuck with 2 cloves

2 carrots, sliced

2 leeks, sliced

1 bouquet garni

Syrup made with 150g (5oz) sugar and 300ml (½ pint) water

300ml (½ pint) chicken stock

Begin 2 days ahead of time by removing the rind from the pork and putting it aside. Spike the pork with the garlic, season well and leave overnight.

Next day, put the meat with its rind and bones into a casserole with the vegetables and bouquet garni, and cover with the syrup, stock and water if necessary. Cover, bring to the boil and simmer slowly for 1 hour. Remove the lid and continue simmering, turning the meat from time to time until all the liquid has evaporated, leaving the fat and vegetables only with the meat (about 1½–2 hours).

Remove the joint from the casserole. Glaze the meat by straining the juices over, and allow the meat to cool for 24 hours. Serve with a salad of *mâche*.

Côtes de porc à la gasconne
Pork chops with olives and garlic

SERVES 4

25 cloves garlic

4 thick pork chops

1 sprig thyme

1 bay leaf

Salt and pepper

2 tablespoons olive oil

1 tablespoon lemon juice

24 green or black olives, stoned

2 tablespoons goose or duck fat

1 glass dry white wine

150ml (¼ pint) beef or chicken stock

Slice one garlic clove and insert slivers into each pork chop. Mix together the thyme, bay leaf, seasoning, oil and lemon juce in a shallow dish. Add the chops, turn to coat and leave to marinate for 2 hours.

Blanch the olives and the remaining garlic separately for 2 minutes, then drain. Chop the garlic.

Heat the fat in a frying pan. Drain the chops and pat dry on kitchen paper. Fry them quickly in the fat for 3 minutes on each side. Add the chopped garlic, cover and reduce the heat. Cook very gently for 30–45 minutes, turning the chops once.

Transfer the chops to a warm serving dish and arrange the olives around them. Add the wine to the pan and stir to deglaze, then add the stock and simmer to reduce slightly. Pour the sauce over the chops and serve immediately.

Market-day In Provence

A fter the seven wonders of the world, there are still some modest experiences which can take away the breath of even the most hardened traveller. The markets of Provence fall into this category.

Visually, the spectacle is always ravishing. The cloudless skies, which are a transparent ultramarine in the early morning and at dusk, become a hot chalky cobalt in the middle of the day. The thick canopies of the plane trees allow just enough sun to filter through to dapple the stalls of food and flowers, the patches of light and shadow repeating the patterns of the peeling tree bark. A gentle breeze rustles the leaves and keeps the produce cool and fresh. The rich greens of the vegetables, the brilliant reds and oranges of the fruits, set against the jet black of the olives and the aubergines, blend and never seem to clash in nature, compared with the brash and lurid displays of man-made merchandise.

The heightened colours are matched by the animation of the people. The stallholders, whether they are professionals or little old ladies who have brought their surplus produce to market so as to be able to chat to their friends, seem to talk more, argue louder, gesticulate more wildly here than anywhere else. The shoppers seem more fussy, more ready to debate with the market-vendors the quality of the produce, and to drive a harder bargain than in any other setting. Even a poodle seems to yap louder and to more purpose than it would in Paris.

It is difficult to be disappointed by any market in Provence; every one you visit seems even better than the last and you would swear it is the best you have ever been to

For the gourmet, the ordinary everyday shopper, or even the hungry tourist, the markets of Provence are more mouth-watering than any others. The peas have not been allowed to swell to the size of marbles in their pods, the broad beans are so young that there will be no need to remove their inner jackets, and the young green haricots snap between the fingers rather than bend in two like sticks of plasticine. The black cherries sparkle and shine in the shade of the trees, not one bad one among them; the strawberries are small and dark red, rather than the size of turnips and a wan orange in colour; the raspberries still have on them the down they bore when picked from the canes.

The olive stalls will carry scores of differently-prepared fruit: plain green and black ones of course, but each may be stuffed with an infinite variety of flavours: garlic and sweet

opposite: the market in Nice

above: the covered market in Ganges

preceding page: the thrice-weekly market in the

Place des Prêcheurs, Aix-en-Provence

peppers, anchovies, basil, fennel, lemon or spices from more exotic lands.

The cheeses will mostly be from goats' milk, and may be sold without name by the wives of the smaller farmers, or may be from well-known areas such as Banon, which produces small cheeses from ewes' milk as well as fresh goats' cheeses. From the Camargue come 'Le Camarguais' and 'La Brique', and they may be flavoured with *sarriette (*summer savory). From the *garrigues* there is a spherical goats' cheese called 'Le Roves', while in the Ardèche and the Drôme, *départements* facing each other across the Rhône valley, the goats' cheeses are called *picodons*. There is even cheese in the style of the Greek feta, and no shortage of more conventional cheeses from cows' milk, even a small round version all the way from the Aubrac.

The range of *charcuterie* can be no less exhaustive; pork *saucissons* of the salami type from all over Provence, the kind from Arles fetching usually the highest price; there are miniature ones called *grelots*, sometimes made with nuts as well as pork; a raucous-looking version is called 'Le Cathare au Vin'. There are *saucissons* made from the meat of other animals too: beef, wild boar, venison and even donkey. As well as pure pork sausages, there are dried ones such as the 'Fouet de Campagne', bent double like a croquet hoop, a miniature version called *amourette* in the shape of chipolatas and made partly with fennel. There are spicy ones too, the

Left: Mormoiron market (basil); *Right:* produce sold from a car boot, Velleron

Camarguaise with hot red pepper and the spice-laden North African *soubressade*. Hams are brought from all over the world – from Parma, Bayonne and Serrano of course, but also from San Danielle in the Friuli area of north Italy.

The spice stalls are no less amazing. Saffron you would expect because it is a staple ingredient of the world-famous bouillabaisse; mace and nutmeg too, ground green and red peppers, fennel, juniper and star anis. The surprises are legion: two kinds of *ras-el-hanout* (yellow and brown), cumin, tandoori mixtures, brown Jamaican pepper, *quatre-épices*, powdered cloves, cayenne, Mexican pepper (large brown grains like peas), green anise, chillis, peppers from Guinea, *niora*, *molokeya*, camomile, green cardamom, mustard seed, *pavot* and *pili pili*.

Courgette flowers for sale, Nice

This list of spices was compiled from a stall in Arles market and is not even complete. Arles is seemingly the mecca for all the shoppers in southern Provence on a Saturday morning. As well as being perhaps the largest and most important of all the Provençal markets, it is one of the most cosmopolitan, reflecting a wide range of cultures and civilizations. The Romans, who made Arles their Provençal capital, also made it their business to bring back foodstuffs and spices from the furthest outposts of their empire, even from as far afield as Senegal. Today the return of so many families from Algeria is having a similar effect on the range of exotic foods being absorbed into contemporary Provençal cuisine.

Marseille too has a fascinating range and variety of markets, one of the most interesting being the small Marché des Capucins, also called Noailles. This is just off the Canebière, a little over a kilometre up from the old Port. It too has a pronounced North African flavour, and the adjoining streets are given over almost exclusively to butchers, fish-mongers and spice shops specializing in produce from the other side of the Mediterranean. In the Capucins I found what I think are the largest apricots I have ever seen, a variety called 'Muscat du Gard', as well as an unusual Spanish melon called 'Brodée', the size and shape of a small rugger ball, sweet and very juicy but not having quite the depth of flavour of a good Charentais. (For more on Marseille, see page 58.)

Aix-en-Provence may not be as large as Marseille, but it has a much more aristocratic feel. Home of the court of the

Clockwise from above: spices at Arles; trading at Arles; Arles market; Les Capucins, Marseille; *opposite:* Les Capucins, Marseille

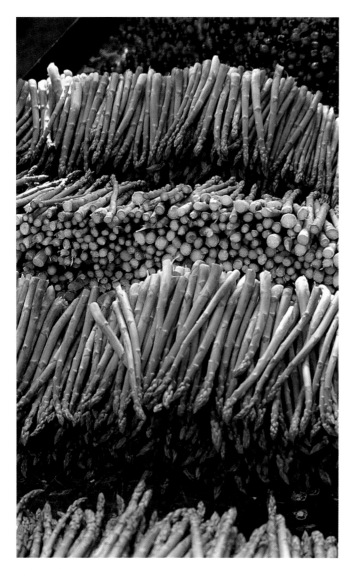

Left: Les Capucins, Marseille (asparagus); *Right:* Arles (olives)

Counts of Provence for many years, Aix has an artistic and literary tradition, reflected in the bookshops which today line its main street, the elegant Cours Mirabeau. The city's most interesting markets are north of the east end of the Cours. The Place Richelme in the old city is small and oblong in shape. The market is intimate, though more important at weekends; there are vegetable stalls round the sides, and in the centre other stalls selling poultry, cheese, honey and herbs.

Every market seems to yield something unusual; here it might for example be the tiny green peppers called *petits marseillais*, or you may find a nun selling courgettes with their flowers still attached. Perhaps it will be the first time you come across a goat's cheese called Arlésienne Gardiane?

The market in the Place des Prêcheurs is much bigger and happens every Tuesday, Thursday and Saturday morning. This is the place to find the famous small strawberries from

Clockwise from top left: Ganges (beans); Ganges (cheese); Nice (*pissaladière*); Monteaux (*fromage apéritifs*)

Mont Ventoux. Cherries too grow on the slopes of Mont Ventoux, a variety called Edelfingen. There is usually one of those typically Provençal stalls selling nothing but different kinds of *tapenade*: plain *tapenade* from green or black olives, green *tapenade* with tuna fish and basil, or with almonds, or variations called *pistounnade* and *anchoïade*. A speciality from the mountains is *tourtous de champsaur*, pastry squares with a wide variety of fillings: apple, prunes, meat, spinach or potato.

Not all the most interesting markets are to be found in the big cities. The true atmosphere of rural Provence is still to be found in the smaller town markets, where once a week the country growers come in to trade with the townspeople and the holiday-makers. Carpentras, famous for its strawberries, is an important agricultural centre, as is Apt, and both have what the Americans call 'farmers' markets'. But even these are large in comparison with some of the village markets, that of

Monteux, between Avignon and Carpentras, being a good example. Here the streets are thronged on a Sunday morning with housewives shopping for lunch, and once a year they try to boost the weekly market into a Fête des Melons, which, with only two stalls selling melons, is pushing things rather. Even more rural is the tiny market, also on Sundays, at Mormoiron, where there are still interesting things to buy – herb plants in particular and also jams and *confits de vin*.

Velleron is an altogether unremarkable town, but every Saturday evening, beginning at six o'clock, there is a truly remarkable farmers' market, with a full range of products of the most excellent quality. There must be the best part of a hundred stalls here, selling everything from baskets to wine, from cheeses to beetroots, and the prices are most competitive. Nearby L'Isle-sur-la-Sorgue is also a famous market-centre, as is Cavaillon a little further south, where the melons come from.

The spirit of Provence has spread east and west of its strict limits, so that stylistically it is hard to say where its cuisine begins and ends. Nice, for example, part of the Kingdom of Savoy and belonging to the King of Sardinia until 1860, is the home of *pissaladière*, adopted by the Italians as pizza. Of all south coast towns, Nice is second in size only to Marseille. At the heart of the French Riviera, you would expect it to have a prosperous feel, and it certainly has that. Its richness is reflected in its various markets, nowhere better than in the Cours de Saleya, just off the waterfront outside the splendid Préfecture. Weekends are the best days here, when a good number of *petits producteurs* bring in their fruit and vegetables, and there is a spectacular display of flowers too. This is a good place to buy some courgette flowers to make fritters with. Note that on Monday the market is given over to antiques.

West of Provence, the *département* of Gard has a Provençal feel though it is strictly in Languedoc; it is hard to say categorically where one begins and the other ends,

The Fête des Melons at Monteux – all two stalls worth – is nonetheless a serious affair

particularly since Nîmes, its principal city, is so rich in Roman influences. It is hard not to regard the Pont du Gard as part of Provence. Nîmes of course has splendid markets, but so do Uzès and Ganges, the latter being a fat little country town on the edge of the Cevennes, where the cherries in particular are big and luscious in May and June.

It is difficult to be disappointed by any market in this part of the world; every one you visit you would swear is the best you have ever been to. (For detailed information on all the markets, see pages 180 to 191.)

La Bohémienne

Savoury gratin of aubergines and tomatoes

SERVES 4

450g (1lb) aubergines

Salt and pepper

Olive oil

350g (12oz) tomatoes, peeled, quartered and deseeded

1 large clove garlic, chopped

2 anchovy fillets

2 teaspoons flour

2 tablespoons milk

Fresh breadcrumbs

Cut the aubergines into 1cm (½in) slices, sprinkle with salt and leave to drain for 1 hour. Pat the slices dry with kitchen paper. Coat the bottom of a frying pan with olive oil and fry the aubergine slices until golden. Add the tomatoes. Season with salt and pepper, add the garlic, and leave to simmer gently for 20 minutes, stirring from time to time.

Pound the anchovy fillets in a mortar with 1 tablespoonful of olive oil. Stir in the flour, then the milk. Add this mixture to the vegetables, and continue cooking for 5 minutes. Check the seasoning.

Transfer to a gratin dish and cover with a layer of breadcrumbs. Sprinkle with oil and brown under the grill.

Artichauts à la Barigoule

Stew of young globe artichokes

Recipe from Erick Vedel.

SERVES 4

4–8 young artichokes, according to size

Olive oil

1 medium-sized onion, chopped

1 slice salt belly of pork, cut into 16 strips (optional)

1 glass dry white wine

1 sprig of thyme

Pepper

This dish should be made with the first, small, tender artichokes which are left whole, but it can be done with young ones up to the size of an apple.

Prepare the artichokes by cutting off any sharp leaf points and pulling off any coarse lower leaves. Break off the stalks. Larger artichokes should be cut into four and their chokes cut out. Peel the stalks and slit them in half.

Cover the base of a thick-bottomed casserole with oil and put in the onion, pork lardons and artichokes with their stalks. Cover and cook over medium heat and lightly brown the contents, then add the white wine, thyme, pepper and a little water. Reduce the heat and cook for up to 1 hour, stirring from time to time and adding more water if necessary.

dip them into the batter to coat well, then deep-fry a few at a time for about 3 minutes until they are crisp and golden, turning them halfway through. Drain on kitchen paper and serve immediately while they are hot and crisp. They need no accompaniment.

Fleurs de courgettes farcies
Stuffed courgette flowers

SERVES 4

stuffing:

1 onion, finely chopped

2 courgettes, finely chopped

2 tablespoons olive oil

1 clove garlic, chopped

2 tablespoons chopped fresh herbs such as parsley and marjoram

4 tablespoons fresh breadcrumbs

Salt and pepper

2 egg yolks

1 bay leaf

8 courgette flowers

2–3 tablespoons chicken stock

Prepare the filling by softening the onion and courgettes in 1 tablespoon of the oil over a medium heat for 2–3 minutes. Remove from the heat and stir in the garlic, herbs, breadcrumbs and seasoning. Allow to cool, then mix in the beaten egg yolks.

Preheat the oven to 180°C/350°F/gas mark 4. Place the bay leaf in an oiled gratin dish. Carefully open each courgette flower and place a spoonful of filling inside, tucking the tops in. Lay each on its side in the dish, add the chicken stock and trickle a little olive oil over each flower. Cover the dish with foil and bake for 15 minutes.

Beignets de fleurs de courgettes
Courgette flower fritters

SERVES 4

fritter batter:

3 tablespoons olive oil

120g (4½oz) plain flour, sifted

Pinch of salt

150ml (¼ pint) lukewarm water

1 egg white

8–10 courgette flowers

Vegetable oil for deep- frying

Prepare the fritter batter 2 hours ahead of time. Make a thickish cream by blending the oil into the sifted flour and salt, then beat in the water until smooth.

Just before frying, fold in the stiffly-beaten egg white. Heat the oil to 190°C/375°F. Spike the flowers on a skewer or knife,

Let Them Eat Cake

A variety of cake called *fouace* is to be found all over the south of France. It is a plain, pale yellow cake, flavoured with vanilla and sprinkled with sugar, and is usually made in the shape of an inflated inner tube. So dry in texture as to be a total conversation-stopper, it needs plenty of liquid accompaniment. Liberally spread with homemade jam and a spoonful of crème fraîche and washed down with a glass of sweet white Gaillac, it is splendid for *le five o'clock*.

In the medieval village of Najac, the *fouace* is something else. It is at the heart of the village fête which takes place each year over the weekend following August 15th. This is no ordinary *fouace* but a giant model, as big as the inside of the biggest baker's oven in the district, and weighing goodness knows how many kilos. This version is more the shape and size of a life-raft and needs a tractor to carry it. As the climax of Najac's three-day event, the outsize *fouace* is hoisted on high and carried from one end of the village to the other and back again before being cut up into bite-sized pieces and distributed to the crowds.

Like the town of Najac itself, the history of its *fouace* is lost in the mists of pre-revolutionary history. How did it come to achieve its obviously symbolic importance? Was it some kind of distribution of food to celebrate the end of a period of famine? Was it a means of avoiding the taxes which you had to pay in the days of the monarchy if you wanted to bake in the public oven? Was it an offering made through the church for the poor? Whatever the explanation, Najac is the only town

> **_Fouace_ is a large cake:**
>
> in medieval Najac it assumes surreal
>
> **dimensions as the children parade**
>
> it through the streets and the grown-ups
>
> **all dance the night away**

in France where such a monstrous piece of pâtisserie is paraded through the streets.

For better or for worse, another feature of the Najac fête is one which has disappeared in recent years. There used to be not just one fête, but two, which took place simultaneously and with the fiercest possible rivalry, often culminating in violence – one year an unfortunate participant swallowed his lighted cigar after being punched on the nose. The reason for this rivalry and division of effort and resources lies partly in the shape of the town and its extraordinary geographical situation.

The Aveyron river gives its name to one of the largest, wildest and least-known of the *départements* of France. It runs most of its course through gorges, with perpendicular banks covered in oaks and sweet chestnuts. In the few places where the river broadens out into a plain, towns have sprung up, and

Sunday is the *fouace* day. The crowd

starts to assemble at the suburban end of

the town after lunch. The action seems

to be centred on a large garage. Inside, two

tractors are ready to tow floats,

each containing a *fouace*.

Each float, dressed overall with the

tricolore, is decked with flowers and

crammed with children who have been

provided with an endless supply of confetti

with which to shower the spectators.

As the procession moves into the

main *place* by the ham-stand, it is joined

by a trio of hurdy-gurdy players in

traditional costume and a group of folk-

dancers in the routine black hats and red

scarves of the Rouergue.

Lanterns amid smoke light up the warm night

The old town gate once stood at the top of this street, where the buildings still nearly meet, allowing only the road to pass between. Beyond this point you are in the modern suburb, which contains the post office, the gendarmerie and the tax office. Here too is the large *place* where the dodgems, merry-go-rounds and suchlike monstrosities are brought at fête time.

The Quartier Bas of course refuses to have any truck with such vulgar pleasures. The rivalry between the two Quartiers existed for centuries, and its origin lay in the extraordinary topography of the town: for those living near the château, it was a half-day's journey to the post office and back. The fête at one time was the highly visible manifestation of this urban separatism. Each Quartier prided itself on making the larger *fouace*, the more impressive torchlight procession, the more spectacular dancing and the louder and more raucous band. But the processions did not confine themselves to their own Quartier. Part of the excitement was the confrontation along the way as each invaded the other's territory.

The duality of the Najac fête continued until the Second World War, during which all fêtes were banned. After the war, there were still two fêtes for a while, but the spirit of rivalry had gone, Najac was losing much of its importance to neighbouring towns, and the population had slowly but surely been falling for years. Finally in 1982 the decision was taken to merge the fêtes officially.

The first day, the Saturday, is a quiet prelude for what is to follow. There are local producers offering specialities such as goats' cheeses. The main street is full of more or less genuine artisans demonstrating ancient crafts and trades. If you need to be reminded how a ball of wool comes into being or how a horse's saddle is made, here is the place to find out. Old farming techniques are on display too, including demonstrations of how to strip maize. Basket-making is a craft which has survived locally and can even be said to be flourishing – the influx of owners of second homes has ensured that no weekender or holiday-maker will be seen at

Najac is one of them. Najac has grown piecemeal. At the furthest extremity, perched on a wholly improbable rocky outcrop, is the ruined medieval château which dominates the surrounding countryside. From here a narrow street, flanked by ancient houses, some in ruins, winds back for a kilometre or so along a narrow ridge until a side-road leads off to the old covered grain market. The main street at this point starts a precipitous climb back towards the plateau. All the town so far described is called the Quartier Bas. Eveything above it is the Quartier Haut. The latter is of course less ancient than the Quartier Bas, which has the snobbery of seniority.

The *bourrée* and the *farandole* are top of the pops at La Loge in the Quartier Bas

market without a suitably rustic basket. The *barriou*, as the main street is called, is fifty metres or so wide, so can contain sizeable displays. The French have a great affection for old cars, and the Najac fête always features a good selection. Giant Peugeot and Citroën saloons display a style of luxurious coachwork and fittings which should make modern manufacturers blush with shame. There are old tractors too, going back to the fifties when these machines made their first appearance on the backward agricultural scene.

It is a pity that there is no trace of the activities for which Najac was once famous and which made it the rich town that it was a hundred years ago. When the hillsides were covered with vines, barrel-making was an important village trade. There were also copper and tin mines in the valley which have been exhausted. Najac's greatest glory though was its hams, which enjoyed a reputation second to none. They used to be weighed in public before being auctioned, and the machine was housed in a kind of kiosk, which remains in the main street today, looking rather like a small bandstand. To prevent fraud the true *Jambons de Najac* were branded as such. Industrialized farming has led to pigs being fed on a less rich diet than their forebears, and so Najac hams are just a folk memory.

Today Najac lives on tourism, and the fête survives as its principal event in the calendar. On the Saturday and Sunday evenings there are two *bals*, one in each Quartier. Needless to say the Quartier Bas limits itself to traditional folk-dancing, while the Quartier Haut favours hard rock. The latter takes place amid all the familiar attractions of a travelling fair, but the Quartier Bas has the benefit of the old covered market, called La Loge. Here the band consists of a fiddler, an accordionist (of course), an all-purpose percussion player and a musician of all talents, who can switch from flute to accordion to a kind of rustic washboard. This dance floor has the added advantage of a large nearby café which also serves good pizzas and does not put up its prices at fête time. You can tell the visitors at once. Whatever the dance – and some have quite intricate rhythms as well as traditional steps – the tourist will be seen determinedly trying to adapt the quickstep. There is obviously still much enthusiasm for local folk-dancing because many Rouergats, including some of the youngest, are very skilful. Some of the dances involve as many couples as can be squeezed into two lines facing each other, each couple having their solo spot as they make their way in the appropriate rhythm and steps to the other end of the line-up.

Sunday is the *fouace* day. The crowd assembles at the suburban end of the town after lunch. The action seems to be centred on a large garage. Inside, two tractors are ready to tow floats, each containing a *fouace*. The amalgamated fête features both. Each float, dressed overall with the *tricolore*, is decked with flowers and crammed with children who have been provided with an endless supply of confetti with which to shower the spectators. There is no civic ceremony or formalities of any kind: the arrival of the band is all that is needed for the procession to start. This particular group has travelled a long way. They are obviously highly experienced at this kind of gig, able to mix in ideal proportions a certain deadpan atonality with a rousing raucousness. Fête fans soon become connoisseurs of this kind of orchestral virtuosity. The leader

of this group told me that bandsmen grew more and more to resemble the instruments they played. His cornettist was a cherry-faced young man with a head as round as his horn, while the bass-drummer would strike fear into the heart of anyone on a dark night. Boum! Boum! Boum! went her long-suffering sheet of parchment, and we were all off past the shooting galleries and dodgem-cars, into the town and down its main street. On a hot day the spectators are crammed under the arcaded buildings, while in the second of the two floats malicious youths squirt them with jets of water from garden-sprays, as if to remind everyone of the true spirit of carnival – the right of every participant to more or less total self-expression. As the procession moves into the main *place* by the ham-stand, it is joined by a trio of hurdy-gurdy players in traditional costume and a group of folk-dancers in the routine black hats and red scarves of the Rouergue. Everyone then funnels down the steep street leading to the Quartier Bas. At this point the way is so narrow that the cacophony of all the combined musical forces and the cheering of the crowd is deafening. We are now approaching the Place St Barthélémy, the lowest point of the saddle of Najac. Here the procession rests to enjoy music and dance, as everyone else fortifies themselves from litre wine bottles for the return journey.

As soon as the sun has set, the *retraite aux flambeaux* (torchlight procession) begins, and it covers exactly the same ground as the *fouaces* have done earlier in the day. *Flambeaux* is a misnomer, because the illumination is by Japanese lanterns, a tradition which started in 1924 when the drought conditions were such that there was no electricity to light the streets. Extra power is added to the charmingly delicate lanterns by modern flares, which give off the most offensive choking fumes as well as a great deal of smoke. But the coughing and spluttering are worth putting up with because of the strangely exotic effect of the fragile lights on the medieval buildings, all seen through a haze of theatrical steam. The cutting of the *fouaces* at the *bal folklorique* comes as something of an anticlimax after this display of oriental impressionism – simply a large table set aside at the edge of the dancing area with pieces of cake and glasses of wine. All the same, the fête would be curiously incomplete without the chance to taste the *pièce de résistance*. The dancing here will go on until all hours, spilling over into the last day of the fête. At the end the music becomes more and more frenzied, making the canned noise from the Quartier Haut seem flat and lifeless by comparison. The sounds from La Loge will linger long in the memory, mingling with Madame's bass drum, the fairy glow of the lanterns on the scalloped slate roofs, and the cement-like texture of the centuries-old *fouace* of Najac.

Croustillant de chèvre
Hot crusted goat's cheese

SERVES 4

1–2 sheets filo pastry

4 rounds of goat's cheese, 5cm (2in) in diameter and
  1cm (½in) thick

Clarified butter, melted

Salad of bitter leaves

2 tablespoons walnut pieces, chopped

Walnut oil vinaigrette

Cut the filo pastry into 8 oblongs, each measuring about 10 x 15cm (4 x 6in). Allow enough pastry round each piece of cheese to make a good parcel.

Place 2 pieces of pastry on top of each other, brush with melted butter and place a round of cheese at one end. Fold the pastry over to make a parcel, fold the edges to seal and brush with melted butter. Repeat with the remaining cheese and pastry.

Arrange the salad leaves on 4 plates.

Heat 1 tablespoon of clarified butter in a frying pan over a medium heat. Add the pastry parcels and fry for 2 minutes on each side, or until crisp and golden. The pastry parcels should have crisp edges and the cheese should be melted through inside.

Lay each parcel on its bed of salad, sprinkle with the walnuts and the dressing, and serve immediately.

Potage Rouergat
Soup from the Rouergue

SERVES 4

125g (4½oz) dried white haricot beans

1½ tablespoons goose fat

1 large onion, coarsely chopped

1 litre (1¾ pints) ham or chicken stock

450g (1lb) potatoes, peeled

Salt and pepper

4 slices French bread

Place the beans in a pan with a tight-fitting lid, cover with cold water and leave to soak overnight. Next day, bring the beans to the boil in the same water and boil hard for about 10 minutes. Reduce the heat, cover and cook for another 45 minutes, or until they have absorbed all the liquid.

Meanwhile, heat the fat in another pan with a tight-fitting lid. Add the onions, cover and cook gently until soft. Add the stock, chop half the potatoes roughly and add to the pan. Bring to the boil, cover and cook over moderate heat for 30 minutes. Pour the soup into a blender or food processor and process until smooth. Dice the remaining potatoes and add them to the soup with the beans. Taste for seasoning: the amount of salt will depend on the stock you have used. Cover and simmer the soup gently for another 30 minutes.

Put a slice of bread in the bottom of each bowl and pour the soup over. A meal in itself.

Hard Cheese

Most fêtes have packed up by four o'clock in the morning. At Chalvignac, in the far west of the Cantal, they are only just starting.

It is the day for celebrating the results of the transhumance and to do honour to the lovingly-made cheeses which represent so many months of hard work.

Most of the milk which the flower-fed cattle have produced is sold to industrial butter and cheese-makers for pasteurization and mass-production. But there still exist a dozen or so artisan cheese-makers, seven of them in the Cantal and the rest in the Aveyron, who use only the milk from their own cows, unpasteurized, to make some of the finest hard cheeses you can buy.

Old-style hand-milking at break of day; a breakfast of cheese soup; a day on the roof of the Massif Central and in the upper reaches of the Dordogne; and finally a celebration of the cheese of Salers

Monsieur Taillé spends the winter with his herd at St Cernin, a few kilometres north of Aurillac. Even at that altitude there is not enough pasture in summer, so at the end of May he brings his cattle up to their summer quarters at a remote mountain plateau called Espinassou, between Mauriac and the Puy Mary. Here, at about 1200 metres high, he has his own *buron* (see page 26), where he has lived since the end of May with his dogs, his only human company being the team of four herdsmen who help him with the milking and droving of the cattle. To pass the long summer days, he has made a small *potager*, where crisp green lettuces rub leaves with petits pois and runner beans. These few vegetables are the only cultivation in sight.

A short way to the north, the Dordogne river has its source in the recesses of the Monts Dore, and it plunges westward through inaccessible gorges below the seemingly unremarkable

village of Chalvignac. Like its peers, Chalvignac has its fête at the end of August. Now it so happens that its Mayor, Monsieur Pradeyrol, is a good friend of Monsieur Taillé. He is also a lover of good cheese and all products of the local *terroir*. He therefore conceived the idea of prefacing the fête with a whole day devoted to a public visit to Monsieur Taillé's mountain retreat, and a celebration back at Chalvignac of the splendid cheeses of the Auvergne.

The visit to the *buron* is to start with the hand-milking of the herd at half-past five in the morning. At the appointed hour of four, when those who have put their names down for this trip may well be doubting their own sanity, about sixty people assemble in the village square of Chalvignac. It is pitch dark. This is no coach-party, except for the school bus which is to lead a procession of cars along tortuous narrow roads, mostly without any surface, meandering beneath the windows of astonished *Auvergnat* farmers who little expect to see so many townies out of bed before them.

The tracks eventually lead to a prairie. Tucked into a fold of ground the *buron* can just be seen, one dim lantern representing the only sign of humanity for miles around. The darkness seems blacker than ever as the party is pointed into the unknown, where the cows and the herdsmen are already into their daily routine. The ground is rough and the air cold.

As day begins to break, the warm milk is carried back to the *buron* by an unaccompanied donkey

After about a kilometre, torches in the void indicate the destination, just as the first suggestion of a very faint pink dawn begins to show the way. Soon a wire enclosure, sixty metres or so square, appears out of the gloom. In one corner is a more substantial triangular wooden pen containing the calves. What first strikes the eye are the strangely lyre-shaped horns of the cows, each wearing a beautiful shiny brass bell. They are of the breed called Salers. Salers is (like Laguiole) a superior *Appellation Controlée* for cheese within the generic type called Cantal. It must be made wholly from milk from the Salers breed. A Salers cheese must by law be matured for at least three months before it is sold, whereas other Cantal requires only one month's compulsory ageing. This explains why this particular fête cannot be held until the end of August, that is to say three months after the transhumance.

Closer examination reveals that there is an outsider in the enclosure. It is the farm donkey, whose job it will be to carry the milk back to the *buron*. In the cart behind him handsome wooden barrels – none of your metal churns – are mounted to receive the fresh milk.

At the _buron_, the cheese is made with rennet and no time is lost in enjoying a breakfast of cheese soup and good red wine

Soon it is light enough to see the milkers at work, each with a bucket. There are sixty-eight cows to be milked and each milking involves a trip to the donkey-cart afterwards, though the milkers willingly offer beakers of warm milk to the visitors. As each cow is done with, an old and highly-experienced cowman is on hand, the _bédélier_. He knows every calf by sight, and, more important, which calf belongs to which mother. He goes into the pen and exhorts each of them one by one to join their mother for whatever is left of her milk, urging them on with a knotted rope and in a loud and totally incomprehensible patois which suggests that he is about to be seriously sick.

The co-ordinated performance of men and beasts is marvellous in its economy of time and energy, and once it is over, the sun is already a fiery ball in the sky and bright enough to cast mauve shadows over the hillside. At half past seven it is time for _casse-croûte_.

The herdsmen hammer the barrels closed and check the harness of the donkey, who heads the procession of cattle, brought up in the rear by two determinedly efficient mongrels, back to the *buron*. They are followed at a respectful distance by the rest of the party. This is an opportunity to take stock of the number of cowpats which the inexperienced have failed to negotiate, but as one cowhand said, *'Ceux-la vous porteront de bonheur...'*

At base, trestle-tables have been laid for all, and from one of the doors of the *buron* a succession of steaming bowls of cheese soup emerges, a wonderfully warming consolation for those whom the still rather feeble sun has failed to warm. This rich meaty stock was poured over generous hunks of country bread on which slices of cheese had been laid to melt in the heat of the bowl. Plastic cups of roughish Auvergne wine were a perfect accompaniment, giving way to hot coffee, laced with limitless supplies of richest Salers cream. Salers butter and Salers cheese wound up this comforting breakfast. Particularly striking was the affinity of taste between the warm milk tasted earlier in the semi-darkness of the hillside, and the unmistakable fresh milk flavour of the cheese, undoubtedly due to the milk not being pasteurized. To add a little local colour, someone started to play the *cabrette*, a kind of bagpipes. By the time breakfast was over, Monsieur Taillé had unloaded the barrels of milk from the wagon and put about ten centilitres (not quite a wine-glassful) of rennet in each one. He told me later that he had collected that morning about 320 litres of milk, which shows how little rennet is needed to start the milk working, to separate the curds from the whey.

The barrels were stood in the middle of the spotless floor, while to one side there was a metal press on rollers, destined to combine all the curd pieces into one homogenous cake. Against the far wall were two green metal presses which would eventually press the finished cheese into the familiar cylinders each weighing forty kilos or so. The cheeses would then be salted and transferred into the cool darkness of the *buron*'s inner sanctum for maturing like a wine – *affinage* as it is called in the trade.

To make his cheese, Monsieur Taillé carefully stirred the milk in each barrel with a large paddle, keeping it in perpetual motion. As the lumps formed, he switched to a coarse flat metal strainer fixed at right angles to a long metal pole: this he raised and lowered to ensure an even distribution of curds and whey within the barrel and uniform operation of the rennet. The work became harder and harder, but Monsieur Taillé had developed powerful biceps. Nor did the physical effort prevent him from keeping up an endless exchange of repartee. Eventually the rennet had done its work and it was time to drain off the whey, first with a bucket and then with a smaller jug. When practically nothing remained except the solids, these were then transferred for the first pressing. As much of the residual whey as possible was then pressed out by bare hands, the curds were wrapped in muslin, and the press was closed. It was surprising how much liquid it still contained. In the Auvergne nothing is wasted, and there were thirsty pigs in a sty below waiting to do justice to the whey.

The first pressing would be complete by evening. The resulting cake-like disc is called *tomme*, and some people eat it as it is. It is slightly sharp and sour but goes down very well with a glass of light country wine. More usually *tomme* is used as the basis for *aligot* (a dish we have already met at Aubrac) and *truffade*, another particularly good local way of preparing potatoes, with garlic and cheese.

The cheese-making over for the moment, it is time to go back to Chalvignac, this time accompanied by a fully mature cylinder of Salers – called locally a *fourme* – which Monsieur Taillé brings to light from the darkness of his *cave*. Monsieur le Maire summons his party and the procession of cars sets off on its return journey. The cortège stops off on the way for a visit to the Château d'Auzers, where the owner Monsieur le Baron has laid on a conducted tour of his charming miniature Renaissance fortress, and a mid-morning snack of homemade buckwheat pancakes called *bourriols*, washed down with a *kir* or two. Soon the party is once more on its way, this time to a full sit-down lunch at a small country restaurant just outside Chalvignac village.

The fête continues in a trip down the Dordogne to La Ferrière

It would be hard to name a single part of the pig which did not feature in this gargantuan but typical *Auvergnat* feast, for pork is the principal meat in this region. Courage nearly failed at the last fence with a *flaugnarde* made from plums, a local kind of Yorkshire pudding. Wine from the slopes of the Auvergne hills was available *à volonté*, and by this time everyone was in a good mood for a trip down the Dordogne in two

gabarres, the kind of flat-bottomed boat once used to ferry cargo up and down the treacherously shallow river. We were accompanied by the ceremonial cheese of course, to demonstrate that, even within living memory, the river was the accepted export route for the produce of the Auvergne.

Down into the gorge, with views of the great Barrage de l'Aigle away to the right, the route led to the landing stage at

La Ferrière, where our *cabrette* player was joined by two accordionists to pipe the cheese aboard and to accompany the boat party on its trip with song and dance. Yes, there was indeed dancing on board.

The boats were soothingly punted, so the hour-long journey downstream and back again was a wonderful chance to recover for those who had lunched too well. It was a chance too to learn from the boatmen what it was like to ply these craft up and down the river to Bordeaux in the old days. It took but a week to drift or be swept downstream with the current, carrying vine stakes, wine in cask, cheeses and timber for furniture-making. But it took three months to make the return journey, hauled by beasts along the dangerous and primitive towpaths, bringing back all kinds of produce which the peasants could not make or grow for themselves.

As the boats returned to La Ferrière, it was time for *le five o'clock*, which consisted of a delicious *friture*, a kind of freshwater whitebait, sharpened with lemon juice and accompanied by ice-cold white wine. This was offered on the river bank by the lady who ran the local fishermens' auberge. I asked her whether she had caught the fish herself, little

thinking that her twinkling response ('*Si! Je péchais toute la nuit!*') would leave so little room for doubt but that her pun was intentional.

Time now to climb back out of the valley to Chalvignac, the cheese slowly borne by two dazzlingly white cart-horses, the accumulating traffic behind showing increasing impatience as the procession took a full hour to reach the village.

Here preparations were already under way for the fête proper, which was due to begin the following Saturday morning. Local artisans and *charcutiers* were setting up their stalls, a barrel-organ player was delighting the children with a free rehearsal and merchants from Laguiole were displaying a selection of their famous knives, as indispensable to a young countryman as a pair of the smartest trainers to a teenage holiday-maker.

In the village square, where a modern covered market had been built in homage to the old-style *halles*, a shout went up as the cheese party, headed by the Mayor, arrived. This mayor is no stuffy dignitary: he is a villager like the rest, not afraid to roll up his sleeves and get his hands dirty; no mayoral chain or chauffeur-driven limousine. He was first out of the cart to help down with the heavy cheese, still in its smart wooden crate, and to carry it across the square to the table of honour beneath the *halle*. Armed only with the professional's wire, he confidently split the forty-kilo cheese neatly into two halves and then into smaller and smaller sections, until it was possible to distribute a generous tasting to the assembled crowd (see opposite). Monsieur Pradeyrol again proved himself model by keeping the speeches short and to the point, praising the virtues of his local *terroir* and the produce of its inhabitants, and then losing no time in declaring the fête open.

Celebrations were then allowed to get under way with two days of events, all holiday-makers conscious that this was the last weekend of the season and that in a few days they would all be back at school or the work-place. Perhaps they reflected upon the day they got up in the dark to savour the daybreak beauty of the Auvergne hills and met the cheese-makers who make their home there for months on end.

Soupe au fromage
Country cheese soup

Steam-baked bread is no good for this recipe: old-fashioned pain de campagne, of which there should be equal quantities of crust and bread, is indispensable. This soup, followed by a green salad, is a meal in itself.

SERVES 4

2 tablespoons duck or goose fat (sunflower oil as a last resort)

2 onions, sliced

2 leeks, finely sliced

Slices of country bread cut 1cm (½in) thick

200g (7oz) Salers, Laguiole or Cantal cheese, otherwise ripe
  Cheddar

1.25 litres (2 pints) chicken stock

Salt and pepper

Heat the fat in a frying pan and add the onions and leeks. Cook them slowly until they are soft but not coloured.

Line the base of an earthenware dish with a layer of the bread. Cover with one third of the cheese, half the leek and half the onion. Repeat the process and finish with another layer of bread, then the remaining cheese.

Preheat the oven to 180°C/350°F/gas mark 4.

Add enough stock to cover, season and cook uncovered in the oven for 1 hour until the stock is almost absorbed. For a thinner consistency, add more hot stock before serving.

Fromage fermier aux amandes
Fresh cows' cheese with almonds and oil

SERVES 4

350g (12oz) fresh cows' cheese

Salt and pepper

60g (2½oz) slivered almonds, lightly toasted

Hazelnut oil

Drain the cheese well and put into small moulds or ramekins to chill for 2–3 hours. Turn them out on to small plates, season with salt and pepper and spike the top with the almonds. Dribble hazelnut oil over all and serve.

The Fête that Almost Never Was

For most people the Camargue conjures up pictures of pink flamingoes, outsize bulls, white horses and cowboys, flaunting themselves under a fierce midday sun and a cloudless ultramarine sky. But in reality the birds are strictly for those who have a pass to the highly-guarded nature reserve, and the ranch life contributes more to special tourist events than to the agricultural economy. Many visitors to the Camargue gaze out over the waters of the Etang de Vaccarès and never see a flamingo, while the most common animal is the sheep rather than the bull. Driving south from Arles in the direction of Les Saintes-Maries-de-la-Mer, the fields, to the extent that they can be seen at all over the top of the giant reed-beds flanking the road, are given over to crops and sheep-grazing. To judge from the smartly painted farmhouses (*mas*), agriculture is clearly prosperous hereabouts, but what is growing in these sun-baked fields? Surely not wheat? It is too short and dense for that. But it is the right golden colour. The answer is given as you flash past a board by the side of the road inviting you to visit 'Le Musée du Riz'.

Rice is a crop which relatively few Westerners know much about. The image they have is probably of waterlogged fields with peasants trudging about up to their knees in water, wearing hats like lampshades. Rice is in fact most intensively planted in the river deltas throughout the world: in the Far East, India and even Italy, which is the largest rice producer in Europe. The Camargue is co-extensive with the former delta

The rice harvest is celebrated with a three-week long fête, finishing at Salin in the Camargue: unfortunately this particular year heavy rains nearly drowned out proceedings altogether

of the Rhône, and is the northern limit at which the crop can be grown – although it must be sown in flooded land, it also needs intense summer heat to ripen it.

The water supply is assured by the river, but in the ecology of a river delta the balance between salt and fresh water is never simple. Until the Second World War, the Rhône delta fanned out south of Arles to form a network of countless waterways which found their way into the tideless sea as best they could, changing course every so often and leaving the hapless farmers at the whim of nature. The Camargue was in those days a pestilential marsh, one of the few areas of Europe where it was possible to catch malaria from the inescapable mosquitoes. It had not always been thus: in the Middle Ages the sea came as far inland as St Gilles, the port of embarkation for the armies of the kings of France going on crusade. Gradually the retreat of the sea left the vast areas of the delta in a state of marine desert, the land dried by the mistral, and the salt brought to the surface by capillary attraction. Because the salt killed most plant life, rice was sown in an attempt to desalinate the ground. It was thought that after a while it would be possible to grow wheat. But the salt killed the rice too, and for a while no way was found of beating the saltiness of the subsoil.

The project of reclamation which was started after the war was ambitious in the extreme. The object was to channel the waters of the Rhône into just two outlets. These are today called the Grand Rhône and the Petit Rhône respectively and they encircle the Etang de Vaccarès which is entirely saline. Because the growing of rice calls for huge volumes of fresh water, it is along these two arms of the Rhône that today's rice fields are planted. Unplanned and unwelcome flooding is avoided by the sophisticated damming of the river upstream (which provides an important source of electricity for southern France) and the enormously high banking of the two rivers once they reach the Camargue. Today there are 25,000 hectares of cultivable land in the Camargue, while at the same time the nature reserve and the traditional *domaines* of the ranchers have been preserved.

At the end of the Grand Rhône lies the small town of Salin-de-Giraud, itself more notable for the mountains of salt which are extracted there from the sea. Between Salin

Despite the weather, the paella, with its daffodil-coloured rice, was a sensation at the fête

and Arles, and sandwiched between the Grand Rhône and the Etang de Vaccarès, are some of the most important rice farms. It is natural that Salin should be the setting for a fête at the time of the rice harvest, and logical that the event should be the climax of three weeks of festivities in the town of Arles based on the theme of rice. 'Les Prémices du Riz' the Arlésiens call it, the first harvest of the rice. But they also manage to fit in to the fête such diverse events as model aeroplane exhibitions, pipe-smoking contests, go-cart races, exhibitions of antiques and, of course, chasing bulls through the streets and inflicting indignities worse still on them. The inhabitants of Arles need little or no excuse to declare themselves *en fête*. For this three-week-long festival in September they appoint an *Ambassadeur du Riz* who holds office for a fixed term of two years.

Robert Bon, rice distributor

But rain can quickly turn the quasi-North African feel of the Camargue into a parody of all that is worst of British wash-outs. When it rains in Provence, inches can fall within minutes. Flash-floods are a genuine fear wherever a river flows. It is hard to parade decorated carts laden with rice, flowers and Provençal produce through such teeming rain and then have them blessed with any decorum by the village priest. This is the usual programme at Salin on the morning of fête day, but in Jessica Bon's second year as *Ambassadeur*, the rain was so heavy that the Mayor of Salin had no alternative but to cancel the procession. Word had spread quickly because the streets of Salin were almost deserted, and the few souls who had ventured out would no doubt have immediately gone back to their firesides if Jessica had not been seen arriving at the chapel in tight black pants and boots, bearing the first sheaf of rice to be blessed (by way of insurance for a good harvest to come) in the dry comfort of the church interior. She was joined by two girls from Salin, dressed in traditional Arlésien costume, representing the salt producers of the village. They bore a large lump of rock salt which they too had brought to be blessed by the *curé*.

In the presence of but a score or so of people, there was a short and rather touching service at which the *curé* gave an unusually brief address ('*La Camargue est comme une belle femme – généreuse et féconde. . .*'), and that might have been the end of the day's celebrations. But Jessica Bon said that there was to be a lunch back at her home, there were bound to be at least one hundred people there, and everyone was welcome for the advertised hundred francs a head. It soon became apparent that Jessica was no ordinary PR appointment by the town council of Arles, though she certainly looked the part, tall with dark Provençal eyes and hair to match. She also happened to be the daughter of Robert Bon, a processor and distributor of rice at the nearby *Mas du Petit Manusclat* where the party was to take place. He also owns and manages the Musée du Riz noted earlier, which is part of his Domaine.

The rain was still pouring down, but not quite as heavily as it had earlier in the morning. At the *Mas* it was possible to have apéritifs in the open air, but the guests were all paddling about in the mud under their umbrellas, like ducks. The *pastis* and wine flowed freely. When the weather became too much, there was always the sanctuary of the Musée, where those who were hazy about how to grow and process rice could put in some useful study. In an old *bergerie* adjoining, trestle-tables and benches to seat 150 or so people were in place, and once tongues had been loosened by Ricard, which does not take long in Provence, everyone moved in to take their place at table.

There were farmers from nearby, not necessarily rice-growers. One of the Bons' near neighbours was a *vigneron* from Marmande in Gascony, who had moved into the Camargue to win the hand of his Provençal wife. There were also townsfolk from Nimes and Arles who come every year, workers from the Salin du Midi up the road, and Monsieur le Curé who had earlier blessed the rice and the salt. The Bon family moved in and out of the rows of tables, shaking hands with the many visitors who were known personally to them.

After appetites had been whetted with pâté, olives and gherkins followed by a salad (often taken as an entrée in Provence), a roar of applause and loud cheers greeted the arrival of the giant paella, carried in a huge round pan, not quite as big as the giant omelette pan at Bessières-sur-Tarn, but very impressive all the same. Mussels shone in their glossy black shells flanked by the pinkest of prawns, tender pieces of chicken and bright red peppers, all embedded in the home-processed rice of the Camargue, daffodil yellow from its dose of saffron.

The music started: discs, many from the early rock'n'roll years, to remind some of the more mature of village fêtes and

His daughter Jessica, Ambassador of Rice

dances they had gone to in their youth. There was not much space for dancing, just the central aisle between the tables, but this scarcely deterred the aficionados any more than it affected either their appetite or digestion. The dancing was interspersed with singing. The three virtual national anthems: 'Coupo Santo' of course (see page 54), then a curious version of 'Roll out the barrel' which is the adopted song of Marseille football club, and finally, as if to remind everyone that even a good Provençal can be a good European too, Beethoven's 'Ode to Joy' led by Monsieur le Curé on the harmonica.

Robert Bon seemed to be everywhere at once: now bopping with his lady guests, now gossiping with them on the benches, now holding forth on the mysteries of rice culture in his museum, a welcome haven of peace from the deafening and ever-increasing noise next door. Had the weather been kinder, there would have been a *pétanque concours* in the yard outside, but it was under water, so when everyone had had enough of the wine and the dancing, the party diminuendoed to a close, and the revellers went home.

Robert had proved such an interesting exponent on everything to do with rice that he kindly agreed to tell me more about it the next morning in a less frenetic setting. The *Mas* was entirely back to normal, the hum of the drying machinery replacing the canned music, and not a trace of the previous day's revelry. Robert corrected several misapprehensions from the day before. First, he is not himself in any serious way a grower of rice. He processes the grains and then sells it on to the big distributors. Second, he is only concerned with rice which passes all the Euro-biological tests. But his family has been in the rice business since the beginning – he is the third generation – so he is expert on all its aspects.

There can be no rice without well-controlled irrigation. The sea water of the Mediterranean has to be kept at bay. Paradoxically it is the big salt-processing plant at Salin which to a large extent achieves this. In order to create the series of salt pans in which the sea evaporates, leaving behind the pure sea salt, a giant breakwater has been built which helps to protect both branches of the Rhône from salt infiltration. Nevertheless the deeper reaches of the river do contain salt, more so than the surface waters. To irrigate the rice fields water is therefore pumped off the top of the river. The buoyancy of salt water has enabled the growers to invent a device whereby, when the saline content rises above an acceptable level, a float rises to cut out the power to the electrically-driven pumps.

Rice can either be planted direct into the flooded fields or in a nursery and then planted out into water. By a combination of natural evaporation and industrial technology the fields are gradually drained, leaving the young plants to enjoy their required 150 days of hot sunshine.

Some rain is welcome from time to time but not at the time when the plants flower for just a few hours in early July, or at the time of the harvest, in the second half of September. The crop is brought in by combine-harvester, but the threshing process is replaced by a kind of combing so as to keep the grain intact. In its natural state the crop is called by its English name, Long Paddy.

The husk-like outer envelopes are removed by heating and the resulting inner grain is called *complet*, or what we would call brown rice. White rice (*blanchi*) is produced by a kind of polishing process which removes more shells of the grain and the vitamin B content with it. This vitamin deficiency is the principal cause of beri-beri in oriental countries where rice is the main starch. Nevertheless, white rice is easier to market

than brown, because of its more attractive colour and because it cooks much faster. Robert Bon produces a compromise version which is only half-polished, called *demi-complet*. Most white rice found on the market has been further processed to remove the amidion which acts to make cooked rice puddingy; the consumer generally expects rice to come out of the pan fluffy and light. In this condition (*étuvé*) it is of little nutritional value.

The hotter the climate the bigger the yield, and the cheaper it is to put rice into production – half the cost in Italy, for example, compared with France (10,000 francs per hectare). The average producer (of whom there about 250) will have about 100 hectares planted in rice and the yield is about 5000 kilos per hectare. Because the rice season is short, and because most farmers like to hedge their bets anyway, they also go in for extensive sheep-farming as well as traditional wheat.

Most rice plantations are divided into rectangular fields, the long sides facing north and south and planted with trees to protect the rice from the excesses of the mistral. The local Co-operative takes more than half the production, the remainder of which is accounted for by a handful of growers. Robert Bon accepts rice only from those whom he knows use no chemicals or fertilizers which are not purely organic. This is a relatively easy discipline in rice fields close to the nature reserve, which is fiercely guarded by the ecologists. The rare species which are protected there would be endangered by the use of noxious sprays or polluted drainage.

It is always good to see green virtue rewarded by commercial success. Robert communicates unbounded confidence in the future of rice as a crop, and the production statistics are there to support him. France is still a net importer of rice: the Camargue produces only about 7 percent of the total European ouput, but as a nation France consumes 17 percent of it. The rice-growers of the Camargue have come a long way in forty years, from being an eccentric production curiosity to one of the principal crops of Provence.

It was fitting that, driving back from Le Petit Manusclat to Arles the sun was once again shining from a clear blue sky and the mistral was blowing hard to dry the rice crop for an abundant harvest. A pity about the previous day's weather.

Gardiane de lapin au riz camarguais

Rabbit Camargue style

SERVES 4

1 rabbit, weighing 1kg (2¼lb), with its liver

300g (11oz) prunes

2 cloves

500ml (17fl oz) red wine

3 tablespoons olive oil

150g (5oz) salted belly of pork, cut into thin strips

400g (13oz) button onions, peeled

Salt and pepper

1 sprig of thyme

2 bay leaves

About 115g (4oz) pork fat, cut into chunks

1–2 shallots, cut into wedges

Joint the rabbit and put it in a shallow dish with the prunes and cloves. Warm the wine slightly in a pan, then pour over the rabbit and leave to marinate overnight.

Drain the rabbit and prunes, reserving the wine, and dry on kitchen paper. Heat the oil in a large casserole and brown the pork pieces. Add the rabbit joints, but not the liver, and brown on all sides. Remove and put in the onions. When these are coloured, put back the meat and season. Add the thyme and bay leaves and pour over the wine from the marinade. Cover and simmer gently for 1½ hours. After an hour add the prunes, reserving 4 for the brochettes.

Prepare 4 miniature brochettes with alternate pieces of liver, pork fat, shallot and half prunes. Before serving, place the brochettes under a hot grill for 2–3 minutes on each side.

Serve the rabbit with a dish of boiled rice, decorated with the brochettes.

Salade de riz aux olives

Mixed Salad of rice with olives

SERVES 4

250g (9oz) rice

3 tablespoons vinaigrette

2 or 3 small tomatoes, deseeded and cubed

1 green and 1 yellow pepper, deseeded and cubed

3 hard-boiled eggs, sliced

6 canned anchovy fillets, cut into pieces

1½ tablespoons capers

110g (4oz) whole black olives

Salt and pepper

Cook the rice in salted water and drain well. Pour on the vinaigrette and toss well, then cover and chill.

Mix in the tomatoes and peppers. Pile on to a large serving dish and decorate with the eggs, anchovies, capers and olives. Season to taste with pepper.

The Typical Country Foire

Ask the average holiday-maker what is his ideal French market. He may well tell you that it has to be in an old medieval town, small enough to feel intimate, but large enough to attract a good variety of produce; reached preferably across a river by an ancient stone bridge, one of those narrow ones with parapets built out over the piers to prevent pedestrians being mown down by the passing traffic. The town will be a *bastide*, built on a criss-cross grid pattern of narrow streets, where the attic storeys of the houses seem to reach out to embrace those opposite.

In the centre there will be a large *place*, with shady arcades on each side, the buildings all around being built out to provide shelter from the burning summer sun and the plentiful rain in winter. The town church will be incorporated into this architectural complex, its tower extending the line of the arcaded frontages, and its buttresses providing a ceremonial arched entrance into the square. The market-place is even better if it is excavated out of slightly rising ground, so that one side will be on a higher level, with a terrace to give an aerial view of the proceedings below. The terrace will naturally have a café where the foot-weary shopper can relax with a mid-morning coffee or an aperitif.

There must be many country towns in the south broadly fitting this description, but the one it fits like a glove is Villefranche-de-Rouergue. Every time you mention the name somebody says: 'Have you been to the wonderful market?'

At an agricultural cross-roads,

Villefranche is a market-town ideally

placed to supply a complete range of

produce throughout the year, as well as

being a beautiful medieval town to visit

Because Villefranche is at an agricultural cross-roads, it has a complete range of produce to offer all the year round. From the mountains of the Auvergne come the wonderful hard unpasteurized cheeses of the Cantal, with their snobby sisters Salers and Laguiole (see page 126 and 24); from the valley of the Lot the most delicious strawberries in France, to say nothing of the *fraises des bois*; raspberries, redcurrants and blackcurrants in their successive seasons and the tiniest young vegetables *en primeur*. From the east of the county come the creamiest Roquefort and the blue cheeses made from the milk given by the flower-fed cows of the Auvergne mountains, and from countless farms nearer at hand come soft cream cheeses (both goats' and cows'), as well as the harder seasoned *cabécous* from Rocamadour and the redoubtable versions of the same wrapped in chestnut leaves and matured in *eau-de-vie*.

the bullets we are used to, but the greenest, tenderest gems no bigger than a cherry stone; a few bunches of tiny carrots, scarcely larger than the pods of the peas, some baby round white turnips, tinged with blue, and a few walnuts. These modest quantities of produce used to provide the poorer peasants with the petty cash needed to buy those few things they were unable to produce themselves such as salt, matches, dried and salted cod to replace meat during Lent, the occasional pair of shoes and basic clothing.

Nowadays, the market habit still subsists, but perhaps less out of economic necessity than a need to meet and gossip with friends and relatives, to relieve the loneliness which is still often the lot of those living on the remoter farms. Wives will have accompanied their husbands who will be hoping to transact rather more substantial business. On every fourth Thursday of the month the market is expanded into a more general *foire*, when farmers bring their animals to the special Foirail de la Madeleine, built out of town specially for the sale of livestock.

Here, in their respective seasons, potatoes from the nearby plateaux and walnuts and chestnuts of premier quality from the ancient local plantations are offered to dealers in huge bulk. Villefranche has become something of a centre for naturally-produced meat; the organically-reared *agneaux*

From the slopes of Bas-Quercy come the most delectable melons of the Charentais type and, in winter, foie gras and all variations of duck and goose. From the Garonne valley there are apricots, peaches and nectarines at knock-down prices, the earliest table-grapes and the blackest, shiniest prunes.

From a radius of sixty kilometres or so around – for such is the catchment area of this important market – small growers will bring from their lovingly-tended *potagers* those vegetables which are surplus to their requirements, and free-range eggs from their own chicken runs, still bearing traces of the nests in which they were laid. A small basket of petits pois perhaps, not

Organic growers are increasingly becoming a feature of country markets

fermiers of the Quercy find their way over the borders into this Aveyron *foire*, as also do the milk-fed calves, *élevés sous mère*, rather than in cramped sheds. Reared in the open air, their meat is pinker and less pallid than most veal one is used to, and the flavour more beefy and pronounced.

The Place Nôtre-Dame is no longer big enough to contain the market as it did a hundred years ago. Even though some of the older sellers have given up (because the bureaucracy of market organization requires them to take up their stalls at six o'clock in the morning), they are partly being replaced by young farmers, many of them producing vegetables organically. The professional market-traders too are gradually taking over some of the places formerly occupied by the *petits producteurs*. It is good to see markets such as this expanding, and providing effective competition to the supermarkets and hypermarkets out of town.

Most of the overflow occupies the length of the Allées Aristide Briand behind the big collegiate church. Tucked in between is the old covered market; it is reserved largely for the sale of fattened geese and ducks in the winter, and has now been glassed in to provide some protection against the cold for stallholders and shoppers alike.

The southern half of the long Allées is mostly given over to clothing, shoes and fabrics, though you can also buy a mantelpiece, tractor or central-heating system if the fancy takes you. The upper half of the street is devoted to food and wine. Here are the travelling *charcuterie* stalls, the prize-winning Guy Cance from Villeneuve d'Aveyron whose *saucisson* called *Rosette* is leaner and moister than most; and the local merchant Laplace from Les Pesquies whose ham is especially good, and who sells bits of the pig that you didn't know the pig had. Here too are the cheese stalls, one of them all the way from Aurillac with Cantal butter off the slab, as well as farmhouse cheeses from St Nectaire, Salers and Laguiole. Then there is the man who sells olives, nuts, dried fruits, spices and other exotica, and who has been coming to Villefranche market for at least thirty years. Some of the best vegetable stalls are on the far side of the street, some selling

organic produce at reasonable prices. Nearby you can buy wine by the *bidon*, and particularly to be recommended are the wines from Philippe and Thierry Romain who travel all the way from Montauban to supply their regular customers.

The sun still shines warm here in autumn when the focus of the market shifts to tomatoes and melons for colour. The last peaches and nectarines of the season, the occasional basket of *cèpes* and the first crop of walnuts serve as harbingers of the colder season to come.

In winter, the market at Villefranche has a quite different feel. Gone are the tourists, the children in push-chairs and men in shorts who should never have been wearing them. Now everyone is wrapped up against the cold, with layers of thick shirts and pullovers, the women's legs well-lagged. The square, much less full than in the summer, echoes less resoundingly to the voices of the reduced crowd. The busy buzz of July is replaced by the soft murmur of January. Huge heads of celery and white chard replace the delicate vegetables of summer; cabbages do duty for lettuces, cauliflowers for spinach. But there is still colour: the orange pumpkins stand out against the old stone houses like Belisha beacons, and the mature carrots are just as brilliant a red as the tender new ones were in June. Spring sees the arrival of the *pointes de choux*, the flowering heads of the cabbages grown specially for animal feed, and the shoots of the wild bryony called *tamier*, or in the local language *répounchou*, of which there are as many spellings as there are sellers. To the local peasants, this modest but reputedly emetic vegetable, not unlike a very thin asparagus to look at, is a guarantee that the winter is over and that sunny days are ahead.

Whatever the season, the shopper will be so laden with purchases that, in the few minutes before *midi*, an apéritif or a cup of coffee at the café in the *place* will be irresistible, just in time to enjoy the carillon from the top of the *collégiale*, nowadays alas electronically controlled rather than hand-rung,

Opposite: flowers are just as much a part of the *foire*

Below: Off to the bar to celebrate a bargain

and which has dropped 'God Save the Queen' from its repertoire. When it is finished, the siren goes for *midi*, there is a brief gridlocking of traffic and soon the *place* is deserted once more. There is relative silence, except for the whooshing sound of the street-cleaners' brushes. Everyone else has gone to lunch. Another *foire* is over.

Ragoût de petits légumes printaniers

Ragout of young spring vegetables

SERVES 4

60g (2½oz) goose fat or butter

110g (4oz) *Jambon de Bayonne* (or other raw country ham cut in one slice), diced

8 button onions

125g (4½oz) young carrots, sliced

1 tablespoon flour

300ml (½ pint) chicken stock

350g (12oz) tiny new potatoes, scrubbed

Salt and pepper

1 sprig *sarriette* (summer savory)

175g (6oz) *petits pois*, shelled

350g (12oz) tiny broad beans in the pod, shelled

175g (6oz) *haricots verts* (French beans)

Heat the goose fat in a pan and add the ham. Cook gently for 10 minutes with the button onions and carrots over very low heat so that they do not colour. Stir occasionally.

Mix in the flour, then add the stock little by little. Cook together slowly for 5 minutes. Add the potatoes. Cover and simmer gently for 20 minutes. Season, but be careful with the salt because of the ham. Add the *sarriette*, peas, broad beans and green beans and cook for another 7 minutes. The potatoes and onions should be well-cooked but the green vegetables slightly *al dente*.

Mellow Fruitfulness

The Eco-Musée of the Walnut is a permanent exhibition in the lee of the romantic castle of Castlenau, hundreds of metres above the river Dordogne. Madame in charge will explain the many different varieties: the small dessert nut Marbot, the two halves of whose dark shell do not always meet perfectly; the Corne, another good table nut; the widely-grown Franquette, used for its high oil content; and the Grandjean, a variety even richer in oil and of which there are at least 45,000 trees in the Sarlat region.

More than half the walnuts sold in France come from the Lot or the Dordogne. You would think that there would be markets and fairs all over these *départements* devoted to the sale of these delicious nuts, but you would be wrong. Today, big-time *négociants* from the cities send their container lorries to collect direct from the specialist producers. Buyers and sellers will deal with each other direct, often *en primeur*, prices being struck in the farm kitchens or, less romantically, by fax. The number of smaller growers is dwindling; those that are left take their surplus nuts, if they have any, to the general market with the rest of their produce.

There still remains a nucleus of farmers who have enough walnut trees to make it worth their while to sustain a local market. Madame speaks of a small market at the village of St Laurent-la-Vallée near Belvès, which 'sometimes happens on Wednesdays'. But it may be wiser to settle for her alternative recommendation of Sarlat, where there is a regular walnut

Some say that autumn is the most beautiful season in the south-west; certainly walnuts and chestnuts are here at their best, while mushrooms perfume the woods and kitchens

market, not in one of the medieval squares, but in a large car park next to the cemetery just outside the town.

Madame suggests you arrive early on a Saturday morning; by nine o'clock, vehicles soon begin to trickle into the car park, sometimes laden with only a couple of sacks of nuts and sometimes with up to a dozen (sacks usually hold about thirty kilos). There are already potential buyers lurking, ordinary members of the public as well as smaller dealers. One couple come to Sarlat every year from their home in the Pyrenees to buy their year's supply. When the dealers arrive in their trucks there is a noticeable heightening of tension. In total there will be about seventy sellers and fifteen or so dealers. All concerned are well known to each other. You may notice a few sellers furtively sprinkling handfuls of prize specimens into the tops of their open sacks, as if that is going to fool anyone.

You can set your watch at ten o'clock by the moment when bedlam breaks out. Dealing is forbidden until the official opening time, though there are many furtive tête-à-têtes. No one tells you when the market has started. The town clocks are too far away to be audible. But suddenly the buyers are to be seen rushing about in a frenzy trying to establish a going rate. They scribble the names of potential sellers on a piece of paper with a price per kilo on it and thrust it into the hands of a seller. If the seller accepts the piece of paper a deal is struck. No experienced seller is going to accept a price in this way until the buyers have been forced up, so it is not uncommon to see a grower tear up the buyer's slip of paper and throw the pieces to the ground in mock disgust. Similarly the prices asked do not come down until that magic moment when everyone seems to know as if by instinct that the two market forces are just about meeting in the middle. At this point there is a flurry of paper and five minutes later the market is over.

Over, that is, bar the settlement and the weighing of the sacks. This last operation takes longer than the whole of the previous proceedings. Each sack is weighed on the official weighing-machine, then emptied into another provided by the buyer. The seller's sacks are not included in the price. The seller then pays his dues to Sarlat Town Council.

Close by you may find Jean-Claude Bordier who, with his wife Francine, owns Le Moulin de La Tour. This pretty walnut-oil mill is astride a stream just east of Sarlat in the village of Ste-Nathalène. The mill goes back to the sixteenth century and its machinery is at least one hundred and fifty years old. It has been in Francine's family for many generations. Jean-Claude comes to market to buy walnuts, because he does not grow enough himself to meet the demand for the exquisite oil which he sells all over the district. When the market is finished, you should not pass up an invitation to his mill to learn how he makes it.

Walnut oil is the traditional oil of the region. Olives are not hardy enough this far north, and until recently sunflower and groundnut oils were unknown here. In any case the last two taste of little or nothing, and the people of Périgord have the

descriptive word *fade* to describe food which has no taste. Walnut oil is used locally where a *Provençal* would use olive: in salads, in mayonnaise and with dishes of salt fish.

Jean-Claude likes to buy his walnuts shelled, but there is no getting away from shelling the nuts he grows himself. He sits on a simple chair with a heavy solid slate on his knees. A wooden mallet is used to hit the nut, years of experience dictating the exact force needed to avoid smashing the nut inside. Shell and nut are allowed to fall into baskets at his feet. It is then a task in the evening for the whole family to sort out the shells from the nuts.

Whole kernels are called *cerneaux*, broken ones *invalides*. The kernels are taken to the mill to be ground into pulp, the machinery at Ste-Nathalène being operated wholly by water power. They are then transferred to a stone basin about a metre in diameter, whose curved sides are silky-smooth after centuries' contact with the juice of the nuts. A wood-furnace is lit below and the crushed nuts are cooked to a paste over high heat for thirty to forty minutes. The paste is then transferred to a press holding up to thirty kilos. Between two wooden blocks, the lower of which is attached for solidity to a steel plate, the paste is pressed to extract the oil. It is filtered through two fine layers of jute. Even so, the oil still needs to rest in a barrel for two or three days before it is totally transparent and can be decanted into bottles or cans. Jean-Claude uses only the first pressing of the paste to make his oil, which has no additives or preservatives. Most walnut oil which is made industrially and sold in supermarkets uses later pressings, and is sometimes 'stretched' through blending with other types of oil. It usually contains additional ingredients, which is why it does not keep. Jean-Claude's oil will keep at least a year in the refrigerator.

Though expensive to buy, walnut oil is more healthy than any other, even sunflower oil. It contains 71 percent polyunsaturates and only 6 percent saturates, compared with figures of 61 and 15 respectively for sunflower oil.

Jean-Claude is interested only in the finest raw materials, which is why he buys from smaller growers at Sarlat market. The nuts which the big dealers buy in bulk are driven away to be kiln-dried. These are the nuts you see in most shops, their shells bleached by the heat and the kernels brittle and like sawdust. The nuts marketed by the locals are quite different, dried by them in the gentler heat of the autumn sun to preserve their oil as well as their natural appearance.

Mushrooms are as much a part of autumn as walnuts. The French are more passionate about mushroom gathering than almost any other form of outdoor activity, even fishing. The finest mushrooms of all are *boletus edulis* – the cèpe.

The cèpe is totally unpredictable, although it usually grows, when it grows at all, in the same place, beneath the same trees. Such places are jealously guarded local secrets. The hunt – for that is what it is really – is carried out with extreme furtiveness, the hunter camouflaging his car by the roadside as best he can, and looking shamefaced when caught in the act with a tell-tale bag in hand.

The unpredictability of the crop makes organized marketing almost impossible, because in some years there are hardly any cèpes at all. The timing of their appearance is also haphazard, depending on a combination of sun and rain, heat and cold, and even the moon. Many say that cèpes are best found on a waning moon five days after heavy rain.

Even so, cèpes are a regular feature of the commercial life of one town, Villefranche-du-Périgord, in the far south of the *département* of Dordogne, and about halfway between Bergerac and Cahors. It is a particularly propitious area for cèpes, because there are so many chestnut trees. There is a general symbiosis between the two, the mushroom relishing the partial shade by the root of the tree. Here too the nights are not yet cool enough to bring frosts which will quickly put paid to mushroom-hunting until another year. September and October are the best months, the cèpes of the summer season not having the flavour of the autumn ones.

Villefranche-du-Périgord is a small medieval *bastide* with many fine old buildings. Its well-preserved stone-flagged *halle* affords a venue for any lucky enough to have picked more

mushrooms than they know what to do with: they can bring their treasure to the market-place and sell it any day of the week. At a hundred francs a kilo, you do not need many mushrooms to go home with some useful pin-money.

Towards the middle to end of October, Villefranche has its annual fête, which, though it is a many-faceted event, gives due prominence to mushrooms. On the Sunday sellers may come at any time of the day, whereas on other days sales are forbidden before four o'clock in the afternoon.

Cèpes are brought to market in trays and are laid on the ground in two rows, the vendors forming an aisle between the rows. You have to bid for a whole tray or nothing. Sellers will not accept

Connoisseurs say that the smaller the cèpe the finer its flavour

almost certainly of an inferior variety. The underside of the cap does not consist of gills like the field mushroom, but of sponge-like spores, which make the genus instantly distinctive. In a fresh specimen the spores will be a pale creamy-white, but they darken and turn yellowish with age. The texture should be quite firm to the touch, any flabbiness indicating that the mushroom is past its best. Cèpes quickly develop small worms, but these are harmless and may be expelled by warming the mushrooms in a very low oven for a few minutes. Cèpes should not be gathered or stored in a plastic bag, as they are very susceptible to condensation. If you go to pick them yourself take a stout stick to poke among the leaves,

a sacrificial price, because the market is a daily event. There is no compulsion to sell: fresh mushrooms will keep in a refrigerator for a few days.

There are many varieties of cèpe, but there is only one truly poisonous kind, a recognisably lurid red, so the cèpe is a safe mushroom to harvest. The size of a cèpe can vary enormously; smaller ones of say five centimetres in diameter are said to have a finer flavour than the bigger ones, although the ratio between cap to stem is smaller.

The stems of cèpes are bulbous in shape; if they are stalk-like and straight, the mushroom is best avoided, because it is

a wicker basket and a sharp knife to sever the cèpe well above ground level, leaving the base of the mushroom as little disturbed as possible in the soil. Confine your search to the edges of the woods, rather than the darker interior, because cèpes like aeration and plenty of warmth during the daytime.

The gastronomic uses of the cèpe are many. With a food processor you can make a smooth *velouté* of cèpes, one of the most delicious of soups. More traditionally, *omelette aux cèpes* is a standby of professional and amateur cooks alike all over the south-west. The meaty taste of the mushroom, combined with its power to recall the scents of the woodland floor, makes it a marvellous ingredient in *civets* and *salmis* of game, while even a few cèpes can elevate a humble dish of potatoes into a gastronomic treat. Cèpes may be dried, bottled, or, best of all, deep-frozen.

Mushrooming can easily be combined with gathering chestnuts, their seasons conveniently coinciding. The sweet chestnut was, until the end of the nineteenth century, one of the most vital of all crops. Even a century after the Revolution the peasant poor could not afford bread made from wheat. The chestnut provided their flour, and, because of its richness in proteins and carbohydrates, much of their other solid food as well. It often did duty for meat. If the chestnut crop failed, famine was widespread.

The chestnut tree yielded more than its fruit. Its trunk was made into fine furniture, into the first of the telephone poles, and into pit-props and railway-sleepers. Its wood was made into doors, floors and windows in most peasant houses and farm buildings. Its leaves provided bedding for cattle as well as a wrap for maturing goats' cheeses. The nuts themselves would be eaten boiled – often a whole breakfast for the very poor – pounded into a soup moistened with milk, roasted in the ashes of the farmhouse fire or wrapped and steamed in cabbage leaves to make a poor man's version of *marrons glacés*.

This seller seems to be proud to have the biggest and most spectacular cèpes in town

But a hundred years ago the chestnut tree suffered a sharp and swift decline. The popularization of the potato and the more ready availability of flour lessened its importance as a food crop. Softer woods gradually replaced the chestnut as timber. Barrel hoops came to be made from metal, and cattle slept on straw. The chestnut plantations, formerly tended with as much care as vineyards, were gradually allowed to grow wild, the young saplings no longer thinned out and the smaller branches no longer collected for firewood. Above all the killer disease called *l'encre* – a kind of fungus which dehydrates the tree from the top downwards and turns the nuts to an inky black powder – gradually conquered the forests.

Today the cycle is starting to be reversed, if only a little. A greater public affluence and discernment has restored the wood of the sweet chestnut to a prized place as timber. Gourmets are rediscovering its virtues as an element in the fashionable *cuisine du terroir*. Suddenly there is an interest in rolling back the tide of *encre* through the development of grafts immune to the disease. Syndicats and co-operatives of growers have been formed to further the process of re-afforestation.

Not even its five hundred inhabitants would claim that Mourjou was the hub of French life. But when the penultimate

weekend of October comes round, you might be persuaded that it is. Whatever the weather, up to 15,000 people come from far and wide to this tiny one-street village for one of the last open-air fêtes of the season: 'La Foire de la Châtaigne', or *Fiera de la castanha* as it is called in Occitan. For Mourjou is in the heart of what was once one of the premier chestnut-growing areas of France, La Châtaigneraie, on the borders between the old provinces of Quercy and the Auvergne.

All the uses of the chestnut are on show at the Mourjou *foire*. Mourjou was not chosen as the home of this event; it chose itself. A small group of local enthusiasts were determined not to see the chestnut disappear. The fact that the success of a chestnut fair might also bring some much-needed revenue to the village was no doubt a secondary consideration.

Mourjou is fortunate to count among its scions Pascal Paganiol, the *locomotive* of the fête. He has played a large part in mobilizing nearly half of the inhabitants of the village to take part in one way or another. Some of them help prepare the sit-down Sunday lunch, each course featuring chestnuts. The first course may be a terrine of rabbit stuffed with them, followed by

a duck sausage with lentils and more chestnuts. After the cheese there may be a chestnut tart. Other villagers help with the preparation of bread and other food-products for sale in the one and only street; and with the roasting of sackfuls of nuts to be washed down with rough cider or red wine. The 'car-parks' – the surrounding fields – are expertly staffed by the young men of the village, whose muscles are much needed to rescue vehicles if there is mud after heavy rain.

This local involvement gives the Mourjou fête its intimate and friendly character. Paganiol maintains that it has a double purpose. Apart from being a convivial and festive occasion, it is also a showcase for the experiments and techniques which are being developed to put the chestnut tree back where it belongs, to restore its place in La Châtaigneraie, and to provide a forum for growers from other chestnut regions.

Visitors to the fair can enjoy chestnuts any way they like: raw, boiled, grilled, transformed into honey, in cooked dishes, *charcuterie*, in *confits* and terrines with and without meat, as jam, a purée, or as the base of flour, bread, buns, cakes, chocolates and alcoholic drinks.

There are also stalls of chestnut furniture, toys and craft products, demonstrations of wickerworking and weaving; the old custom of communal bread-baking in the village oven is revived. You can also learn how to dry chestnuts over a slow fire in a special little building called a *sécadou*. This is equipped with wooden slats on which the trays of nuts are laid over the smouldering embers. In the old days smoking ensured a good supply of nuts all winter.

Exhibitors at Mourjou come from far and wide: from the Lozère, Gard, Aveyron, Corrèze, Dordogne and the Lot, and they will demonstrate how to graft and prune the trees, how to use gadgets which will both spray and gather the nuts, or remove their prickly shells and sort them into sizes. They will explain the different varieties, those which are resistant to *l'encre*, those which grow better on higher ground, and the difference between *marrons* and ordinary chestnuts. They will also sell you young trees up to two metres in height to take home.

There is also a cookery competition open to all, and lessons for the modern cook on how to use chestnuts. The recipe for chestnut terrine at the end of this chapter comes from the Mourjou fête. There are demonstration dishes donated by well-known chefs of the region, as well as spit-roasted pork on the Sunday evening, served with chestnuts in the open air.

The *foire* looks forward more than it looks back. Creativity is encouraged. A specially invented aperitif, that is now produced commercially, consists of three parts dry white wine and one part chestnut liqueur. Local wine makers are usually at hand to supply bottles of their delicious pink and red wines, as well as their white Entraygues.

The chestnut apéritif goes under the unlikely name of 'Pélou Tonic', *pélou* being the dialect word for the prickly outer shell of the chestnut. There is a Confrérie of the Pélou, which has become one of the promotional bodies of the fête. In ceremonial robes of green and yellow, the official colours of the fête, they enthrone new members at the fête each year in the little *place* outside the *mairie*. They also invite similar *confréries* from other regions.

An exciting project for the future is the creation of a Maison de La Châtaigne, intended to be a living museum and a centre for visitors. It could also become a chestnut *conservatoire*, with an orchard containing as many different varieties as possible; and perhaps a specialist restaurant. A site for this project has already been identified in the commune of Mourjou itself.

The positive, forward-looking *animation* of this event is wholly admirable, but the visitor does not come only to be lectured and educated. It is the heart-warming ambiance of the *foire* which is so memorable, enhanced by the burning braziers of nuts, the sight of thousands of cars negotiating the tiny single-tracked lanes of this countryside, the thronged village street with only two tiny squares opening off it, the single café more crowded than the *métro* at rush-hour, the groups of country musicians playing strangely modern sounding versions of old folk-songs on distinctly anachronistic instruments. All these combine to make this one of the most memorable of all the country fêtes, especially if the visitor is lucky enough to be blessed with one of those perfect Indian summer days, when, even in the unreliable climate of the Auvergne, the sun shines from a cloudless sky.

Terrine de castanhas
Terrine of chestnuts and mushrooms

SERVES 4

300g (11oz) chestnuts in their shells

  or 250g (9oz), shelled

Salt and pepper

1 tablespoon sunflower oil

110g (4oz) onion, chopped

110g (4oz) chestnut mushrooms, chopped

6 juniper berries, crushed

Pinch of nutmeg

70g (3oz) melted butter

Slit the chestnuts, put them into boiling water for 5 minutes, then peel them, removing both skins.

Put the nuts back into salted water and boil gently for 15 minutes. Drain them, then liquidize in a food processor, moistening them with a little water if necessary.

Heat the oil in a pan, add the onion, and soften for 5 minutes. Add the mushrooms with a little salt. Cover and cook slowly for 10 minutes. Add pepper, juniper berries and nutmeg and purée the mixture in a food processor.

Combine the two mixtures and add the melted butter. Mix all together and put it into a terrine. Smooth the top and chill.

Serve chilled with wholemeal toast.

Salade de noix aux gésiers
Walnut salad

SERVES 4

200g (7oz) *confit de gésiers* (preserved duck gizzards)

1 head of chicory, sliced

3 medium oranges, peeled and sliced

16 walnuts, shelled and broken into pieces

Walnut oil dressing

Place the opened tin of *gésiers* in a bain-marie or low oven until the fat has melted. Drain off the fat and pat dry with kitchen paper. Cut the *gésiers* into small cubes.

Arrange some chicory in the centre of each plate and surround with slices of orange. Scatter the chopped *gésiers* and walnut pieces over the chicory and sprinkle with walnut oil dressing just before serving.

Tarte aux noix
Walnut tart

SERVES 8–10

400g (13oz) sweet shortcrust pastry

250g (9oz) shelled walnuts

120g (4½oz) sugar

4 slices crustless brown bread

3 eggs, separated

120g (4½oz) Chocolat Menier

2 tablespoons Grand Marnier or brandy

2 tablespoons water

10 walnut halves

Preheat the oven to 200°C/400°F/gas mark 6.

Roll out the pastry as thinly as possible, and use to line a greased 23cm (9in) flan tin. Prick the bottom with a fork.

Pulverize the walnuts in a food processor and mix in the sugar. Crumble the bread, moisten the crumbs with water and squeeze them dry. Mix the crumbs into the nuts. Beat the egg yolks and stir them in. Whip the egg whites until stiff and fold them in, then pour the filling into the flan case.

Place the flan tin on a baking sheet and bake for about 40 minutes, until the top is golden brown and set. Leave to cool a little, then ice the top while it is still warm.

Heat the chocolate gently in a pan with the Grand Marnier and water until it is melted and smooth, then pour evenly over the tart. Decorate the top with the walnut halves.

Confiture de figues vertes aux noix

Walnut and fig jam

Adapted from a recipe of Lucia Macdonald, who must have the biggest walnut tree in the Tarn-et-Garonne.

SERVES 4

1 large lemon

700g (1½lb) sugar

300ml (½ pint) water

1kg (2¼lb) fresh, slightly under-ripe green figs, quartered

200g (7oz) fresh walnut pieces

Pare off the lemon rind and cut it into fine julienne strips. Cut away all the white pith and thinly slice the lemon.

Place the sugar and water in a heavy-bottomed saucepan and stir over a moderate heat until dissolved. Cook the syrup without stirring until it reaches a temperature of 104°C, 220°F, then add the figs, lemon rind and slices. Bring back to the boil and cook over moderate heat until the mixture is thick – up to 2 hours – adding the walnuts after 1 hour.

Fill sterilized jars and seal while the jam is hot.

Pommes de terre aux cèpes

Potatoes with cèpes

SERVES 4

450g (1lb) waxy potatoes, peeled

2–3 cèpes

1 clove garlic, chopped

1 tablespoon parsley, chopped

1–2 tablespoons goose or duck fat

Salt and pepper

Cut the potatoes into thinnish rounds. Cut off the stalks of the cèpes and chop them finely. Slice the caps of the cèpes.

Heat the fat in a large, thick-bottomed frying pan. When it starts to smoke, add the potatoes and the sliced caps. Keep the heat high and turn the slices continuously until they start to colour. Watch them carefully as they tend to stick.

When they are sealed, add the chopped stalks, garlic and parsley, with plenty of salt and pepper. Lower the heat and cover the pan with a tight-fitting lid or foil. Leave to cook for 30 minutes, turning the mixture every 10 minutes to crisp all sides and to ensure it is not sticking on the bottom of the pan. This is excellent with a pork roast or a steak.

Confit de petits oignons aux châtaignes et aux noix

Garnish of onions, chestnuts and walnuts

SERVES 4

2 tablespoons goose or duck fat

12–20 small onions, according to size (allow 3–5 per person)

16 walnuts

Salt and pepper

120ml (4fl oz) dry white wine

4 tablespoons chicken stock

24 chestnuts, peeled (frozen or vacuum-packed)

Melt the fat in a heavy frying pan, add the onions and cook gently for about 10 minutes, until softened but not brown.

Crack the walnuts, keeping their kernels in quarters if possible. Add to the onions, season, add the wine and stock, and simmer gently, uncovered, for 40 minutes.

When the onions are cooked the liquid should have reduced by about one-third and be slightly syrupy. Add the chestnuts and let them absorb some of the juices for a further 10 minutes over a low heat. Check for seasoning. This is an excellent accompaniment to roast game or pork.

Pasta Party

Ravioli may be an Italian word, but this form of pasta (or *pâte* in French) may well have been invented in the mountains of the Vercors, the frontier territory between the Savoy Alps and Provence. This is wonderful cheese country: the cows and sheep spending the summer months here provide an extensive range of soft rather than hard cheese, and the goats' cheese from St Marcellin typifies a style of production to be found all over the region.

This was once very poor country, and the local peasants in the Middle Ages had little chance to eat meat, but in addition to their farm cheeses they did produce good flour and the mountains were covered in herbs. From these simple ingredients they evolved, perhaps as long ago as the fifteenth century, a flour and water paste, enriched with a little egg, which they stuffed with cheese and flavoured with herbs – today parsley is the most commonly used. The result is what the French call *ravioles*.

These are a far cry from the familiar Italian pillows, because, as well as being entirely vegetarian in content, they are but a fraction of the size, less than 2.5cm square. It is interesting to speculate on how the farmers' wives in the mountains went about making them. Perhaps they simply took a sheet of pastry, spooned little piles of stuffing at suitable intervals, and covered it with another sheet, pressing down between the stuffing, then cutting it up. Today the production is fully mechanized and fairly sophisticated .

The 'Ravioles du Dauphiné' are the pride and joy of the Isère valley. To help with their promotion (as well as that of the cake called *la Pogne*), Romans holds a fête towards the end of September

Ravioles may nowadays be found all over France, but they remain a speciality of the Isère valley. Production is centred round the old town of Romans, strategically placed on both the river and the main road leading from Valence to Grenoble. The vineyards of Hermitage are not far away. Romans boasts some 32,000 inhabitants, but, at least out of season, the old *quartier* sloping down to the river is peaceful. Except, that is, on fête-day. Towards the end of September each year, the town decides to make the most of the last warm days and to celebrate and promote its specialities. These include a bread-like cake called 'La Pogne', which is not unlike the *fouace* of Najac in taste and appearance (see page 118). There is a related version called 'St Génix', small and round like a cottage loaf, but slashed open at the top before baking, the gaps being filled with sweet almonds coloured a vivid red, to make the cake look as if it is bleeding.

La Pogne plays very much second fiddle, though, to the *ravioles* whose fête is entirely centred round the Tour Jacquemart. This medieval relic marks the centre of the town, all that is left of a fortress long since demolished. It is topped by a carillon operated automatically by a statue clad in Napoleonic costume, called Jacques, the instrument with which he strikes the bell being a *marteau*, hence Jacquemart.

In the Place Général de Gaulle, adjoining the Tour Jacquemart, a stand is set up by the Association de Défense pour la Véritable Raviole du Dauphiné. The elegant lady in charge explained that the principal producers had grouped together because they were anxious to counter the confusion between the modern Italian ravioli and the old-style *ravioles* of

Romans. The French version differed fundamentally in that it was made from soft wheat as opposed to the hard kind used in Italy. So as to protect the composition of the *pâte*, its method of manufacture and the area of its production, the Association obtained in 1989 a kind of *Appellation Contrôlée* for the 'Raviole du Dauphiné'.

The Association has eight members, of whom four operate in Romans itself. The nearest to hand was the doyenne of them all, representing a firm called 'Ravioles Madame Maury'. I had the good fortune to persuade the present-day Madame Maury, despite the pressures of fête-day, to tell me a little more about the *ravioles* of Romans. She recalled the days of her parents when the *ravioles* were an essential part of any celebration, as well as a popular local dish. No village fête or sporting occasion in the area was complete without an expert on hand with the *ravioles*. In private homes, the day before a wedding or christening, the *ravioles*-makers, called to this day *les Ravioleuses*, would arrive to prepare the stuffing and roll out the *pâte* on wooden planks. They would then cut up the *pâte* to make the *ravioles* by hand. The next day, the *ravioles* were poached in the stock from the *poule au pot*. They are still served in the same way today, plunged into the boiling stock and then simmered over a much reduced heat for no more than two minutes. They must be eaten without delay, and need nothing more except a little melted butter or grated cheese.

The experts say that this is still the best and only real way to enjoy *ravioles*; but imaginative and talented chefs are not going to be put off by this kind of purism from inventing their own *ravioles*-based specialities. Some stuff them with tapenade, some serve them with *girolles* or other wild mushrooms; other recipes call for puff pastry and a stuffing of chicken livers, while one of the simplest and most delicious ways of presenting them is to deep-fry them in oil for no more than a minute and a half and serve them on a crisp green salad. Our own recipe (see opposite) tries to recreate them as remembered from the Auberge des Remparts at Venasque further south in Provence; the sweetness of the leeks marries beautifully with the tang of the cheese hidden in the *ravioles*.

You can if you like try to make your own *ravioles*, and delicious they will doubtless be. But there is really little point because the shop-bought product loses nothing in quality and the presentation is inevitably more professional. Typically the *pâte* calls for nothing more than flour, water, eggs, a little butter and salt, while the stuffing maintains the traditional mix of cows' and goats' cheeses, parsley butter and seasoning. It is in the cutting of the *pâte* that modern technology beats the home cook every time.

Chez La Mère Maury, Madame works front of house and has seven chefs in the *atelier* behind her. One mixes the *farce*,

A member of the Confrérie sports his bronze plaque of *ravioles*

another beats the *pâte* in a mechanical dough-mixer. Another rolls it out in a kind of press which goes backwards and forwards until the required thinness is reached. It then goes to another machine to be cut into large squares. Yet another process coats one surface with the stuffing and then enfolds it within another square, while the last operation is to harden off the squares in cold cabinets.

The squares are called *plaques*, each of which contains forty-eight *ravioles*. Three *plaques* are called not surprisingly a *grosse*, and ten *grosses* are packed together into a carton. This is how they are despatched to shops and supermarkets, but private customers may buy one *plaque* at a time. The *ravioles* will keep fresh for up to a week but they freeze well and do not need to be defrosted before cooking. According to Mère Maury, you should allow two or three *plaques* per person, but it is difficult to imagine anyone getting through one hundred and forty-four *ravioles*, however small they may be.

A visit to the producer encourages the appetite no end, and the thirst even more. Down in the Place Jacquemart, the *intronisations des nouveaux ambassadeurs* are already under way, each recruit being adorned with a bronze plaque of *ravioles* to hang round his neck. Pogne candidates are each decorated with a miniature cake. The master of ceremonies must also be feeling thirsty because he has one eye on the clock and the other on the rows of bottles of delicious white Crozes-Hermitage which are to be offered as the *vin d'honneur*. The Confrérie's stand is the nucleus of the Fête, and here all the visiting worthies are gathered; wholesalers and supermarket representatives jostle with the bourgeoisie of Romans, while the women vie with each other for the smartest hats. Anyone can join in the fun, and the atmosphere is rather like that of a street party, everybody appearing to know everyone else, whether they have ever met before or not.

The Association's stand does a roaring trade in *ravioles*, to be consumed on as well as off the premises, and there isn't a café or restaurant in town which is not serving *ravioles* in one form or another. Once the *ravioles* have been digested there will be camel-rides for the young and not so young, folk-dancing by invited groups, a vintage-car rally, falconry and trips around

Chez la Mère Maury *ravioles* are turned out by the *grosse*

the town on *le petit train*. In the evening, le Crazy Hot Jazz Band will try to restore jaded appetites for yet more *ravioles*; the energetic can rock the night away, while the more lazy can enjoy the mock-burning of the Tour Jacquemart – and yet more *ravioles*, a slice of La Pogne and home to bed.

Ravioles de Romans sauce poireaux

Ravioles in a leek sauce

SERVES 4

2 medium-sized leeks

150g (5oz) butter

2 litres (3½ pints) chicken stock

Salt and pepper

5 sheets of ready-made *ravioles de Romans*

First prepare the leek sauce. Trim the leeks, using mainly their white parts, and wash them carefully. Slit them lengthwise into two then divide each half. Cut up the lengths finely. Melt 50g (2oz) of the butter in a pan and add the leeks. Cover and sweat gently until they are quite soft, about 20 minutes. Transfer them to a food processor and process to a smooth purée.

Return the leeks to the pan and add about 300ml (½ pint) of the chicken stock to make a sauce. Reheat gently, then remove from the heat and whisk in the remaining butter. Season and keep warm.

Just before serving, bring the rest of the stock to the boil and add the *ravioles* 1–2 sheets at a time. When they come to the surface, stir them gently to separate. Reduce the heat and allow to cook for 1–2 minutes – not more. Drain the *ravioles* and transfer to a heated gratin dish. Pour the sauce over, turn the *ravioles* in it and serve immediately.

Hung Out to Dry

In the months which one generally thinks of as autumn, the Basque country enjoys a seemingly indefinite extension of summer. The brilliant sunshine reflects dazzlingly off the whiter-than-white stucco buildings, but, as October progresses, their façades become covered with what look like carpets of coral. It is the time when the small red peppers of Espelette are hung out to dry on strings, a brilliant crimson to start with, but darkening as they mature to the kind of soft Indian red which matches perfectly the colour of so many Basque window-shutters.

The *piment d'Espelette* is a strange phenomenon when considered in the context of French agriculture and cuisine, but in the Basque country it is the essential condiment or spice on which their culinary repertoire is based. No *poulet basquaise*, *ttoro* (fish soup), *charcuterie* or *pipérade* would be considered at all authentic unless suffused with this special red pepper, while it appears in a number of other dishes seldom found outside the region: *axoa*, a sort of *ragoût parmentier* or shepherd's pie made with veal instead of lamb and generously dosed with the ubiquitous pepper, and *tripoxa*, a boudin also made from veal and similarly seasoned, are but two examples. We have already met it as a preservative for *jambon de Bayonne* (see page 20).

When used fresh, the pepper is finely chopped, the fiercely hot seeds being carefully avoided. When the peppers are dried, they are ground to a powder, apricot in colour with red flecks. The *piment d'Espelette* is hot, but not nearly as fierce as, say,

The Basque town of Espelette has long been associated with the red hot pepper (*piment*) which bears its name. The annual fête in its honour is one of the last of the season

Cayenne pepper. Its flavour is quite distinctive, like that of no other spice. It is a condiment as well as a seasoning.

The growing of the Espelette pepper (*capsicum annum L.*) is an old tradition in the region surrounding the little town. The plant seems to have been brought back from Mexico to Spain by Christopher Columbus. By the seventeenth century it was grown all over Castile, as a garden crop and in window-boxes by the farmers' wives. It was also esteemed for its medicinal qualities. According to one eighteenth-century commentator, it 'excites the appetite, expels the wind, sharpens the wits and hastens the digestion'. Today it is still held to be a cure for a heavy cold or bronchitis.

By the time of the Revolution, the *piment* was an important element in the economy of Espelette. Because of its position at the foot of one of the passes into Spain, between St Jean-de-Luz and St Jean-Pied-de-Port, the town was a lively trading centre which was host, among others, to chocolate manufacturers who are said to have included the pepper in their recipes. It had yet another use as church incense, an association which is continued today as part of the Mass on fête day.

Traditionally, the seeds of the pepper were sown on St Joseph's day, March 19th. A month later the little plants were thinned and planted out in the sunniest spots. The plants grew into bushes not more than half a metre high and the bright red fruit was ready to harvest from the end of September until the first frosts. The peppers were strung up the evening they were picked, and hung to dry either in the warmth of the kitchen or on the front of the house. Six to eight weeks later, they were taken to the village bread-oven to be roasted and later ground

to powder in a large mortar. The heat of the oven is critical, and the experts still plunge their hands inside as it is the only sure way to test the heat.

Today, pepper-growing is big business, and some growers have no other crop, having given up their sheep and maize. They are sufficiently concerned to protect their product that they are working to obtain an *Appellation Contrôlée* for *piments* grown in Espelette and a handful of neighbouring communes. Methods of cultivation have been modernized to enable growers to sell fresh peppers throughout the summer season. Sowing now takes place as early as February under glass, with

As October progresses, the buildings seem to be covered with carpets of coral as the red peppers of Espelette are hung out to dry

the seedlings grown on under plastic. In this way the harvest can start in August, and by the time of the fête, there are already ample supplies of the precious powder.

The fête at Espelette is always held during the last weekend in October. There is a kind of preview on Saturday with displays of products of the *terroir* and noisy dancing in the evening. The real fête begins on the Sunday morning with Mass in the unusually beautiful church. The building is in the typical Basque style. Its interior is lined with three tiers of carved and painted oak galleries round a central aisle. At the east end an elaborate decorated altarpiece of the seventeenth century contrasts with the simple rusticity of the rest of the building, with its stone-flagged floor and square bell-tower. The ceiling is painted in delicate shades of red, gold and blue and the church is lit by small windows fitted with wooden shutters. It is packed for Mass with about seven hundred and fifty people, the galleries so crowded that steel columns have had to be fitted beneath to give the necessary support. Attendance on this scale makes one realize what Sunday Mass must have been like when all the village went to church.

Most of the nave is reserved for the local Top People and their guests, the rest having access to the galleries via the bell-tower. The local school-children are all dressed up for the occasion, some in pepper-and-salt shirts, others like young nuns, and yet others with garlands in their hair. The boys are in white shirts with red Basque sashes and the choirboys have red cummerbunds too. At the back of the church, laid on a fine oak table, are six wicker trays containing choice specimens of the *piment d'Espelette*, attended by sixteen older girls in long-sleeved dresses with shawls, and wearing Basque espadrilles.

It is claimed that there can be representatives of no fewer than twenty-two *confréries* from round about, all invited by the Confrérie du Piment d'Espelette of course, who carry black canes and wear decorated berets, green cloaks with red trimmings and red and gold collars. You may recognize among the guests the Confrérie du Jambon de Bayonne and the Omelette Géante de Bessières-sur-Tarn (see pages 18 and 10). Other gastro-celebrities can include the Jurade du Sel de Salies, the Confréries of the Eels of Hendaye, the Garbure of Anglet, the Trouts of St Pée-de-Nivelle, the Ttoro of Ciboure as well as the Pirates of St Jean-de-Luz.

This riot of colour is augmented by two groups of musicians, one led by an exceptionally rotund tambour-player and a standard-bearer with a Groucho Marx moustache.

The real fête begins on the Sunday morning with Mass: the church is filled to bursting with people in the galleries as well as the nave

The other group in white with green belts and hats carry most known examples of brass instrument, including an imposing and highly-polished sarrusophone. The Mass begins, Monsieur le Curé dressed in white with a green surplice. The singing is outstandingly simple and beautiful, strangely reminiscent of Maori music. Just before the communion, the sixteen girls at the back of the church come forward with the trays of peppers and lay them on the altar. At this point there is an elaborate folk-ballet before the altar, the dancers carrying an apple in each hand. The priest then blesses the *piments* and all those who have had a hand in their growing. The seeds from these privileged peppers will be kept

to plant for next year's crop. Choir and congregation join in singing the chorus to the *chanson des piments*, in Basque of course, each verse being taken solo by a small girl from the choir. This is followed by more dancing, two men with daggers wrapped in white handkerchiefs indulging in dangerously high kicks to the accompaniment of drum and fife. Communion is taken while the organ plays a movingly simple blues-style folk-song which perhaps Christopher Columbus also brought back with him from his travels to the New World.

Mass is followed by a splendid procession through the town, ending with the inevitable *intronisations*, which take place in the grounds of the seventeenth-century château, today the home of the Mairie. There is little shade when it is fine, or shelter when it is wet, so the temptation is strong to slope off in the direction of the village in search of refreshment. The choices available include the new, still fermenting white wine from Jurançon, fizzy, yeasty, cloudy and musty, and with a taste which some may acquire more easily than others. Or hot dogs, which in the Basque country consist of really delicious sausages with old-fashioned French bread. The more foresighted may repair to one of the local restaurants at which the possibility of getting a table is zero unless you have booked at least a month in advance. The Euzkadi, the principal hostelry in town, owned by its uncrowned king Monsieur Darraïdou, was already taking bookings during the August holidays.

The afternoon is given over to singing and dancing in the streets with the many bands and spectators who have come from the coastal towns for the day. There are stalls selling Basque cheeses made from mountain-ewes' milk, *charcuterie* and even a kind of *fouace*. The *épicerie fine* in the village offers a variety of goodies based on the pepper: what they call a *compôte* which is a purée with other condiments and very hot indeed; a hot pepper sauce with vinegar; jars containing strips of *piment* preserved in vinegar and other purées diluted with fresh tomato to cool down the strength though not the colour; pâtés with extra powdered *piment*; and tins of *palombes*, a famous variety of local wild pigeon, well spiced with the familiar pepper. Nor are the children forgotten. At the north end of the village, a breeder of *pottoks*, an enchanting local breed of wild mountain pony now in danger of extinction, lets the young ones in to see his stable and pat the *pottoks*.

Just to walk up and down the main street, listening to the bands, and enjoying the singing and dancing of the good-humoured crowd does not lose its novelty until one realizes that it is beginning to get dark, a reminder that Toussaint (All Saints' Day) is only a week away and winter will soon descend. Everybody in Espelette has been determined to make the most of what may be their last Sunday outing of the year.

The afternoon is given over to singing and dancing in the streets with the many bands and spectators who have come for the day

Pâtes au Piment

Pasta with a peppery tomato sauce

SERVES 4

4 tablespoons extra virgin olive oil

½ small *piment*, deseeded, finely chopped and pounded

2 large ripe tomatoes, peeled and chopped

2 large cloves garlic, finely chopped

Salt

350g (12oz) spaghetti or other pasta

Grated Parmesan or hard ewes' milk cheese

Warm the oil in a heavy-bottomed pan over a very low heat and add the *piment*. Leave for 15 minutes without allowing it to brown. Add the tomatoes and mash all together in the pan with the garlic. Season with salt and allow to cook very slowly for up to 30 minutes. The sauce should be the consistency of a purée.

Cook the pasta in boiling, salted water until *al dente*. Drain and serve with the sauce and the grated cheese.

Ttoro
Basque fish soup

SERVES 4

5 tablespoons olive oil

2 onions, finely chopped

Head, skin and bones of hake or other white fish

2 cloves garlic

1 bouquet garni

Salt

6 peppercorns

Small piece *piment d'Espelette*

1.5 litres (2½ pints) water

600g (1¼lb) hake, cut into 4 cutlets

Seasoned flour

4 langoustines or scampi tails (optional)

12–16 mussels (optional)

4 rounds of French bread for croûtons

1 tablespoon parsley, chopped

Heat 2 tablespoons of the olive oil in a large casserole, and gently cook the chopped onions until golden. Add the fish head, skin and bones, 1 clove garlic, cut up, bouquet garni, salt, peppercorns, piment and the water. Cover and simmer for 30 minutes, then strain the stock and return to the casserole.

Dip the cutlets in the seasoned flour until evenly coated. Heat 2 tablespoons of olive oil in a frying pan and fry the cutlets for 1 minute on each side. Transfer the fish to the hot fish stock with the langoustines and mussels and simmer gently for 15 minutes.

Meanwhile, heat the remaining oil in a frying pan and fry the bread croûtons until golden brown. Rub the croûtons with the remaining clove of garlic and keep hot.

Chop up the garlic clove. Put a croûton in each soup bowl, sprinkle with the chopped parsley and garlic, place

a hake cutlet on top and ladle over the fish stock. Aficionados will want to add additional ground *piment d'Espelette*, which does for *ttoro* what *rouille* does for Provençal fish soups.

Chou-fleur au piment
Peppered cauliflower

SERVES 4

3 tablespoons extra virgin olive oil or walnut oil

1 *piment d' Espelette,* deseeded and finely chopped

1 cauliflower, divided into florets

Salt

1 large clove garlic, finely chopped

Cover the base of a sauté pan with the oil and gently sweat the pepper over a low heat for 15 minutes. This will extract some of the flavour from the pepper as well as turning the oil a pretty orange colour.

Meanwhile, steam or boil the cauliflower in salted water for 8 minutes, then drain.

Transfer the cauliflower to the pan with the pepper, raise the heat slightly and stew gently, uncovered, for another 5 minutes or so. Just before serving, add the garlic and toss all together.

Amazing Graisse

The Egyptians and the Romans knew all about the force-feeding of geese and ducks. But it was only in the eighteenth century that the appreciation of *oies et canards gras* became widespread in France. It seems that, until then, even pâtés were made of game birds, rather than domestically raised geese and ducks. Foie gras as we now know it was first made fashionable in Alsace in the 1750s, where the Governor's chef was responsible for introducing it to the tables of Paris. Today much of the production is based in the south-west, although the techniques have spread nationwide in response to the demand.

Although a fine foie gras is held to be 'without equal, only comparable with itself, the pearl, the jewel, the diamond, the supreme fruit of gastronomy'[*], its enjoyment is today within the reach of those with quite moderate incomes. This is because the raising of the birds is largely mechanized, modern feeding methods cutting by nine-tenths the traditional feeding time. Birds raised and fed in such a way no doubt satisfy the industrial *charcutiers*, but no restaurateur or *épicier* of quality would ever admit to dealing in industrialised foie gras, just as they would never admit to using anything but free-range poultry! But those who vaunt the merits of the traditional one-old-lady-to-one-bird approach are not just nodding in the direction of the folklore. The knowing gourmet will insist that

[*](Hugues Robert, *Le Grand Livre du Foie Gras*, Editions D. Briand-R. Laffont, Toulouse 1982)

Everywhere in the south-west there are *marchés au gras* between November and March dedicated to the sale of fattened geese and ducks; Sarlat and Caussade are two important examples

the quality of a good foie is pre-ordained almost from the bird's birth and, as far as force-feeding is concerned, there is no substitute for the personal relationship which develops between the stuffer and the stuffed.

The old farmers' wives say they have real empathy with the geese and ducks which they raise. Geese at least have a tendency to monogamy and are fiercely protective of their families, an attitude with which a peasant-farmer can identify. She will maintain that a goose is a living creature, by no means stupid, and that it has a capacity for grief just like a human being. Force-feeding, if properly carried out, will not allow of brutality, but rather calls for complicity, connivance and co-operation. For this reason the skill of the *gaveuse* who understands the ways of her birds makes all the difference. The final days of the bird may be uncomfortable or painful even,

but for most of its life it has been spoilt, fed on the fat of the land and brought up almost as one of the family.

It is no aim of this chapter to convert those who are opposed to force-feeding; theirs is an understandable position, but they will probably have stopped reading by now. One wonders however how many of them are content to buy supermarket eggs or battery chickens, industrialized lamb or pork, all of which are reared under conditions which make the *élevage* of ducks and geese look paradisaical? While one wrong does not justify another, it is well to keep these matters in perspective.

For the first months of their lives the conditions enjoyed by these birds are idyllic. They need plenty of rich green vegetation (nettles and wild garlic are much appreciated) in the early stages. For their first five or six months they are led about their *domaine* by their loving parents, supervised by the *gardeuse*, traditionally the grandmother of the farming family, or during school-holidays the children. Sometimes there is a dog to help keep them in order. In October, Grandma will start to level her sights on Christmas and the festivities of the year-end. The next step is to encourage the birds to grow as fat as possible naturally. They are taken to the richest pastures, fed on oats and maize. Flour is added to their drinking water. This preliminary diet will strengthen the digestive system, and will identify any birds which are not going to be suitable for force-feeding.

After a fortnight, the process of *gavage* starts. The geese are fed manually with maize three times a day. A farmer's wife can

Both private and trade buyers consider the fattened geese at Caussade

and restaurateurs who are not too worried about provenance. But the typical *grand'mère*, alas a dying breed, has no such outlets ready to hand. So she will take her produce, or as much of it as she does not need for family consumption, to one of the country *marchés au gras* – markets dedicated exclusively to the sale of these special ducks and geese.

Nature, by one of her happier coincidences, has arranged that these birds are market-ready at just the time when they are most needed. From November to March, neatly covering the traditional feasts at Christmas and New Year, there is a lively trade at these markets. There are some trade buyers who will want to insist on quality products, and these can be identified as they leave in pairs, heaving a groaning tray with seven or eight geese in it, weighing in all a good forty kilos. There are also a great many more private customers who come to stock up their larders to see them through the festivities, and to make enough foie gras or *confits* for the cold winter months.

The larger towns in the south-west – Brive, Pau and Périgueux for example – have extensive markets which attract big crowds, but smaller towns such as Sarlat also specialize in a more private and intimate style. Sarlat has a small square towards the north end of the old town called Place des Oies, though the market itself has moved towards the larger squares in the middle.

Caussade, halfway between Cahors and Montauban, is a town which has a dedicated *marché au gras*, and it is held rather improbably every Monday during the winter season. In the architecturally non-conscious years after the Second World War, this purpose-built *marché au gras* was built just to the south of the town centre in honour of M. Bonnaïs, a former mayor. There are strict rules about what can and cannot be sold here. The only produce available is either the whole bird, or its liver. In other markets you can sometimes find birds without their liver (called *manteaux* or *paletots*), or joints from birds, magrets or legs for example. Here at Caussade it is all or livers. The birds

feed six or seven in an hour, so it is clear how labour-intensive manual *élevage* is. One of the reasons why ducks have become more popular to raise than geese is that they never need feeding more than twice a day.

Birds which are raised industrially or by specialist farmers as a monoculture will be sold directly to the trade: the bulk canners of *confits*, the makers of *cous farcis*, the wholesalers who parcel up and pack magrets vacuum-sealed, the pâté manufacturers must have been *gavés* by the seller, though the means of *gavage* is not specified. The birds must have been plucked and the produce prepared on the farm where they were raised. All produce must carry the official stamp of approval of the market organizers. The birds must have been killed not more than twenty-four hours prior to the market, and must have been kept chilled in the meantime, never frozen, because that ruins the livers. The separate livers must be wrapped in material appropriate for food-contact, which in practice means that livers are film-wrapped and displayed on plastic trays. These regulations, when first introduced, upset the conservatively-minded peasant-farmers, who felt their traditional standards to be under criticism, but today the red tape seems to have been accepted.

The municipality offers a free weighing service. Generally the ducks weigh up to four and a half kilos and the geese up to seven; the ducks' livers on their own weigh on average four hundred grams and the goose livers double that or more. Sometimes the sellers slit open the breastbone of the birds to show the quality of the liver. Nowadays there are many more ducks than geese, largely because, apart from the livers, the

The Place des Oies in Sarlat, once given over exclusively to the sale of geese

duck meat is easier to sell than that of the goose. Gourmets insist all the same that the goose yields the more delicately-flavoured liver, while duck livers lend themselves well, because of their stronger flavour, to cooked preparations. Do not be fooled by the fact that duck livers are about half the price of goose livers. They shrink much more during cooking.

At Caussade market no customer is allowed in until nine o'clock in the morning, and an hour later the market is over. An inexperienced customer has little time in which to make what may be his first purchase. It is important to know what to look for. One whole bird looks very much like another, but the breasts (magrets) should be firm and plump to the touch. Unless the liver is exposed, you are buying very much on a hunch, which is why so many buyers keep going back to the same producers time after time. The liver is easier to assess, especially when it has been removed from the bird, although contact has to be through the transparent wrapping. The texture should be even, firm without being hard. The surface should be evenly coloured, without spots of extraneous colour or any marks which make it look as if it has been

smeared with mud. Livers which are reddish in colour should be avoided because they will probably have lost their tenderness (*fondant*).

All produce is sold by weight. Since 80 percent of the cost of a whole bird is attributable to the liver, it is important to satisfy yourself by feel that the liver is of an appropriate size. Ideally, take an experienced friend with you. Otherwise you may or may not be able to get some views from bystanders; it is hard to get people to stick their necks out when there is so much at stake!

Whether you leave the market with a whole bird or part of one, deal with it at the earliest possible moment, particularly the liver. The fresher the liver the better the pâté. After the liver, don't forget that the most precious part of the bird is the quantity of golden fat, which you can either use to make *confits* with the flesh, or simply render down for cooking. It is the most delicious medium there is.

Foie gras frais aux câpres

Fresh foie gras with capers

SERVES 4

1 fresh foie gras of duck, about 450g (1lb)

Salt and pepper

2 tablespoons brandy

1 tablespoon duck or goose fat

60g (2½oz) chopped shallot

1 tablespoon flour

120ml (4fl oz) white wine

4 tablespoons veal or chicken stock

60g (2½oz) capers

Check that the liver is clean and free from gristle or blood-vessels (see recipe opposite), then soak for 1 hour and dry on kitchen paper. Season and sprinkle with the brandy, then leave in the refrigerator for 2–3 hours.

Heat the fat in a casserole. Dry the liver on kitchen paper, then place in the casserole and cook gently for 10 minutes until it changes colour, turning it carefully. Remove the liver from the casserole and reserve. Add the shallot to the casserole and cook until softened, then add the flour and stir until it starts to brown. Stir in the wine and stock and leave to simmer for 30 minutes over a very low heat.

Raise the heat, put in the foie gras, and reduce the heat immediately and simmer slowly for another 10 minutes. Rinse the capers, if they have been preserved in vinegar, and add them at the end of the cooking time.

Slice the foie gras, arrange on a serving plate and coat with the sauce. The foie gras should be so tender that it can, as is traditional, be eaten with a spoon.

Foie gras entier mi-cuit

Terrine of foie gras

This pâté should be prepared several days ahead of time, as it improves significantly.

SERVES 6–8

2 fresh foie gras of duck, weighing 900g (2lb) or 1 fresh foie gras
 of goose, weighing 600g (1¼lb)

2 teaspoons armagnac

2 teaspoons *vin doux naturel* or port

2 teaspoons medium-sweet white wine

Pinch of nutmeg

Pinch of cinnamon

Salt and pepper

Aspic jelly:

150ml (¼ pint) strong chicken stock

1 teaspoon gelatine

Separate the lobes of the liver(s), removing all the stringy veins and traces of green and dark red. Soak them in warm water for 1 hour.

Drain and pat the liver dry with kitchen paper. Open pockets in each lobe with a small sharp knife, so that you can remove all the remaining veins. This is essential if the finished pâté is to cut easily and not tear.

Place the liver in a shallow dish with the armagnac, wines, spices and seasonings. Turn to coat well, then leave to marinate overnight in the refrigerator.

Next day allow the liver to come to room temperature for an hour. Preheat the oven to 150°C/300°F/gas mark 2. Choose a terrine that the livers will fit into when tightly packed, getting the top surface level to within 2cm (¾in) of the top of the terrine. Pour the marinade over.

Fill a roasting tin to a depth of 2cm (¾in) with water heated to 70°C/158°F – the temperature of the water and oven are important. Put your terrine into the roasting tin and cook uncovered for 35 minutes.

Remove the terrine from the oven and allow to cool at room temperature, then refrigerate until required. It should be left untouched for at least 4–5 days. It will keep for a week more in your refrigerator.

Well ahead of serving-time, make the aspic jelly by warming the chicken stock. Add the gelatine, stir vigorously, then remove from the heat and pour into a shallow glass dish. Leave to cool, then chill.

To serve the pâté, unmould it on to a serving dish. Garnish with the aspic, chopped into tiny pieces. To divide the pâté, dip a knife into a jug of hot water before cutting each slice. Serve with fresh walnut bread or toast.

The Pig At the Lion d'Or

The truffle is one of nature's most mysterious productions. Scientists took centuries to decide whether it was vegetable or mineral. A creature of the dark, it grows only underground, no trace of it appearing above the surface. To draw from the daylight world the carbons vital to its survival and reproduction, it needs another plant to feed it these precious things, converted into sugars and proteins by photosynthesis. So it forms a symbiotic relationship with certain kinds of tree, most famously oak and hazel, on whose newest and tiniest roots it establishes a permanent grasp; an iron handshake in a glove which looks like insulating tape.

For most people the most extraordinary feature of the truffle is its smell. Nothing remotely resembles it. Sometimes reminiscent of an old country-house dairy, it suggests also the rough scrubland where it grows, with thyme, juniper berries and heather, the ash of the country fireplaces where it was traditionally cooked and the perfumes of the soil in which it spends its life.

Truffles are fussy. They insist on chalky ground, rich in organic matter. It is a mistake to think that the poorer the ground the better the truffle. They must have suitable host-trees nearby, but they also need aeration, hot sun in summer punctuated with heavy showers or storms, and excellent drainage in wet weather. A cold winter suits them well enough, though spring frosts will literally nip them in the bud. The most propitious areas are where the oak tree grows wild:

Lalbenque is home to the foremost truffle-market in the south-west. Here, in the winter months, one can sample the famous *omelette aux truffes* at the Hôtel du Lion d'Or

the *garrigues* of Provence and the province of Quercy, itself named after *quercus*, the Latin word for oak tree.

Madame Berthier can therefore be said to be at the hub of French gastronomy. Her Hôtel du Lion d'Or is the only one in the otherwise unremarkable village of Lalbenque in the Quercy, which hosts the premier truffle-market in the south-west. The restaurant over which she presides with both magisterial authority and great charm is not however a wall-to-wall carpeted, candle-lit temple of gastronomy. It is rather the archetypal French village auberge, where, every Tuesday during the winter months, Madame Berthier feeds one hundred and thirty truffle-hungry mouths: people who have come many miles to deal in the local treasure, to buy for restaurants or the *charcuterie* trade, to preserve in tins and jars for the finest groceries of the world, or simply to take home as an extravagant treat. Even at source, the truffle lives up to its reputation as the most expensive foodstuff in the world. Here it changes hands at a mere £100 a pound, about 1,900 francs a kilo, if you can drive a hard bargain. But by the time it has been marked up by the *négociants*, the wholesalers, the canners and the retailers, to say nothing of the restaurants, the truffle is beyond the reach of all but the very rich .

This has not always been so. A hundred years ago, truffles were fairly commonplace. Although never the daily food of the poor, they enjoyed a brief period of fashion when they featured regularly and unremarked on the tables of the bourgeoisie; even the humblest farmer's wife would manage to slip a few chopped truffles beneath the skin of her Christmas turkey. The oak plantations, where the truffles grew, were often adjacent to vines which relished much the same growing conditions and climate. When phylloxera struck in the 1880s, it was logical for the peasants to replant with new oak trees, and even to let the existing plantations spread naturally into the abandoned vineyards.

The short-lived truffle boom came abruptly to an end with the First World War. The decline was due largely to lack of knowledge about the product. Truffles will not grow beneath oak trees which are more than 30–35 years old, so that the trees planted after the phylloxera epidemic were useless for trufficulture by the time the war broke out. The woods needed constant attention and the trees severe pruning, but this was mens' work and they had gone to the Front. The diminished numbers who returned found the truffle woods in a derelict state and there were more important priorities on the

family farms. There was much poverty and hardship; many emigrated or went to the cities to seek work. The *truffières* witnessed the same decline as had befallen the vineyards.

Our present interest in the *cuisine du terroir* has produced a demand for truffles which cannot be met by the supply. Hence the explosion in prices, which have increased 200-fold since the Second World War. While the more entrepreneurial are trying hard to find means of recreating the truffle plantations, a truffle oak will not act as host until it is fifteen years old, so the time-lag is inevitable. Even so, there is nothing certain about the truffle, and perhaps many hundreds of hectares of oak have been planted which will never see a truffle.

If you are minded to experience the truffle-market at Lalbenque, you should book in to Madame Berthier's the night before. The peace and quiet of the previous evening is a better environment in which to savour her *omelette aux truffes*, which is endowed with sufficiently generous quantities of truffle to raise it to the level of a rare treat.

She told me all I needed to know about the truffle season. I asked her whether it had been a good year, and she said that the truffles had been slow to ripen; there had been thirteen moons during the previous year. The January moon was late and everybody knew that truffles were not fully ripe until the time of the January moon. This was confirmed by Madame Berthier's waitress, Madame Delon, herself a *trufficulteur*, who said that the demand for truffles at Christmas and the New Year was leading to a premature gathering of unripe truffles; in the old days, she said, you never even bought your truffling pig until the middle of November.

The one thing that everybody knows about truffles is that you need a pig to find them for you, for they grow beneath the ground. Many growers today use dogs, and I also found two *folklorique* old-timers who relied on a particular type of fly to point to the place where the truffle might be. This technique involves the grower lying flat on his stomach waiting for the tell-tale insect for hours on end, and is somewhat uncertain, because, at the end of the vigil, he may find nothing but stones and earth if he has been studying the wrong kind of fly.

You will not be able to persuade Madame Delon to take you out

with her pig on market morning, because her services are pre-empted by Madame Berthier for the one hundred and thirty lunches at the Lion d'Or. However, the local Tourist Office is next door, and during the season they organize a truffling-pig show for the curious. I went to a spot ten minutes walk out of Lalbenque, in full view of the open road, where Madame Aymard had a small *truffière* with a dozen or so oak trees. There she was with Titou, a delicious adolescent piglet, the palest of pinky white, and spotlessly clean except for her snout, which was covered in earth and grass. Bursting with excitement, snorting and snuffling with pleasurable anticipation and straining at her tough canvas harness, Titou was only too anxious to demonstrate her skill. She did not seem to mind that she was cheated of the product of her labour, satisfied instead by a few grains of maize and some cats' biscuits. She had unearthed the best part of a kilo of black diamonds within half an hour, all from beneath one single oak tree.

Meanwhile, back in the town, the market was about to get under way. About thirty trestle-tables had been lined up along one side of the street opposite the Lion d'Or, each able to accommodate two or three exhibitors. The market starts officially at two-thirty, but already by about two o'clock the tables were manned and the visiting crowds swarmed around. The proceedings are conducted in an air as mysterious as that which surrounds the life of the truffle itself. Each grower brings his specimens wrapped in a napkin or tea-towel, usually in a suitably-sized basket. He stands behind his exhibit with the air of one offering dirty postcards in Soho or the Place Pigalle. This conspiratorial mood is partly traditional, partly due to the threats of the French tax authorities to require the peasant-producers to register for TVA and to file complete accounts of their transactions. Wandering around the market, notebook in hand, I was asked by one worthy peasant whether I was a representative of Le Fisc, and when I replied: 'Certainly not', he said: 'I am very pleased to hear that, because otherwise I would have spat at you.'

The market is intended principally as a forum for growers and the trade. The amateur buyer intervenes at his peril. It has been said that unscrupulous growers would wrap pebbles in soil and mix them in with their truffles to fool the mug, but the presence of professional buyers has weeded out this kind of fraud. All the same, purchase can be a hazardous business. To begin with, the truffle is still surrounded with earth which makes detailed scrutiny a difficult business. An hour or so's study of the various stalls can give you some idea of what to look for. Size is in theory unimportant, though the very smallest truffles will carry more than their fair share of soil, and will lose more weight than larger specimens in canning or bottling. Regularity of shape does not mean much either. Perfectly round specimens have probably

come from more sandy soil, while the knobbly kind owe their irregularity to the pebbles among which they have grown. What is important is that they should be firm in texture, like a potato, and should give off plenty of the essential aroma without which a truffle is no more than a piece of rotting vegetation.

You need a cool head at the market, and inexperienced amateurs like myself are scared that, if they do not look out early for their truffles, they will miss the boat. The amateurs were busy seeking out the growers who had small lots of good quality; you have either to buy the whole lot or nothing at all, because the growers will not divide up their produce. Soon after two o'clock I made it my business to choose my vendor and stand by his precious napkin. I was not the only one and, terrified that someone would get there before me, I tentatively asked him whether it was possible to buy before the official opening time. Monsieur X – he was keen not to give me his real name – looked at me for a long while before he said: *'Vous n'êtes pas français, Monsieur?'* I confessed that I was not and, after another long pause, he asked: *'Vous êtes particulier?'* and I replied that I was very much so. *'Vous n'est pas dans le commerce?'* he asked. I said: 'Definitely not.' After weighing up the situation very carefully, he said: 'Let's go round the back.'

I had heard a great deal about what happened behind the scenes at this market; some people had suggested that only a fraction of the trade took place in public, and that most truffles were sold out of car boots on the church steps or outside the post-office away from the prying eyes of the gendarmes. Monsieur X's proposition did not surprise me, but I felt a slight *frisson* of criminality in acceding to his proposal.

We set off down a side street, he clutching his pretty yellow basket containing about three hundred and fifty grammes of truffles in a snow-white damask napkin. Once out of the main thoroughfare he asked me if I had a car. It so happened that it was parked nearby, and I took this as an invitation to open the boot to provide shelter for our nefarious commerce. 'Oh, no,' he said, 'we're getting inside.' By this time I was getting nervous, fearing I might never again emerge in one piece. We sat in the front and he formally exhibited his beautiful truffles while I contemplated the awful prospect of paying for them. 'You are of course paying in cash?' By this time I rated the question as insultingly obvious, but I did not have the right money, nor did he have any change. I needed to go to the bank to change a note. He said quite charmingly but firmly: 'I keep the truffles here while you are gone.' I came suddenly to understand that expressions such as 'black market' and 'underground' might have originated here in Lalbenque.

After concluding our transaction, we returned to the main street where there were still a few minutes to go before the official opening of the market. At two-thirty sharp, a whistle blew, chaos ruled as all the trestle-tables were swept clear, but in five minutes there was not a sign of a truffle. Growers and dealers had all flocked to the official weighing-machine, the deals had been struck and all that remained was for Madame Berthier to do the washing-up for her one hundred and thirty *couverts*. I was not surprised when Monsieur X came up to me and asked whether I would like another hundred grammes. I knew then that I had paid over the odds, but I was past caring. My purchase proved to be worth every franc.

Salade de pommes de terre aux truffes

Potato salad with truffle

This recipe was kindly supplied by Gilles Marre, chef-proprietor of Le Balandre, Cahors.

SERVES 4

50g (2oz) whole truffles, brushed and washed

3 tablespoons sunflower oil

1 tablespoon extra virgin olive oil

450g (1lb) waxy potatoes such as Charlotte or Roseval

1 tablespoon verjuice or mild white wine vinegar

Salt and pepper

Clean the truffles in running water, as described opposite. Slice them as thinly as possible and place in a bowl with the sunflower and olive oils. Leave to marinate for 2 hours.

Meanwhile, boil the potatoes in their skins until they can be pierced with a skewer. Peel and then slice them.

Drain the truffles and make a dressing with the oil and verjuice or vinegar. It should be quite mild. Season with salt and pepper.

Toss the potatoes in the dressing while they are still warm, sprinkle the sliced truffle on top and serve.

Omelette aux truffes de Madame Berthier

Madame Berthier's truffled omelette

SERVES 1

30g (1¼oz) fresh truffle, brushed, washed and finely chopped

2 eggs

1 knob of butter

Salt and pepper

Chop the truffle finely and then place in the bottom of a bowl, break in the eggs and stir lightly without beating. Leave to stand in a cool place for 2 hours or more.

Season the mixture and beat it lightly. Heat the butter in a frying-pan and make the omelette in the usual way.

Truffe en chausson

Truffles in puff pastry

This recipe is based on one supplied by the Office du Tourisme du Pays de Lalbenque .

SERVES 4

4 truffles, about 15g (½oz) each

350g (12oz) puff pastry

30g (1¼oz) butter

Salt

1 egg yolk

Preheat the oven to 220°C/425°F/gas mark 7.

Wash the truffles in running water, using a very soft nail-brush to remove any earth clinging to them.

Roll out the puff pastry to a thickness of 5mm (¼in), and cut out 4 circles about 10 cm (4in) in diameter.

Place a truffle on one half of each circle, cutting it in half if necessary in order to fold over the other half to make a complete seal. Before sealing, put a knob of butter on top of the truffle and sprinkle a little salt over. Brush the edges of the pastry with beaten egg, fold over and pinch the two edges together to seal. Knock up the rim with the back of a knife, and brush the top with beaten egg.

Place the *chaussons* on a greased baking sheet and bake for 17 minutes, until the 'cushions' have risen and are golden and crisp.

The Food Markets of Southern France

• Markets in bold type are the more important ones • Numbers after a place name denote which weeks in the month a market takes place, e.g. 'St Cyprien (2)' under Monday means the market happens only on the second Monday of each month • Asterisks denote those markets which occur only during the summer season • *alt* means alternating weeks; *pl* stands for *place*, *ave* for *avenue*, *bd* for *boulevard*

DORDOGNE

MONDAY	TUESDAY	WEDNESDAY	THURSDAY	FRIDAY	SATURDAY	SUNDAY
Champagnac Bel Air (1)	Beaumont-du-Périgord (2)	Bergerac	La Coquille	Bergerac (Pl Barbacane)	Beaumont-du-Pér.	Creysse
Les Eyzies	Lanouaille	Le Buisson	Domme	**Brantôme**	Belvès	Eymet*
Le Fleix	Mareuil	Gardonne	Excideuil	Le Buisson	**Bergerac**	Gardonne
Hautefort (1)	Neuvic	Hautefort	Eymet	Le Lardin	Le Bugue	Issigeac
Miallet (3 except Paques)	Payzac (1+3)	Jumilhac-le-Grand	La Force	**Ribérac**	La Roche-Chalais	Pressignac-Vicq*
St Cyprien (2)	Pt-Ste-Foy-Ponchapt	Montignac	Lalinde	Salignac-Eyvigues (last)	Montignac	Prigonrieux
Ste Alvère	Prigonrieux	Montpon-Ménestrol	La Roche-Chalais (1)	Sigoulès	Mussidan	Rouffignac
Tocane St Apre	Ribérac*	**Périgueux**	Monpazier	St Aulaye	Neuvic	St Cyprien
Villamblard	St Aulaye (last)	Piégut-Pluviers	Mouleydier	St Léon-sur-l'Isle	Nontron	Singleyrac*
Villefranche-de-Lonchat	St Pardoux (2)	Ribérac	St Astier	Sorges*	**Périgueux**	
	Thénon	Siorac	St Pardoux		St Aulaye	
	Trémolat (last)	Vélines	St Saud Lacoussière		St Léon-sur-l'Isle	
			Sarlat		**Sarlat**	
			Terrasson-le-Villedieu		St Pardoux	
					Tocane St Apre	
					Verteillac (pm)	
					Villefranche-du-Périgord	

GIRONDE

MONDAY	TUESDAY	WEDNESDAY	THURSDAY	FRIDAY	SATURDAY	SUNDAY
Arcachon	Ambes	Arcachon	Arcachon	Ambares	Arcachon	Arcachon
Bordeaux (St Michel)	**Andernos**	Bègles	Bordeaux (la Bastide)	Andernos	Bazas	Barsac
Braud St Louis	Arcachon	**Blaye**	Branne	Arcachon	Bègles	**Bassens**
Captieux	Ares	Bordeaux (Pl Cauderan)	Carbon-Blanc	Bègles	Biganos	Bordeaux (Cours V. Hugo)
Carcans*	Bordeaux (Pl Buisson)	Castres	**Cavignac**	Belin Béliet	Blanquefort	Castelnau-Médoc
Castillon	Bourg (1)	**Cenon**	Hourtin	**Blaye**	Bourg	Eysines
Hourtin*	Braud St Louis (1)	Coutras	Listrac	Bordeaux (Bacalan)	Bordeaux (St Michel)	**Libourne**
St Savin Blaye	Hourtin (pm)*	**Créon**	Lussac	Braud St Louis	Branne	Pessac
St Loubès	Lesparre	**Gujan-Mestras**	Le Porge	Cadaujac	Bruges	**St Christoly-de-Blaye**
Targon	Libourne	Le Haillan	St André-de-Cubzac	Carcans Ville	**Cadillac**	St Emilion
	Monségur	Lacanau-Ville	Salles	**Cenon**	Coutras	St Seurin sur l'Isle
	Pellegrue	Maubuisson	Soussans	Gensac	Gradignan	St Sulpice
	Pessac	Mérignac	La Teste-de-Buch	Hourtin-Plage*	Hourtin	La Teste-de-Buch
	Sauveterre	Portets	Villandraut	**Langon**	Léognan	
	La Teste-de-Buch	Pugnac		**Libourne**	Lesparre	
		St Emilion		Lormont	Ludon	
		St Symphorien		Monsegur	Mérignac	
		La Teste-de-Buch*		Podensac	Pauillac	
				St Aubin	Pessac	
				St Laurent	**La Réole**	
				Targon	St André-de-Cubzac	
				La Teste-de-Buch	St Loubès	
					St Médard-de-Guizières	
					St Médard-en-Jalles	
					Ste-Hélène	
					La Teste-de-Buch	
					Villeneuve d'Ornon	

LANDES

MONDAY	TUESDAY	WEDNESDAY	THURSDAY	FRIDAY	SATURDAY	SUNDAY
Biscarosse-Plage*	Aire-sur-Adour	Biscarosse-Plage*	Biscarosse-Plage*	Biscarosse-Ville	Aire-sur-Adour	Amou
Capbreton*	Azur	Capbreton*	Capbreton*	Capbreton*	Biscarosse-Plage*	Biscarossse-Plage
Grenade-sur-Adour	Biscarosse-Plage*	Eugénie-les-Bains	Castets	Léon*	Capbreton*	Capbreton*
Léon*	Capbreton*	Gabarret	Geaune (alt)	Lit-et-Mixte*	Dax	Léon*
Lit-et-Mixte*	Léon*	Hagetmau	Léon*	Mimizan	Labenne	Lit-et-Mixte*
St Julien-en-Born*	Lit-et-Mixte*	Léon*	Lit-et-Mixte*	Moliets-et-Maa*	Léon*	Parentis-en-Born*
St Saturnin	Moliets-et-Maa*	Lit-et-Mixte*	Magescq	St Julien-en-Born*	Lit-et-Mixte*	St Julien-en-Born*
Soustons	**Mont-de-Marsan**	Morcenx	**Mimizan**	St Vincent-de-Tyr.	Moliets-et-Maa*	Seignosse*
Tartas	St Julien-en-Born*	**Peyrehorade**	Moliets-et-Maa*	Vielle-St-Girons*	**Mont-de-Marsan**	Vielle-St-Girons*
Vielle-St-Girons*	Sanguinet*	St Julien-en-Born*	Mugron	Vieux-Boucau*	Morcenx	Vieux-Boucau*
Vieux-Boucau	Seignosse-le-Penon	Sanguinet*	Parentis-en-Born	Morcenx	**Peyrehorade**	Ygos
	Vielle St Girons*	Seignosse-Bourg	Sabres		Roquefort	
	Vieux-Boucau*	Vielle-St-Girons*	St Julien-en-Born*		St Julien-en-Born*	
		Vielle-St-Girons	St Paul-lès-Dax		Saint-Sever	
		Vieux-Boucau	Seignosse-le-Penon		Sanguinet	
		Villeneuve-de-Marsan	Sore		Vielle-St-Girons*	
			Soustons		Vieux-Boucau*	
			Vielle-St-Girons*			
			Vieux-Boucau*			

LOT-ET-GARONNE

MONDAY	TUESDAY	WEDNESDAY	THURSDAY	FRIDAY	SATURDAY	SUNDAY
Agen	**Agen**	**Agen**	Agen	Agen	**Agen** (also Pl Jasmin)	**Agen** (also
(Pl Durand daily)	(Pl 14 juillet)	(Pl Durand)	Clairac	Aiguillon	Astaffort	Pl 14 juillet)
Astaffort	Aiguillon	Castelmoron	Duras	Barbaste	Casteljaloux	Fumel
Barbaste	Casteljaloux	Houeilles	Le Mas d'Agenais	Buzet	Duras	Mézin
Cancon	Fumel	Lavardac	Mézin	Castillonès*	Lauzun	Penne-d'Agenais
Cocumont	Monflanquin	Monclar-d'Agenais	Miramont*	Fumel	Monclar-d'Agenais	Prayssas
Duras	Sos	Penne-d'Agenais	Monflanquin	Layrac	Monflanquin	Pujols
Lacapelle-Biron	**Villeneuve-sur-Lot**	**Tonneins**	**Monsempron-Libos**	Ste-Livrade-sur-Lot	Nérac	Puymirol
Miramont		Villeréal*	Tournon*	Seyches	St Sylvestre-sur-Lot	
				Vianne (eve)	**Tonneins**	
					Villeneuve-sur-Lot	
					Villeréal	

PYRENEES-ATLANTIQUES

BAYONNE

Covered market in Halles Centrales every morning and Friday all day
Open markets in the mornings:
Balichon: Wednesday
Halles Centrales: Tuesday, Thursday and Saturday
Place des Gascons: Wednesday and Saturday

Place de la République: Friday and Sunday
Polo Beyris: Friday

BIARRITZ
Daily in the Halles Centrales

Others

MONDAY	TUESDAY	WEDNESDAY	THURSDAY	FRIDAY	SATURDAY	SUNDAY
Monein	Arudy	Artix	Bedous	Morlaas (alt)	Arthez	Ciboure
Mourenx	Hasparren (alt)	Eaux Bonnes	Lembeye	**Oloron**	Arudy	
Pau	Mauléon(haute-ville)	Espelette	**Pau**	**Pau**	Arzacq (alt)	
St Jean-Pied-de-Port	Mourenx	Garlin (alt)	St Etienne-de-	St Jean-de-Luz	Boucau	
Salies-de-Béarn (am)	**Nay**	Hendaye	Baïgorry (alt)	St Palais	Espelette*	
Sauvagnon	Orthez	Lons	Salies-de-Béarn	Soumoulou	Hendaye	
Tardets (alt)	**Pau**	Mourenx	Urrugne		Mauléon (basse-ville)	
	St Jean-de-Luz	Navarrenx			**Mourenx**	
		Orthez			**Nay**	
		Pau			**Pau**	
		St Jean-de-Luz			Pontacq	
		St Palais (Jan/May)			St Jean-de-Luz*	
		Sauveterre			Sauvagnon	
					Sauveterre (pm)	

GERS

MONDAY	TUESDAY	WEDNESDAY	THURSDAY	FRIDAY	SATURDAY	SUNDAY
Aignan	Fleurance	Auch	Auch	Cazaubon	**Auch**	Bassouès
Mauvezin	Saramon	Barbotan-les-Termes	Cologne	Lectour	L'Isle-Jourdain	Cologne*
Mirande		**Condom**	Eauze	Montréal	Nogaro	
Samatan		Gimont	Miélan	Riscle		
		Marciac	Plaisance	Seissan		
		Nogaro	St Clar	Vic-Fézensac		

HAUTES-PYRENEES

MONDAY	TUESDAY	WEDNESDAY	THURSDAY	FRIDAY	SATURDAY	SUNDAY
Lourdes	Gazost	**Lannemezan**	Arreau	**Lourdes**	Bagnères-de-Bigorre	Arrens-Marsous
Luz-St-Sauveur	Capvern*	**Lourdes**	Campan*	Loures-Barousse	Castelnau-Magnoac	Esquièze-Sèze*
Rabastens-de-Bigorre	**Lourdes**	Ste-Marie-de-Campan	Cauterets*	**Tarbes**	**Lourdes**	La Barthe-de-Neste
Tarbes	Maubourguet	St Pé-de-Bigorre	**Lourdes**		Pierrefitte-Nestalas	**Lourdes**
	Sarrancolin	**Tarbes**	**Tarbes**		St Lary-Soulan	**Tarbes**
	Tarbes	Tournay			**Tarbes**	
		Trie-sur-Baïse			Vic-en-Bigorre	

HAUTE-GARONNE

Toulouse

Daily: Boulevard de Strasbourg
Daily except Monday: Cristal-palace; Pl du Marché aux Cochons; Place Rétaille; Place St Georges; Marché Arnaud Bernand
Tuesday: Place du Capitole; Place du Salin (small growers)
Wednesday: Place de la Croix de Pierre
Friday: Place du Ravelin
Saturday: Place du Capitole; Place St Etienne; Place du Salin (small growers)
Sunday: St Sernin; Place St Aubin (small growers)

Covered markets every am except Monday: Carmes, Victor Hugo, St Cyprien

Open markets in the suburbs:
Tuesday: Marché de la Faourette; Marché de la Coquille; Marché de l'Ormeau
Wednesday: Marché de Rangueil; Marché Bellefontaine; Marché d'Empalot
Thursday: Marché de Reynerie
Friday: Marché de la Faourette; La Coquille; Marché Ancely (4–7 pm)
Saturday: Marché de l'Ormeau; Marché des Pradettes

Outside Toulouse

MONDAY	TUESDAY	WEDNESDAY	THURSDAY	FRIDAY	SATURDAY	SUNDAY
Bagnères-de-Luchon*	Auriac-sur-Vendinelle	Aspet	Bagnères-de-Luchon*	Auterive	Aspet	Bagnères-de-Luchon
Bessiéres-sur-Tarn	Aurignac	Bagnères-de-Luchon	Caraman	Bagnères-de-Luchon*	Bagnères-de-Luchon*	Montgiscard
Montréjeau	Bagnères-de-Luchon	Boulogne-sur-Gesse	Carbonne	St Béat	Baziège	Plaisance-du-Touch
	Blagnac	Cadours	Colomiers	St Martory	**Blagnac**	Tournefeuille
	Castanet-Tolosan	Le Fousseret	Fronton	Villefranche-de-Lauragais	Cazères	**L'Union**
	L'Isle-en-Dodon	Nailloux	Rieumes		Colomiers	Villemur-sur-Tarn
	Martres-Tolosane	Ramonville-St Agne	**St Gaudens**		Cugnaux	Villeneuve-Tolosane
	Montesquieu-Volvestre		Villeneuve-Tolosane		Fenouillet	
	Muret				Garidech	
	St Béat (1)				**Grenade**	
	St Lys				L'Isle-en-Dodon	
	Verfeil				Montesquieu-Velvestre	
					Muret	
					Nailloux (4)	
					Plaisance-du-Touch	
					Ramonville-Ste-Agne	
					Revel	
					St Alban	
					St Jean	
					St Orens-de-Gameville	
					Villemur-sur-Tarn	

ARIEGE

MONDAY	TUESDAY	WEDNESDAY	THURSDAY	FRIDAY	SATURDAY	SUNDAY
Bélesta	Ax-les-Termes	Bélesta	Ax-les-Termes	Bélesta	Ax-les-Termes	Bélesta
Foix (1,3+5)	Bélesta	**Foix**	Bélesta	Daumazan-sur-Arize	La Bastide-de-	Verniolle
Mirepoix	Castillon (3+5)	Le Fosset (3+5)	Larroque d'Olmes	**Foix**	Sérou (1)	
St Girons (2+4)	Pamiers	Lavelanet	Massat (2+4)	Lavelanet	Bélesta	
	Varlhes (2+4)	Lézat-sur-Lèze	Mazères	Saverdun	Larroque d'Olnes	
		Le Mas d'Azil (2+4)	Mirepoix		**Pamiers**	
		St Jean du Falga	**Pamiers**		St Girons	
		Seix (2+4)	Rouze		Tarascon-sur-Ariège	
		Tarascon-sur-Ariège	Seix (1+3)		Varilhes	
		La Tour du Crieu	Vicdessos			

TARN-ET-GARONNE

MONDAY	TUESDAY	WEDNESDAY	THURSDAY	FRIDAY	SATURDAY	SUNDAY
Caussade	Caylus	Grisolles	**Castelsarassin**	Albias	Beaumont-de-	Lafrancaise*
St Nicolas de la Grave	Montech	Labastide-St Pierre	Monclar-de-Quercy	Lavit-de-Lomagne	Lomagne	Lamagistère
	Nègrepelisse	Lafrançaise		Montricoux	Caylus	Moissac
	Valence d'Agen	Laguépie (3)		Verdun-sur-Garonne	Lauzerte	Montbeton
		Montauban			Moissac	Monclar-de-Quercy*
		(Pl Lalaque)			Montaigu-de-Quercy	Réalville
		Septfonds			**Montauban**	Roquecor
					(Pl Nationale)	St Antonin
					Valence d'Agen	St Etienne-de-
					Varen	Turmont

TARN

MONDAY	TUESDAY	WEDNESDAY	THURSDAY	FRIDAY	SATURDAY	SUNDAY
Briatexte	**Albi** (Pl F.	**Albi** (Cantepau)	Aussillon	Brassac	**Albi** (Pl Ste-Cécile)	Graulhet
	Pelloutier)	Cagnac	Blaye	Carmaux	(Pl F.Pelloutier)	Lacaune
	Blaye	Cahuzac	**Castres** (Pl J.Jaurès)	**Castres**	(Bd de Strasbourg)	Lisle-sur-Tarn
	Brassac	Castres (Lameilhé)	**Graulhet**	(Pl J.Jaurès)	Brassac	**Mazamet**
	Castres (Pl J.Jaurès)	Montredon-	Labastide-Rouairoux	Gaillac	**Castres** (Pl J.Jaurès)	Murat-sur-Vèbre
	Mazamet	Labessonnie	St Amans-Soult	Labruguière	(Les Quais)	Pampelonne
	St Paul Cap-de-Joux	Puylaurens	St Juéry	Lacrouzette	Cordes	Trébas
	Vielmur-sur-Agout	Réalmont	Soual	Lautrec	Lavaur	
		St Sulpice	Vabre	Marssac	**Mazamet**	
		Salvagnac		Roquecourbe	Murat-sur-Vèbre	
					Rabastens	

AVEYRON

MONDAY	TUESDAY	WEDNESDAY	THURSDAY	FRIDAY	SATURDAY	SUNDAY
Cassagnes-	Brousse-le-Château*	Arvieu*	Bozouls	Aubin	Capdenac-Gare	Baraqueville*
Bégonhès (3)*	**Capdenac-Gare**	Aubin	Canet-de-Salars*	Cassagnes-Bégonhès	Cransac (pm)	Belmont-sur-Rance
St Christophe- Vallon	**Decazeville**	Camarès (4)	Mur-de-Barrez	**Decazeville**	Firmi	Couvertoirade
	Entraygues*	Couvertoirade	Olemps (pm)	Entraygues	**Laguiole**	Grand-Vabre*
	Espalion	**Millau**	St Affrique	**Espalion**	Naucelle*	Lanuéjols
	Rignac	Montbazens	St Amans des Cots	**Millau**	Pont-de-Salars*	Marcillac
	St Affrique	Montredon*	St Jean-du-Bruel	Onet-le-Château	Réquista	Najac*
	Roque-Ste-	Pont-de-Salars*	Villefranche-de-Panat	Rodez (pm)	**Rodez**	La Primaube
	Marguérite*	Rodez	**Villefranche-de-**	St Saturnin-de-	St Affrique	Rieupeyroux
		Sévérac-le-Château	**Rouergue**	Lenne (4)	St Côme d'Olt*	Villefranche-de-
		St Parthem (soir)*	Viviez	Salles-Curan*	St Géniez d'Olt	Panat
		Ste Geneviève-sur-	Villefranche-de-Panat	Viviez		
		Argence				
		Villecomtal*				

LOT

MONDAY	TUESDAY	WEDNESDAY	THURSDAY	FRIDAY	SATURDAY	SUNDAY
Assier (1+3)	Bretenoux	Bagnac-sur- Célé	Brengues*	Floirac	Bretenoux	Biers-sur-Cère
Souillac*	Catus	Cahors	Mercuès	Gramat	Cajarc	Castelnau-Montratier
	Floirac	Latronquière	Montcuq*	Latronquière	**Cahors**	Cazals
	Gourdon	Livernon (5pm)	Sauzet	Miers* (5pm)	Duravel	Concots
	Gramat	Luzech	Sousceyrac	Prayssac	**Figeac**	Douelle
	Lacapelle-Marival	Martel		St Germain-du-Bel-Air	Gourdon	Gramat
	Leyme*	Payrac*		Salviac	**Martel**	Labastide-Murat
	Marcilhac-sur-Célé	Souillac*		Souillac	Pradines	Lacapelle-Marival
	(5pm)	**Sousceyrac (2)**			Puy L'Evêque	Lalbenque
	Puy l'Evêque				St Céré	Limogne
	St Céré				Vayrac	Montcuq
	Salviac					Prayssac*
	Vayrac					Puybrun
						St Germain-du-
						Bel-Air
						St Géry*
						Thédirac
						Le Vigan

CORREZE

MONDAY	TUESDAY	WEDNESDAY	THURSDAY	FRIDAY	SATURDAY	SUNDAY
Le Lonzac	Bort (2+4)	Aubazine	Argentat (1+3)	Beaulieu (1+3)	**Beaulieu**	Aubazine
	Brive	Beaulieu	Brive		**Brive**	Tulle
	Marcillac-la-Croisille	Larche (2)				Ussel
		Lubersac (1+3)				
		Tulle				
		Ussel (1+3)				

PYRENEES-ORIENTALES

MONDAY	TUESDAY	WEDNESDAY	THURSDAY	FRIDAY	SATURDAY	SUNDAY
Argelès-Plage*	Argelès-Plage*	Argelès Plage*	Amélie-les-Bains	Argelès-Plage*	Argelès-Plage*	Argelès-Plage*
Bourg Madame	Canet-en-Roussillon	Argelès-Ville	Argelès-Plage	Canet-en-Roussillon	Argelès-Ville	Banyuls
Canet-en-Roussillon	Cerbère	Arles-sur-Tech	Banyuls	Cerbère	Canet-en-	Canet-en-Roussillon
Elne	Le Soler	Canet-en-	Canet-en-Roussillon	Elne	Roussillon	Collioure
Estagel	Millas	Roussillon	Millas	Estagel	Céret	Perpignan
Le Soler	**Perpignan**	Collioure	**Perpignan**	Ille-sur-Tet	Le Soler	**St Laurent-de-
Perpignan	**Prades**	Elne	St Cyprien (village)	**Perpignan**	**Perpignan**	la-Salanque**
Rivesaltes	Sorède	**Font-Remeu**	**St Laurent-de-	Pollestres	Port Vendres	
		Perpignan	la-Salanque**	St Cyprien	St Estève	
		Pollestres	Toulouges	Sorède	St Laurent-de-Cerdans	
		St Estève		Toulouges	St Paul-de-Fenouillet	
		St Paul-de-Fenouillet				
		Toulouges				
		Vinca				

AUDE

MONDAY	TUESDAY	WEDNESDAY	THURSDAY	FRIDAY	SATURDAY	SUNDAY
Argeliers	Argeliers	Argeliers	Argeliers	Argeliers	Argeliers	Argeliers
Castelnaudary	Carcassonne	Belpech	Carcassonne	Cuxac d'Aude	**Carcassonne**	Coursan
Gruissan	Couiza	Bram	Coursan	Fabrezan	Chalabre-Corbières	Durban-Corbières
Port Leucate	Cuxac d'Aude	Cuxac d'Aude	Durban-Corbières	Laredorte	Gruissan	**Narbonne**
	Fabrezan	Durban-Corbières	Espéraza	Leucate	Port la Nouvelle	Salles sur l'Hers
	Leucate-Village*	Gruissan	Fabrezan	Limoux	Rieux-Minervois	
	Rieux-Minervois	Leucate Port	Leucate-Village	Narbonne		
	Sigean	Leucate-Plage*	**Narbonne**	Sigean		
	St Pierre-la-Mer*	Lézignan-Corbières	Rieux-Minervois			
		Quillan				

HERAULT

MONTPELLIER
Daily: Cours Gambetta
Daily except Sunday: Avenue Pompignane; Marché Jean Jaurès; Place des Beaux Arts
Daily exceptTuesday and Sunday: Place des Arcaux
Daily except Sunday and Monday: Avenue Pédro
Tuesday, Friday, Saturday: Place Jean Baumel
Tuesday and Friday: Avenue du Professeur Gras
Sunday only: Avenue St Champlain, near Eglise Dom Bosco (small growers)

BÉZIERS
Daily except Monday: Allées Paul Riquet
Monday: Place du 11 novembre
Tuesday: Cité de la Devèze, Place Emile Zola
Wednesday: Place du 11 novembre, L'Iranget
Thursday: Cité de la Devèze
Friday: Place David d'Angers
Saturday: Place du 11 novembre, Cité de la Devèze

Others

MONDAY	TUESDAY	WEDNESDAY	THURSDAY	FRIDAY	SATURDAY	SUNDAY
Abeilhan	Abeilhan	Abeilhan	Abeilhan	Abeilhan	Abeilhan	Abeilhan
Bédarieux	Baillargues	Alignan-du-Vent	Agde	Baillargues	Alignan-du-Vent	Bessan
Frontignan	Balaruc-les-Bains	Camplong-Canet*	Aniane	Balaruc-les-Bains	Castelnau-de-Léz	Capestang
Lespignan	Bessan	Capestang	Castelnau-le-Léz	Camplong d'Orb	Cazouls-lès-Béziers	Ceilhes
Maureilhan	Castelnau-le-Léz	Castelnau-le-Léz	Cazouls-lès-Béziers	Capestang-le-Léz	Cessenon	La Grande Motte
Montady	Castries	**Clermont**	Cers	Castries	**Frontignan**	Lattes
Montblanc	Cazouls-les-Béziers	**l'Hérault**	**Frontignan**	Caux	**Gignac**	Maureilhan
Pérols	Cers	Juvignac	Graissessac	**Ganges**	Lodève	**Palavas-les-Flots**
Pomerols	Cessenon	Lespignan	Lansargues	Juvignac	Maureilhan	St Chinian
Le Pouget	Cruzy	Lignan	Laurens	Lespignan	Murviel-lès-Béziers	
Sauvian	**Ganges**	Loupian	Magalas	Maureilhan	Nissan-lès-Enserune	
Sérignan	Gigean	Montblanc	Marsillargues	Montagnac	Servian	
Sète	Lamalou-les-Bains	Palavas-les-Flots	Mèze	Montblanc	St Gély-du-Fesc	
Valras-Plage	Lansargues	Le Pouget	Murviel-lès-Béziers	Le Pouget	St Jean-de-Védas	
	Marsillargues	St Pons-de-	Nissan-lès-Enserune	Poussan	**Vias**	
	Murviel-lès-Béziers	Thomières	Paulhan	Puisserguier	Villeneuve-lès-Béziers	
	Nissan-lès-Enserune	**Sète**	Le Pouget	Sauvian		
	Olonzac	**Vias**	St Gély-du-Fesc	Sète		
	Le Pouget	Villeneuve-lès-	St Jean-de-Védas	Valras-Plage		
	St Martin-de-	Maguelonne	St Matthieu-de-	Villeneuve-lès-		
	Londres	Villevayrac	Tréviers (pm)	Béziers		
	St Pangoire		Salvetat-sur-L'Agout	Villeneuve-lès-		
	Servian		Servian	Maguelonne		
	Thézan-lès-Béziers		Thézan-lès-Béziers			
	Villeneuve-lès-Béziers		Villeneuve-lès-Béziers			

GARD

MONDAY	TUESDAY	WEDNESDAY	THURSDAY	FRIDAY	SATURDAY	SUNDAY
Alès	Aimargues	Aigues-Mortes	Alès	Aimargues	Alès	Aigues-Mortes
Clarensac	Alès	Alès	Anduze	Alès	Bagnols-sur- Cèze	Beaucaire
Concoules*	Bezouce	Aramon	Beauvoisin	**Barjac**	Bernis	Alès (pré St Jean)
Grau-du-Roi (at	Bouillargues	**Bagnols-sur-Cèze**	Beaucaire	Bezouce	Caissargues	Beaucaire
le Boucanet)	Codognan	Collias	Bellegarde	Le Cailar	Colognac*	Bellegarde
Lasalle	Genolhac*	Gagnières	**Bessèges**	Calvisson	Genolhac	Bréau and
Méjannes-le-Clap*	Grau-du-Roi	Goudargues	Caveirac	Générac	Grau-du-Roi	Salagosse*
Montfaucon	Langlade	Grand Combe	Codolet	Génerargues	Grand Combe	St Gilles
Orsan	Ledenon	Grau-du-Roi	Comps	Grau-du-Roi	Langlade	St Michel d'Euzet*
St Laurent d'Aigouze	Le Vigan	(at Le Boucanet and	Grau-du-Roi	(at Le Boucanet	Le Vigan	
Vergèze	Marguerittes	Port Camargue)	Le Vigan	and Port Camargue)	Marguerittes	
	Montfrun	Manduel	Mialet	Les Mages	Millaud	
	Nîmes	**Nîmes**	Nîmes (mas de Mingues)	Marguerittes	Sauve	
	Redessan	Quissac	Pujaut	Molières-sur-Cèze	Sommières	
	Roquemaure	St Génies-de-	Sauve	Nîmes (bd J.Jaurès)	**Uzès**	
	St Ambroix	Malgoires	Vergèze	Remoulins	Vauvert	
	St Hippolyte-du-Fort	Sumène	Villeneuve-lès-	Salindres	Valborgne*	
	St Jean-du-Gard	Vauvert	Avignon	St Hippolyte-du-Fort		

ARDÈCHE

MONDAY	TUESDAY	WEDNESDAY	THURSDAY	FRIDAY	SATURDAY	SUNDAY
Ariebosc*	Ariebosc*	Ariebosc*	Ariebosc*	Ariebosc*	Ariebosc*	Alba-la-Romaine
Mauves*	Jaujac	Annonay	Chomérac	Charmes-sur-Rhône	Annonay	Annonay (2)
St Agrève	Lalevade-	Antraigues (pm)	Lalouvesc	Cruas	Aubenas	Lablachère
St Paul-le-Jeune	d'Ardèche	Baix	Lavilledieu	Davézieux (pm)	Bourg St Andéol	Le Lac
St Pierre-de-	Lamastre	Bourg St Andéol	Mauves*	Guilherand	Lamastre	d'Issariès*
Colombier*	Mauves*	Coucouron	Montpezat	Jaujac	Privas	St Martin-
	St Etienne-	Joyeuse	St Martin-de-Valamas	Labégude	Ruoms	d'Ardèche*
	de-Lugdares	Le Lac d'Issariès*	St Pierre-de-Colombier*	Mauves*	St Pierre-de-	St Pierre-de-
	St Pierre-de-	Mauves*	Sarras	St Félicien	Colombier*	Colombier*
	Colombier*	Le Pouzin	Vallon Pont-d'Arc	St Paul-le-Jeune	Tournon	St Pierreville
	Satillieu	Privas	Vernoux-en-Vivarais	Soyons	Les Vans	Vals-les-Bains
	Viviers	St Jean-de-Muzols		St Pierre-de-Colombier*		
		St Pierre-de-Colombier*		Serrières		
		Tournon		Thueyts		
		Villeneuve-de-Berg		La Voulte-sur-Rhône		

BOUCHES-DU-RHONE

MARSEILLE

Daily: Le Prado et Michelet; Place Jean-Jaurès; The Old Port (fish); Place Notre Dame du Mont; Jules Guesde; St Lazare; Boulevard Michelet; Place Etats Unis; Capucins (also called Noailles)
Monday: La Belle de Mai; Place Sébastopol; Cours Pierre Puget
Tuesday: La Plaine; Cours Pierre Puget
Wednesday: La Belle de Mai; Place Sébastopol

Thursday: La Plaine
Friday: La Belle de Mai; Cours Pierre Puget
Saturday: La Belle de Mai; Place Sébastopol; Cours Pierre Puget

AIX-EN-PROVENCE

Daily: Place Richelme; Place Prêcheurs
Daily except Tuesday and Thursday: Marché Encagnane et du Val St André

Others

MONDAY	TUESDAY	WEDNESDAY	THURSDAY	FRIDAY	SATURDAY	SUNDAY
Fontvieille	Alleins	Allauch	Aubagne	Aubagne (pm)	Arles	Aubagne
Fuveau	Aubagne	Arles	Aureille	Carry-le-Rouet	Aubagne	Berre-l'Etang
St Etienne-du-Grès	Berre-l'Etang	Barbentane	Auriol	Cassis	Auriol	Bouc-Bel-Air
Stes-Maries-	Bouc-Bel-Air	Cassis	Berre-l'Etang	Ceyreste	Cabannes (2)	Châteaurenard
de-la-Mer	Cabannes	Cuges-les-Pins	La Bouilladisse	Châteauneuf-	Carnoux	Gardanne
Sénas	Carry-le-Rouet	Fos-sur-Mer	Carnoux	les-Martigues	Charleval	Gignac-la-Nerth
Venelles	La Ciotat	Fuveau	Ensuès-la-Redonne	La Destrousse	La Fare-les-Oliviers	Jouques
	Coudoux	Gardanne	La Fare-les-Oliviers	Eguilles	Fos-sur-Mer	Martigues
	Eguilles	Gémenos	Fuveau	Eyragues	Marignane	Pélisanne
	Eyguières	Jouques (pm)	Maillane	Fontvieille	Miramas	Plan d'Orgon*
	Fuveau	Mayrargues	Marignane	Gardanne	Les Pennes-Mirabeau	Port-de-Bouc
	Gréasque	Peyrolles	Martigues	Grans	Plan-du-Cuques	Le Puy-Ste-
	Istres	Port St Louis-	Maussane-les-Alpilles	Gréasque	Port St Louis-du-Rhône	Réparade
	Lançon-Provence	du-Rhône	Miramas	Lambesc	St Chamas	St Victoret
	Marignane	Port-de-Bouc	Les Pennes-Mirabeau	Mallemort	Salon-de-Provence	Salon-de-
	Meyreuil	Rognac	La Roque-d'Anthéron	Mouriès	Sénas	Provence
	Les Pennes-	Rognes	Roquefort-la-Bédoule	Peynier	Septemès les Vallons	Vitrolles
	Mirabeau	Rousset	Salon-de-Provence	Port-de-Bouc	Simiane-Collongue	
	Peypin	St Cannat	Sausset-les-Pins	Roquevaire	Velaux	
	Port-de-Bouc	St Etienne-du-Grès	Sénas	St Andiol	Vitrolles	
	Rognonas	St Mitre-les-	Velaux	St Etienne-du-Grès (pm)		
	St Paul-Lez-Durance	Remparts	Vitrolles	St Martin-de-Crau		
	Salon-de-Provence	Salon-de-Provence		Salon-de-Provence		
	Tarascon	Sénas		Sénas		
	Ventabren	Trets		Ventabren		
	Vitrolles	Vitrolles		Vitrolles		

VAUCLUSE

MONDAY	TUESDAY	WEDNESDAY	THURSDAY	FRIDAY	SATURDAY	SUNDAY
Bedarrides	Avignon (Montfavet)	Avignon (Rocade)	Avignon	Avignon	Avignon	Coustellet
Bedouin	(Ave de la Trillade)	(Eglise Jean XXII)	(HLM St Jean)	(Pont des 2 Eaux)	(Pte Magnanen)	Isle-sur-Sorgue
Bollène	(Monclar Sud)	(Châteauneuf-	Caumont-sur-Durance	(Monclar Sud)	Grillon	Maubec*
Cadenet	Beaumes-de-Venise	de-Gadagne)	Orange	Bonnieux	Orange	Monteux

Cavaillon
Goult
Lauris
Mazan
Orange
Pernes-les-Fontaines
Piolenc
St Didier
Velleron

Caderousse
Carombe
Cucuron
Lapalud
Mondragon
Orange
Pernes-les-Fontaines
St Saturnin-lès-Apt
La Tour d'Aigues
Vaison-la-Romaine
Velleron

Entraigues-sur-Sorgues
Malaucène
Mérindol
Morières
Orange
Pernes-les-Fontaines
Sault
Le Thor
Velleron

Pernes-les-Fontaines*
Le Pontet
Roussillon
Vacqueyras
Velleron

Carpentras
Cavaillon
Châteauneuf-du-Pape
Courthézon
Loumarin
Velleron

Pernes-les-Fontaines
Ste-Cécile-les-Vignes
Le Thor
Velleron

Mormoiron*
Sorgues

VAR

MONDAY	TUESDAY	WEDNESDAY	THURSDAY	FRIDAY	SATURDAY	SUNDAY
Bandol	Bandol	Aups	Les Adrets	Aiguines	Aups	Bandol
Le Beausset	Le Beausset	Bagnols-en-Forêt	Les Arcs-sur-Argens	Bandol	Bagnols	Bauduen
Belgentier	Bormes-les-Mimosas	Bandol	Aups	Le Beausset	Belgentier	Le Beausset
Grimaud	Brue Auriac	Le Beausset	Bargemon	Carnoules	Bormes-les-Mimosas	Bras
Roquebrune-sur-Argens	Callas	Bormes-les-Mimosas	Le Beausset	Châteaudouble	Brignolles	La Croix Valmer
St Raphael	Le Cannet-des-Maures	Bras	La Cadière-d'Azur	Correns	Brue Auriac	Forcalqueiret
Ste-Maxime	Claviers	Camps-la-Source	Fayence	**Cuers**	Callas	Fréjus
La Valette du Var	Correns	Carces	Forcalqueiret	La Farlède	Carces	La Garde Freinet
Varages	Cotignac	Cavalaire-sur-Mer	Fréjus	Flassans-sur-Issole	Claviers	Grimaud
	La Farlède	Cogolin	Gonfaron	Fréjus	Cogolin	Hyères
	Fayence	La Crau	Grimaud	La Garde-Freinet	**Draguignan**	La Londe-les-Maures
	Figanières	Draguignan	Hyères	Ginasservis	Evenos	Nans-les-Pins
	Fréjus	Fréjus	Le Lavandou	Grimaud	Fayence	Ramatuelle
	La Garde-Freinet	La Garde-Freinet	Méounes-les-Montrieux	Hyères	**Fréjus**	St Cyr sur Mer
	Garéoult	Hyères	Ollioules	Le Luc-en-Provence	La Garde-Freinet	St Julien-le-Montagnier
	Hyères	Nant-les-Pins	Pignans	Montferrat	Hyères	Salèmes
	Lorgues	St Mandrier*	Plan de la Tour	Montmeyan	Ollioules	Six Fours-les-Plages
	Mazaugues	St Maximin-la-Ste-Baume	Pourrières	La Motte	Pierrefeu-du-Var	Tanneron
	Montauroux	St Raphael	Ramatuelle	Pontèves	Puget-Ville	Salernes
	Montmeyan	St Zacharie	St Raphael	Rians	Roquebrune-sur-Argence	Taradeau
	Pierrefeu-du-Var	Salèmes	Les Salles-sur-Verdun	Roquebrune-sur-Argens	La Roquebroussanne	Trans
	Roquebrune-sur-Argens	**Sanary-sur-Mer**	Ste-Maxime	St Raphael	St Mandrier-sur-Mer	Vidauban
	St Julien-le-Montagnier	Sollies Pont	Six Fours-les-Plages	Sollies-Tourcas	St Tropez	Vinon-sur-Verdon
	St Tropez	Taradeau	Le Thoronet	Toulon	Six Fours-Les-Plages	
	Six Fours-les-Plages	Tourtour	Varages	Le Val	Tourtour	
		La Valette-du-Var	La Verdière		La Verdière	
		Vidauban	Villecroze			

DRÔME

MONDAY	TUESDAY	WEDNESDAY	THURSDAY	FRIDAY	SATURDAY	SUNDAY
Allex	Anneyron	Ancone	Allan	Bourg-de-Péage	Alixan	La Batie Rolland (4)
Châteauneuf-du-Rhône	La Bégude de Mazenc	Aouste-sur Sye (pm)	La Beaume-de-Transit	Chanaret	Aouste-sur-Sye (pm)	Beaufort-sur-Gervanne*
Loriol	Chabeuil	Beaufort-sur-Gervanne	Beauvallon	Châteauneuf-du-Rh	Beaumont-lès-Valence	Beauvallon
La Motte Chalençon	Crest	Bourg-lès-Valence	Bourdeaux	Châtillon-en-Diois	Buis-les-Baronnies	Bourg-de-Péage
Saint-Donat	Grignan	Buis-les-Baronnies	La Chapelle-en-Vercors	La Coucourde	La Chapelle-en-Vercors	Bourg-lès-Valence
St Sorlin-en-Valloire	Hauterives	Crest	Grane	Dieulefit	Crest	Colonzelle
Tulette	Livron	Die	Montélimar	Le Grand Serre	Die	Génissieux
Valence	Montbrun-les-Bains	Erome	**Nyons**	Loriol	**Donzère**	La Laupie-Nyons*
	Montmeyran	Etoile-sur-Rhône	Peyrins	Luc-en-Diois	Livron-sur-Drôme	Romans-sur-Isère
	Romans-sur-Isère	Lus-la-Croix-Haute	**Portes-lès-Valence**	Montélimar	Montbrun	Saillans
	St Paul-Trois-Châteaux	Malissard	Romans-sur-Isère	Romans-sur-Isère	Montélimar	Séderon
	Valence	Montélimar	St Vallier-Valence	**St Rambert d'Albon**	Romans-sur-Isère	Saint-Uze
		La Roche-de-Glun	Taulignan	Suze-la-Rousse	St Jean-en-Royans	
		Romans-sur-Isère		St Barthélémy-Tulette	St Marcel-lès-Valence	
		St Nazaire-en-Royans		**Valence**	Sauzet	
		Valence			Tain-l'Hermitage	
					Valence	

LES ALPES-MARITIMES

NICE
Markets daily, except Monday, as follows:
Cours Saleya; Saleya; Avenue Malausséna (Libération); Place Fontaine
du Temple (Ray); Boulevard Virgile Barel (St Roch); Boulevard Paul Montel

(St Augustin);

Friday: Place San Niccolo
Saturday, Sunday and public holidays: Nice Village

Other than in Nice

MONDAY	TUESDAY	WEDNESDAY	THURSDAY	FRIDAY	SATURDAY	SUNDAY
Le Bar-sur-Loup	Breil-sur-Roya	Cagnes	Cagnes	Cagnes	Beaulieu	Cagnes
Caille	Cagnes	**Cannes**	**Cannes**	**Cannes**	Cagnes	**Cannes**
Cannes*	**Cannes**	Le Cannet	Carros-le-Neuf	Grasse	**Cannes**	Le Cannet
Le Cannet	Le Cannet	La Colle-sur-Loup	Grasse	Menton	Le Cannet	Grasse
Menton	Grasse	Grasse	Mandelieu-la-Napoule	Monaco	Grasse	Menton
Monaco	Menton	Mandelieu-la-Napoule	Menton	Pégomas	Mandelieu-	Monaco
Peymeinade	Monaco	Menton	Monaco	Roquebrune-	la-Napoule	Puget-Thémiers
Roquebrune-	Mouans-Sartoux	Monaco	Mouans-Sartoux	Cap-Martin	Menton	Roquebrune-
Cap-Martin	Roquebrune-	Roquebrune-	Pèone	St Etienne-de-Tinée	Monaco	Cap-Martin
St Laurent-du-Var	Cap-Martin	Cap-Martin	Roquebrune-	St Laurent-du-Var	Pèone	St Laurent-du-Var
	St Cézaire-sur-Siagne	Roquesteron	Cap-Martin	St Vallier-de-Thiey	Roquebrune-	Vallauris
	St Laurent-du-Var	Tende	Sospel	Tende	Cap-Martin	
	La Trinité	Tourrette-sur-Loup	Turbie	Théoule-sur-Mer*	St Cézaire-sur-Siagne	
	Valbonne	Vallauris	Valbonne	Valbonne	Vallauris	
	Vallauris	Villeneuve-Loubet	Vallauris	Vallauris	Villefranche-sur-Mer	
	Vence			Vence	Villeneuve-Loubet	

MISCELLANEOUS FOIRES AND FÊTES
in calendar order

Mimosa: Cannes (Alpes-Maritimes)	January
Citrons: Menton (Alpes-Maritimes)	February
Boeufs gras: Bazas (Lot-et-Garonne)	Thurs before Quinquagesima
Boeufs gras: St Donat sur l'Herbasse	Mon before Palm Sun
Boeufs gras: Le Grand Serre (Drôme)	last Sat March
Boeufs gras: Turenne (Corrèze + Drôme)	Thurs before Palm Sun
Salé: Toulouse (Haute-Garonne)	Thurs before Easter
Jambons: Bayonne (Pyrénées Atlantiques)	Thurs, Fri and Sat before Easter
Goats/cheese: Arles sur-Tech (Pyrénées Orientales)	Sat after Palm Sun
Seeds and plants: Crest (Drôme)	3rd April
Lambs: Chaumeil (Corrèze)	10th April
Goats and calves: Aubazine (Corrèze)	Sun nearest to 23/4
Asparagus: Mormoiron (Vaucluse)	end April
Plants: Forcalquieret (Var)	1st May
Wine and cheese: Condrieu (Rhône)	1st May
Jambons: Bédarieux (Hérault)	2nd May
Plants: Hyères (Var)	3rd May
Flowers: Lavardac (Lot-et-Garonne)	1st Wed May
Goslings: Valence d'Agen (Lot-et-Garonne)	approx 6th May
Cheese: Thuir (Pyrénées Orientales)	8th May
Plants: St Nicolas de la Grave (Tarn et Garonne)	end May
Wool: Grimaud (Var)	Ascension Day
Cherries: Itxassou (Pyrénées Atlantiques)	May/June
Organic fair: Rabastens (Tarn)	two days early June
Flowers: Mirepoix (Ariège)	Whit-Monday
Picodons (cheese): Taulignan (Drôme)	Sun after Whitsun
Foire de l'Aïoli: Les Mayons (Var)	Ascension Day
Silk cocoons: La Garde-Freinet (Var)	15th June
Salé: Toulouse (Haute-Garonne)	24th June
Goats: Nespouls (Corrèze)	June
Goats' cheese: Roaix (Vaucluse)	lst Sun July
Tuna fish festival: St Jean-de-Luz (Pyrénées Atlantiques)	1st week July
Cherries: Malemort-du-Contat (Vaucluse)	1st w/end July
Vaches grasses: Beaulieu sur Dord.(Corrèze)	mid-July
Chipirons: Hendaye (Pyrénées Atlantiques)	mid-July
Goats' cheese: Plaisance (Gers)	14th July
Fête de l'olivier: Peymeinade (Alpes-Maritimes)	mid-July
Wool: Martel (Lot)	23rd July
Olives: Les Vans (Ardèche)	4th Sun July
Ponies and donkeys: Roquecor (Tarn-et-Garonne)	end July
Oysters: Mèze (Hérault)	6th August
Oysters: Marseillan (Hérault)	3 days in August
Oysters: Goujan-Mestras	mid-August
Turkeys: La Laupie (Drôme)	August
Fruit: Prayssas (Lot)	24th August
Onions: Coutras (Gironde)	last Wed August
Onions: Tournon (Ardèche)	29th August
Rams: Naucelle (Aveyron)	end August
Garlic: La Crau (Var)	last Sat August
Garlic: Hyères (Var)	4th Sat August
Garlic: La Garde (Var)	1st September
Onions: St Donat sur l'Herbasse (Drôme)	1st Mon September
Prunes: St Aubin (Lot-et-Garonne)	1st Sun September
Garlic: Sollies Pont (Var)	1st Thurs September
Ttoro: St Jean-de-Luz (Pyrénées Atlantiques)	early September
Garlic: Draguignan (Var)	1st Sat September
Saucisses: Le Val (Var)	2 days early Sept
Sel: Salies-du-Béarn (Pyrénées Atlantiques)	7th/10th September
Onions: Guitres (Gironde)	2nd Wed September
Olives: Mouries (B-du-Rhône)	2nd w/end September
Sheep: Guillaumes (B-du-Rhône)	16th September
Apples: Peyruis (Alpes de Haute-Provence)	end September
Lavender: Montbrun (Drôme)	last Sat September
Cheese (Pyrenees): Laruns (Pyrénées Atlantiques)	last Sun September
Apples: Châtillon-en-Diois (Drôme)	Sun after All Saints
Fête des tripoux: Naucelles (Aveyron)	2 days November
Turkeys (fête du glouglou): Varaignes (Dordogne)	11th November
Poultry: Baraqueville (Aveyron)	3rd Fri December
Turkeys: Le Grand Serre (Drôme)	2nd Sat December
Turkeys: Ardancette (Drôme)	Sat before Christmas
Foire des **gourmands**: Valréas (Vaucluse)	Sat before Christmas
Capons: Grignols (Gironde)	Sun before Christmas
Poultry: Molières (Dordogne)	Sun before Christmas

MARKETS & FAIRS FEATURING PARTICULAR PRODUCTS

N.B. Verify dates locally, especially where approximates only are given below

FOIE GRAS   November to end of March inc.

(and fattened geese and ducks)

FOIRES

Eysines (Gironde)	3 days end November
Ludon (Gironde)	November
Thuir (Pyrénées Orientales)	3rd week November
Verniolle (Ariège)	1st Sun December
Mazères (Ariège)	December
Brive (Corrèze)	2nd week December
Belpech (Aude)	2nd week December
Castelnaudary (Aude)	1st Sun December
Montbazens (Aveyron)	3rd Tues December
Vic-en-Bigorre (Haute-Pyrénées)	1st/2nd December
Monségur (Gironde)	2nd Sun December
Fumel (Lot)	2nd Mon December
Vergt (Dordogne)	2nd half December
Sauvian (Hérault)	Sun before Christmas
Gaillac (Tarn)	beginning December
Lavardac (Lot-et-Garonne)	2nd week Jan
Piégut-Pluviers (Dordogne)	2nd or 3rd Sun January & February
Issigeac (Dordogne)	3rd Sun January
Vic-en-Bigorre (Haute-Pyrénées)	end Jan/beg. February (concours)
Brive (Corrèze)	1st Sat February
Vergt (Dordogne)	February
Monségur (Gironde)	2nd Sun February

WEEKLY MARKETS AU GRAS   November to February/March

Pau (Pyrénées Atlantiques)	daily except Sun
Vic-en-Bigorre (Hautes-Pyrénées)	Mon
Mirande (Gers)	Mon
Fleurance (Gers)	Tues
Gimont (Gers)	Sun
Caussade (Lot-et-Garonne)	Mon
Cahors (Lot)	Wed and Sat
Périgueux (Dordogne)	Tues, Wed, Sat
Thénon (Dordogne)	Tues
Piégut-Pluivers (Dordogne)	Wed (January and February)
Ribérac (Dordogne)	Fri
Sarlat (Dordogne)	Wed, Sat
Terrasson (Dordogne)	Thurs
Vergt (Dordogne)	Fri
Thiviers (Dordogne)	Sat
Montclar de Quercy (Tarn et Goronde)	Sun

GARLIC   June/October

FOIRES

Uzès (Gard)	24th June
Sauzet (Drôme)	last Sun July
Lautrec (Tarn)	1st Fri August
Cadours (Haute-Garonne)	last w/end August
Toulouse (foire au salé + Haute-Garonne)	24th August
Mauvezin (Gers)	1st Mon after 15/8
Hyères (Var)	24th August
Piolenc (Vaucluse)	last w/end August
Draguignan (Var)	1st Sat September
Sollies Pont (Var)	2nd Mon September
Toulouse (Haute-Garonne)	15th October

MARKETS

Beaumont-de-Lamague (Tarn et Goronde)	Tues & Sat July–January

STRAWBERRIES

FOIRES AND FETES

Beaulieu-sur-Dordogne(Corréze)	1st w/end May
St Géniez d'Olt (Aveyron)	July

MELONS

FOIRES AND FETES

Ligueuil (Dordogne)	3rd week August
Jouels (Aveyron)	3rd September
Pont de l'Arn (Tarn)	1st Sun September

MARKET

St Laurent Lolmie (Lot)	Mon to Sat August to October

TRUFFLES

FOIRES

St Paul les-trois-Châteaux (Drôme)	mid-February
Sorges (Dordogne)	21st January
Martel (Lot)	approx 25th January

MARKETS

Lalbenque (Lot)	Tues 2.30pm
Limogne (Lot)	Fri 10.30am
Sauzet (Lot)	Thurs 1.00pm
Périgueux (Dordogne)	Sat
Thénon (Dordogne)	Tues
Sarlat (Dordogne)	Sat
Saint Alvère (Dordogne)	Mon
Richerenches (Vaucluse)	day not stated
Chamaret (Drôme)	Mon
Carpentras (Vaucluse)	27th November

WALNUTS and/or CHESTNUTS   October, November

FOIRES

Villardonel (Aude)	Sun nearest All Saints' Day
Villefranche-de-Rouergue (Aveyron)	4th Thurs October*
Lanouaille (Dordogne)	Sun before 4th Tues October
Alès (Gard)	2 days October
Sauveterre-de-Rouergue (Aveyron)	w/end before All Saints
Mourjou (Cantal)	3rd w/end October
Dournazac (Haute-Vienne)	end October
Bédarieux (Hérault)	2nd November
Lavardac (Lot-et-Garonne)	1st Wed November
La Garde-Freinet (Var)	23rd November
St Etienne-de-Tinée (Alpes-Maritimes)	2 days November
Collobrières (Var)	last 3 Sundays in October
Les Mayons (Var)	Sundays in October

MARKETS

Sarlat (Dordogne)	Saturday
Belvès (Dordogne)	1st Wed October, November, December
Sauveterre-la-Lemance (Lot-et-Garonne)	Wed

WINE HARVESTS

FOIRES AND FETES

Marcillac (Aveyron)	Whit Monday
St Emilion (Dordogne)	mid-June
Gaillac (Tarn)	1st w/end August
Châteauneuf-du-Pape (Vaucluse)	end August
Madiran (Gers)	15th August
Ruoms (Ardèche)	2nd Sun August
Montagnac (Hérault)	29th August
Nice (Alpes-Maritimes)	September
Gimont (Gers)	September
Tende (Alpes-Maritimes)	September
Nîmes (Gard)	end September
Elne (Pyrénées Orientales)	October (2 days)

Recipes